D0613875

FOINAVON

FOINAVON

THE STORY OF THE GRAND NATIONAL'S BIGGEST UPSET

DAVID OWEN

WISDEN SPORTS WRITING

First published in 2013
Wisden Sports Writing is an imprint of
Bloomsbury Publishing Plc
50 Bedford Square
London WC1B 3DP

www.bloomsbury.com
www.wisden.com

ISBN 978-1-4081-5475-5

A CIP catalogue record for this book is available from the British Library.

Typeset in Sabon by seagulls.net

Printed and bound in Great Britain by CPI Group (UK) Ltd,
Croydon CR0 4YY

To Molly

'Foinavon has no chance. Not the boldest of jumpers, he can be safely ignored even in a race noted for shocks.'

Daily Express, 8 April 1967

Contents

8 April 1967 …

I remember not the smallest detail of my seventh birthday on 7 April 1967, but one moment from the following afternoon has remained with me.

It was 3.32pm as I now realise. I don't think I was watching the Grand National exactly, but it was on in our bay-windowed Taunton house. I could hear the commentary chattering away in the background, 'Rutherfords, Castle Falls, Castle Falls, Rutherfords … ' like an incantation. Surely one horse or the other would win. Then, abruptly, everything changed. Where previously all had seemed settled, at least to a distracted seven-year-old, now chaos reigned. Michael O'Hehir's irrepressible voice acquired an incredulous tone as he rattled out his now famous roll call of fallen horses. That is when I looked up at the television picture and saw a thrilling mêlée. It looked like every single horse had been stopped in its tracks. A few jockeys, thrown onto the landing side, were flapping around like beached fish. There was, as O'Hehir said, a 'right pile-up'. But then, after an improbably long interlude, just as it seemed that the whole race had ground irretrievably to a halt, one horse and rider approached the fence, slow as you like, on the wide outside, plopped over and trundled away to a sort of immortality. 'Foinavon has gone off on his own,' announced O'Hehir.

My eyes never left the screen until he passed the winning-post three minutes later.

The Grand National got me at an impressionable age. From that afternoon, for years to come, I used to stage versions of the race in my bedroom, laying out an assortment of pencil boxes, biscuit tins and the odd cuddly toy for the fences. The horses were those small collectable picture cards that Brooke Bond used to give away with PG Tips tea, in sets numbered, handily enough, from one to fifty. Cards landing picture side up when tossed over a 'fence' were deemed to have fallen. Even today, I can remember the specific cards that represented a few of the horses. Bassnet was a redstart from a British birds series; Anglo was *kallima inachus*, the orange dead leaf butterfly, from tropical Asia; Vulcano was a De Dion Bouton from a vintage car series given away with packets of sweet cigarettes.

What can I say? It was a long time ago. Xboxes were few and far between. In some ways, I liked to think, my imaginary Nationals were an improvement on the real thing. The biggest field in a real Grand National, for example, was 66 in 1929. As the years went by, though, I added the new runners to my original field of 44. By the time football claimed me, I regularly had 'Nationals' with 80 or 90 horses charging pell-mell up and over the cunningly angled shortbread tin standing in for Becher's Brook. Let me tell you, it was quite a spectacle.

I wasn't the only impressionable youngster on whom Foinavon's Grand National left its mark. Two girls called Carol Mills and Sally Williams composed a poem in red ink, in eleven four-line verses. They posted it to Foinavon, 'Oh! What a lucky horse!' John Kempton, who trained him, still has the poem (see page 259).

I suppose it was the train-wreck quality of the 1967 race, pure and simple, that grabbed me that first afternoon. It was a black and white television set, so it wasn't the bright race-day colours appealing to me. I was wary of donkeys, never mind clunking great thoroughbred horses, and blissfully ignorant that there was any chance of anyone or anything getting hurt charging over those big, dark fences.

With the passage of time, though, I came to realise that Foinavon's incredible victory struck other personal chords. For one thing, like many people, I love an underdog – and upsets don't come much bigger than Foinavon's Grand National triumph. But whereas nearly every sports-lover cheered when Ronnie Radford's Hereford United dumped Newcastle out of the FA Cup, or Jim Montgomery's Sunderland beat the dastardly but once awesomely powerful Leeds at Wembley, that's not really how it works in racing. So many of those watching the National have bet on the outcome that, in contrast to football, when a rank outsider comes in, people tend not to be too thrilled. This offends my sense of fairness. I must admit it is lucky I was too young to bet on Foinavon's race or I might have taken as dim a view as any other losing punter. As it was, I was able to enjoy his win as wholeheartedly as any FA Cup giant-killing.

Foinavon's National is also one of those sports stories that comes with its own life-lesson. I suppose you could interpret it as a horsey reworking of the fable of the hare, or in this case hares, and the tortoise, though I prefer to see it as the parable of why you should never give up. In sport, as in life, you just don't know what lies around the corner.

Of course, now I realise that the National is a dangerous business – for riders and their mounts. I am soft-hearted to a fault about animals. So I watch the race with intakes of breath and gritted teeth. But still I watch. Engaging in something as deliberate as writing this book has obliged me to ask myself why.

I don't think you can justify exposing a racehorse to danger in a scientific or mathematical way. If you take the view that it is unacceptable to put an animal avoidably at risk and you shun animal products yourself then it strikes me as both logical and perfectly respectable to contend that the race should be stopped. What I think the rest of us can do is assess what is to be gained and what lost from that particular course of action.

If you stopped the Grand National, it would prevent perhaps one handsome animal a year from suffering a life-ending fracture in the course of competing in the most physically demanding event in the British horse-racing calendar. You might also spare an indeterminate number of people the undeniably distressing sight of the stricken animal endeavouring in vain to right itself or to carry on galloping. It is hard, in all honesty, though to think what else you might put in the 'gains' column. I certainly don't believe that the animals spared the rigours of competing in the National would instead live out long lives in sun-dappled pastures. If the National disappears, along with its copious prize money, it will be much less worthwhile devoting time and attention to training horses, like Foinavon, with a proclivity for endurance events. In the long term, 'National-type' horses would no longer be produced. In the short term, a great many would drop out of racing. These are, on the whole, high-maintenance animals with a very specialised skill-set. Even when they can be retrained for, say, eventing or leisure-riding, this takes time, money and an owner or benefactor willing to take a chance. The supply of all three of these vital ingredients is limited and eminently exhaustible. If you stop the National, in short, I think that far fewer of the current crop of long-distance specialists would live out long, purposeful, reasonably well-cared-for lives than if the race keeps going.

Nor do I believe that halting the National would put a stop to the public relations war between horse-racing interests and the animal rights movement that nowadays erupts every year around the time of the Aintree meeting. It would just move to new battlegrounds. Two weeks before the 2012 Grand National, which led mortifyingly to the deaths of two of the forty runners, a high-profile Flat race in the Middle East eventually claimed the lives of three of just 13 horses entered for it. Horses will occasionally suffer life-ending injuries in any form of horse racing, no matter how well regulated the sport is, no matter what steps are taken to protect them. For those who find it immoral to place any animal purposely and unnecessarily at risk, no form of horse racing can truly be acceptable. The Grand National is just the juiciest target.

I would not proffer it as an inescapable conclusion in any way, but horse racing is still a pursuit I feel comfortable supporting on certain conditions. One of these is that all reasonable measures to protect racing horses, consistent with the character of a race, are put in place. Another is that animals in training are well looked after, with, for example, strict and effective policing of medicines administered in the days before a race. I was quite struck by the measured reply I got back from Australian philosopher and animal rights campaigner Peter Singer a few years ago when I approached him for a comment about the ethics of horse racing. 'I think that animals are often subject to unnecessary stress and abuse in the racing industry,' Singer stated. 'And jumps racing is definitely worse because of the high rate of injuries ... But I also think that, given the relatively small number of animals involved, and the more individualised attention racehorses get, the suffering of racehorses is insignificant compared to, say, the suffering of factory-farmed chickens and pigs. That's why I've never made much of an issue about it.'

I must admit, though, that I don't look at this purely in terms of horse welfare. The Grand National is thrilling. It is spectacular. There is an aesthetic beauty about a big field pouring over the spruce-dressed Liverpool fences, just as there is about a Dennis Bergkamp goal or a Roger Federer passing-shot. The courage and skill required to excel make those who succeed, equine and human, among the most revered figures in all of sport. But the National is about so much more than the clinical business of winning. For most, the adrenalin rush of tackling those fences is more than enough. After the race, one former jockey told me, the eyes of everyone who had completed the course would be 'ablaze with the experience'. This is what makes the race an inexhaustible fount of stories. The National, in short, has its own very considerable intrinsic value – and this is partly because of the demands it poses and the heavy price it can exact.

For all of the controversy that dogs it, for all that football has become an ever more dominant sporting superpower, for all that our attitude to horses has changed since they ceased to be indispensable for farming and waging war, the National still embodies Britain in ways that have something in common with the way the Tour de France embodies France. The bicycle race goes to the country, turning its best-known landmarks, natural and man-made, into the amphitheatre in which the action unfolds. With the Grand National, it is the other way around: the country goes to the race. But this happens in a number of ways.

Firstly, and most obviously, horses from all over the country (and beyond) head to Liverpool to compete. In 1967, Honey End and What a Myth came from Sussex, Red Alligator from County Durham, Kilburn from Kent, Foinavon from Berkshire and so on. A horse called Freddie flew the flag for Scotland – even though, like Foinavon and so many of the 44 runners, he was foaled in Ireland, in County Offaly. Secondly, a high proportion of the population – something like one in six – makes a point of watching the National and often making a small bet. The race's appeal, moreover, embraces town- as well as country-dwellers and stretches from top to bottom of society. Freddie's biographer Vian Smith, indeed, went as far as to explain his subject's huge 1960s popularity in terms of class struggle. The secret of Freddie's command over the hearts of men, he wrote, 'lies in his furious refusal to give in. Men and women see in him the proletariat tackling the aristocrats and somehow winning when it seems he cannot.'

Lastly, it is part of the charm of racing that features of the national landscape (and many other things) can be brought to life and assembled in one place through the medium of the horses' names. This was never plainer than in the 1967 Grand National, whose narrative, by one interpretation, could be summarised thus: a valley in Hampshire (Meon Valley), brings down a hill in Wiltshire (Popham Down), which later causes the pile-up that hands victory to a towering Scottish mountain (Foinavon).

Few racehorses in history have been named after a more striking geographic feature than the 1967 Grand National winner. Foinaven, as the Gaelic is usually anglicised today, is a great lummox of a mountain in Sutherland on the Grosvenor estate of Reay Forest. With its long multi-summited ridge, it is not a classical mountain shape like Ben Stack, its near neighbour. But at a whisker under 3,000 feet, it glowers over the ruggedly scenic local landscape with its white-faced sheep, properly sulphurous gorse and ten weather changes an hour. From her summer base at Lochmore Lodge, Anne, Duchess of Westminster, Foinavon's one-time owner, would have struggled to see his mountain namesake behind the contours of the smaller, but nearer Arkle. But it would often have brooded in the background as she fished the Laxford river or stalked red deer. And on the road back from Oldshoremore beach, on a clear day, the three mountains – massive Foinaven, squat Arkle and shapely Ben Stack – stand out in majestic line, just as they once did in Tom Dreaper's famous stable north of Dublin.

Conquering a mountain is an obvious metaphor for realising an ambition. The Grand National has metaphorical power too. With its obstacles and colour, its feats of raw courage, its elation, its despair and, above all, its outrageous twists of good and bad fortune, it is the perfect sporting metaphor for our passage through life. That, more than anything, is why I keep coming back to it. And it is why I will never forget Foinavon. This is his story.

Chapter 1

VULGAN

In spring 1942, France was under German occupation as far south as the Loire. The United States had entered the war and its troops were about to start using the wide-open spaces of Aintree racecourse as a transport depot. But the tide of history had not yet turned decisively against Hitler in North Africa and the Soviet Union, and the Normandy landings were more than two years away. It was against this unpromising backdrop that a ten-year-old mare called Vulgate made the 120-mile journey from her stable near Evreux, west of Paris, to the La Potardière stud farm near the town of La Flèche, between Le Mans and Angers.

With petrol scarce and the atmosphere in the countryside at best tense, this was not a trip to be undertaken lightly – not least because a union with the same stallion, Sirlan, the year before had failed to produce any offspring. This time, however, the mating proved fruitful. The following spring Vulgate gave birth to a male foal who would go on to leave as big an imprint on National Hunt racing as any horse in history.

The yard where the foal, Vulgan, was raised was presided over in wartime by Madame Jacques Lambert, daughter of Count André d'Ideville, a past president of the French Sport Society, and a woman with more on her mind, clearly, than dreaming up over-elaborate names for her livestock. Madame Lambert's husband was away in North Africa at the time with the French army. Having landed back in his homeland at Toulon at the head of his squadron in August 1944, Commander Lambert was wounded fighting German troops in Lorraine, eastern France on 11 October. He died about a month later.

This turbulent start to his life did not prevent Vulgan, whose relatively short frame was belied by an imperious eye and fiery temperament, from compiling an impressive race record. Starting with a third-place finish in an 800-metre (four-furlong) dash at Maisons-Laffitte, he clocked up five wins over three seasons (1945–7) on the Flat in France. These included the Group 4 Prix Major Fridolin and Prix de la Goutte d'Or, both run at Longchamp's famous racecourse in the Bois de Boulogne on the edge of Paris. He also finished second in his final French season in the Group 2 Prix de Strasbourg at Saint-Cloud.

Horse racing continued in Britain as well as France through the war years, but with more disruption. This may help to explain the success enjoyed by French-bred horses on English courses in the immediate post-war period. Vulgan himself was acquired by a Mr H. Coriat, a Wiltshire farmer who, according to *Sporting Life*, 'hitherto has always preferred to go hunting, rather than to watch racing'. Trained at Childrey, near Wantage, by Captain John de Moraville – who was awarded the Military Cross in 1941 but was a prisoner of war by the time his future charge was foaled – the five-year-old bay colt in March 1948 gave Coriat his first winner – in Cheltenham's prestigious Gloucestershire Hurdle. Sent off at 9/2 second-favourite, he came through with a sweetly timed challenge after the final flight to win by three-quarters of a length. It was to be his only race over obstacles, the branch of the sport at which so many of his progeny would excel.

For most of his last two years as a racehorse, Vulgan competed in long-distance Flat races requiring the stamina that his pedigree suggested he should possess. At Royal Ascot in June 1948, he made the frame twice in a week, coming second in the Gold Vase over two miles before winning the marathon Queen Alexandra Stakes, a feat he came close to repeating the following year when finishing second as odds-on favourite. He ran his last race on 12 November 1949. Fittingly, it was at Liverpool.

It was during his spell at Childrey that the stallion's explosive temper nearly cost him his future fame. A trademark bite inflicted a nasty cut on de Moraville's thumb, prompting him to threaten to have the aggressor gelded. As the trainer observed in later years, had he carried out his threat, he would have changed the course of jumps-racing history.

Happily for scores of future owners and trainers, including Foinavon's connections, millions of racegoers (and, many might add, Vulgan himself), the emasculator was never deployed and by 1951 the stallion was installed at the yard where he would spend the rest of his life.

His path to the white-walled driveway of Frank Latham's Blackrath Farm in County Kildare, just a few miles south-east of The Curragh, Ireland's premier Flat racecourse, was not straightforward, however. In October 1950, he was sold for 510 guineas at Newmarket to the British Bloodstock Agency, which specialised in buying horses for export. As Dermot Whelan, a former stud groom who started working at Blackrath in 1958, recollects, the horse was earmarked for a buyer in a 'foreign country' (he cannot remember which one), but the deal, he says, fell through because of a dock strike. This enabled Latham to snap him up for £520 and move him to Kildare's rich pastureland.

Latham had not even intended running Blackrath as a stud. When he bought the property in 1944, he was planning to rear young horses there. He already had a training establishment in North County Dublin, where he still lived. He therefore advertised for a head lad to take charge of his new acquisition. One of those who replied to the ad was a stud groom from Mallow whose stud farm was closing down. He told Latham that, as a result, a stallion called Flamenco was available for nothing. Latham said, 'OK, bring him up with you.'

Vulgan took up residence in the first box inside Blackrath farm's sturdy black steel gates. So aggressive was he that a false ceiling eventually had to be built into his stable to discourage him from rearing. The walls were padded with coconut matting to try and stop him hurting himself in his fits of temper. Whelan, a former jockey, had to use a piece of wire to reach over the stable-door and catch hold of his head-collar to mini-mise the risk of getting kicked or bitten. The stallion's short stature caused him difficulties with the bigger mares and a platform was built in the soft-surfaced inner yard to help him accomplish his assigned duties. There was no doubting his vitality, though, and he would still buck around like a playful young colt during exercise sessions right up until the day he died.

His initial fee for servicing a mare was just 25 guineas, but as his reputation grew, so did this charge. By 1956, it was up to 47 guineas (£49 7s, or £49.35); in 1960 it was 59 guineas; in 1964 it was 121 guin-eas; and in 1966 it hit 149 guineas. In his last few years at Blackrath, Vulgan's offspring were winning so many races that Latham was able to insist that his star resident was available only to mares whose owners would also pay for a second horse to see a less garlanded stallion. By the time he died, his fee had risen all the way to £250 – a fraction of the £50,000-plus fees commanded by the top Flat stallions today, but enough to recoup Latham's initial investment every couple of visits.

Between 1966 and 1974, the stud that wasn't intended to be a stud was responsible for the leading National Hunt sire – Vulgan – each and every year. It often had another stallion in the top five leading sires of jumpers too. This was Escart III who is best remembered as the sire of L'Escargot, a winner in the 1970s of both the Cheltenham Gold Cup and the Grand National. L'Escargot it was who, in 1975, prevented Red Rum from notching a hat-trick of three consecutive Grand National victories.

Vulgan was leading National Hunt sire on at least 11 occasions in all, fathering a string of high-class hurdlers and steeplechasers whose names are instantly recognisable to horse-racing enthusiasts even today: Larbawn, Kinvulgan, Kinloch Brae, Castleruddery, all were Vulgan foals. He produced winners of both of Cheltenham's most prestigious races: the Champion Hurdle (Salmon Spray) and the Gold Cup (the giant The Dikler). And he sired the winners of the 1964, 1967 and 1970 Grand Nationals. In 1970, indeed, the first two past the winning-post (Gay Trip and Vulture) were Vulgan offspring, while the 1967 race saw Foinavon line up against two more of Vulgan's sons (Vulcano and Penvulgo). More prosaically, Latham's champion stallion was single-handedly responsible for the disproportionate number of racehorses whose names began with the letters 'Vul' that were active in this period. The 1967/68 jumps racing season featured well over twenty.

This, then, was Vulgan's destiny. In 1957, though, he was still just another waspish stallion doing his thing in the racehorse country west of the Wicklow Mountains. This was the year that a 19-year-old mare called Ecilace was brought up from County Limerick to be impregnated by him – in return for the 47-guinea fee.

Chapter 2

ECILACE

The village of Pallasgreen straddles the main N24 road between Limerick and Tipperary in rural Munster. It boasts a pub called The Chaser, a branch of St Ailbe's Credit Union and it played host to the team from Kyrgyzstan ahead of the 2003 Special Olympics, which were staged in Ireland. An out-of-the-way spot, it appears little marked by the vainglory of the Celtic Tiger years.

It can be scarcely more than 30 miles from the famed Coolmore stud, but this is also cattle country – and Ryan country. The local celeb, a hammer-thrower who won gold for the United States at the 1920 Olympic Games in Antwerp, was called Ryan. The local honey farm is called Ryan's. And the man who owned Ecilace at the time of her assignation with Vulgan in 1957 was called Ryan.

Timothy H. Ryan ran a dairy farm of 80 acres about a mile back towards Tipperary from the centre of the village. An easy-going man whose family had lived in the area for more than 200 years, he was not much involved with racehorses. Indeed, Ecilace was the only broodmare he ever owned. He had inherited her from his father-in-law Michael Fitzgerald, a more serious horse-breeder based at Straffan, County Kildare, a village best known nowadays as home of golf's so-called 'K Club'. Fitzgerald's Kildare connection could explain why Ecilace was sent to Vulgan, a Kildare-based stallion.

Though never raced, Ecilace had form as a brood-mare before her trip to Blackrath. A decade earlier she had foaled the oddly named Umm, winner in 1955 of both the Irish Grand National and the coveted Galway Plate. Ecilace was also half-sister to a number of winners, among them a horse called Millennium, which won more than twenty times, three of these victories coming in the same week. A photograph exists of Fitzgerald with his mare and the foal Umm in a Kildare meadow in 1947. Fitzgerald stands straight-backed, decked out in hat, suit and tie, as the leggy foal sticks close to his mother. Ecilace eyes the camera warily.

Eleven years later, and around eleven months after visiting Vulgan, the mare had another son to tend to. The foal, which would eventually be named Foinavon, spent roughly the first year and a half of his life on Timothy Ryan's Limerick farm. His first stable, just up the road from a level-crossing, was a solid, stone affair with a narrow door, timber roof-beams and whitewashed inner walls. There were six stables in the block, though these were not all used for horses. A small back window, at about shoulder-height for a man and fitted then as now with dark metal bars, overlooked the lane and a good-sized field on the other side of the road.

This field, with its view of local landmark the Hill of Nicker, mythological home of the ancient Irish goddess of love, is now given over to cattle. In the summer of 1958, though, the foal, like thousands of others in Ireland's lush, green meadows, would have spent long days here with the fitful Irish sun beating on his back. Another photograph taken not long before his sale the following year shows a flat-capped handler with the yearling in classic side-on pose. The man holds the lead-rein at arm's length in his left hand while in his right he holds up a short stick, like a conductor's baton, to fix the horse's attention. The horse looks handsome and nicely relaxed, as evidenced by the slack in the lead-rein. In the background, Timothy Ryan, dressed much like his father-in-law 12 years before and gesturing with his right arm, is neatly framed by the yearling's powerful neck and forelegs. So carefully composed is the photograph you cannot help but conclude that the young thoroughbred was a patient sitter.

In September 1959, the colt made the more than 100-mile trip to Dublin, most likely by train, and, on the 21st of the month, he was sold at Goffs in Ballsbridge to a Mr H. J. Rooney. The price paid was 400 guineas, so farmer Ryan made a tidy margin over Vulgan's 47-guinea fee for impregnating his mare.

Harry Rooney worked for Captain Charles Radclyffe, a well-known schooler of young jumpers whose father-in-law, Major Gilbert Cotton, was Aintree's long-time course inspector. It was Radclyffe's custom to bring a small number of yearlings over from Ireland each season and to raise them on his property at Lew in Oxfordshire. Successful Grand National horses bought by Radclyffe as yearlings include Corbiere, Zongalero and State of Play. A former High Sheriff of Oxfordshire, he schooled the Queen Mother's young horses for many years.

It is hard to be certain because Radclyffe's young purchases were generally not named until after he sold them on, but it is probable that Foinavon spent his second birthday in this delightful corner of the Oxfordshire countryside. This may even have been where he was gelded. Orchard Paddock – where the youngsters were kept – with its gnarled fruit-trees, was the only field on the farm that had never been ploughed. Fertilisers, moreover, were used only sparingly, so as to safe-guard the health of its original old grasses.

If the colt was housed here, though, his stay was brief; in May 1960 he again changed hands, being bought by the owner for whom he would later make his racing debut, Anne, Duchess of Westminster. A County Cork-born general's daughter, the duchess would go on to become, along with the Queen Mum, the best-known owner of steeple-chasers of her era, although this owed little to Foinavon's efforts.

Three months after sealing the Foinavon deal, Radclyffe found himself bidding in the Ballsbridge sales ring for a gangly bay gelding against the duchess and her trainer Tom Dreaper. County Meath-based Dreaper won the auction with a bid of 1,150 guineas. The duchess had just bought Arkle.

Foinavon was taken to Bryanstown, the duchess's 700-acre farm near Maynooth, a few miles west of Dublin, where her racehorses were accustomed to spend their summers grazing and resting valuable limbs. It was not for another 16 months, in September 1961, at an age when many Flat horses have the bulk of their racing careers already behind them, that he was sent to Dreaper's Greenogue yard to be broken.

Chapter 3

THE ROAD
TO BALDOYLE

In a pocket of rural charm not yet shunted away by the boom-bust materialism of the north Dublin suburbs, lies one of racing's holy places. It looks modest enough: a compact collection of whitewashed, red-doored stable-blocks behind a bright red gate, with the first stable so close to the road that its occupant could practically take up hitch-hiking. Yet any racing fan with a passing interest in football might testify to the aptness of the colour-scheme; if there was a Manchester United of 1960s steeplechasing, this was it.

It was here at Greenogue that a pipe-smoking cattle farmer who was getting on in years nurtured, more or less simultaneously, the two most highly rated steeplechasers that ever drew breath. Arkle, as sweet-tempered as he was intelligent, with his three Gold Cups and his widely publicised penchant for Guinness, became the sport's poster-boy. But the vicious Flyingbolt, who suffered from brucellosis, a contagious disease that can cause joint and muscle pain, is reckoned to have been only 2lb Arkle's inferior and much better than champions of more recent vintage, such as Desert Orchid and Best Mate.

When Foinavon arrived in September 1961 and took up residence in box number 4, Tom Dreaper's school of steeplechasing excellence had still not quite attained its absolute peak of pre-eminence. This came in 1964, the year in which the trainer celebrated his 66th birthday. All told, he collected stakes worth £41,849 in England and Ireland for patrons such as the Duchess of Westminster, with Arkle responsible for nearly half the haul. (This at a time when Dreaper could have bought an ounce of Ogden's tobacco for his pipe for 5/5½d – 27p.) Nevertheless, Fortria, the yard's star turn, had already reeled off consecutive victories in the Queen Mother Champion Chase, Cheltenham's premier two-mile steeplechase, and the trainer's astonishing run of seven successive Irish Grand Nationals – a feat achieved with seven different horses – between 1960 and 1966 was under way. He had already won that race five times in all, starting in 1942 at around the time Vulgan was conceived in war-torn France. So the stallion's three-year-old son was certainly entering the jumps game at the very top of the pile.

Dreaper's training regimen could be characterised by the aphorism 'less is more' – unlike his racehorses' diets, which consisted of four oats-laden feeds a day. According to Ivor Herbert, former trainer and Arkle biographer, 'In contrast to almost every other important stable in Western Europe, Tom Dreaper's horses are hardly ever out of their boxes for more than thirty minutes. Forty-five minutes would be the absolute longest.'

'We used to go out at nine and were back in at half-nine,' says Peter McLoughlin, a long-time member of the tight, devoted Greenogue team, who rode Fort Leney, another Dreaper star, in the 1967 Cheltenham Gold Cup. 'Twice a week we would school. We had four little jumps on the way to the gallops, which were across the road and about three fields away. Then we had six fences on the gallops. Two of these fences had ditches on the landing side. Fairyhouse fences. They taught the horses to stretch out as they jumped.' According to Pat Taaffe, Arkle's regular jockey, schooling over the four 'baby' fences was 'Mr Dreaper's big thing'. They were about three feet thick and three feet high, composed of loosely packed furze held in by a tree trunk on either side. They were very close together and frequently used, so the ground around them was what the soft-spoken Taaffe once described as 'you know … mucky'. It was Dreaper's contention that, if it was to be a steeplechaser, a horse needed to know how to jump even before it knew how to gallop.

With his arrival at the stable coming in the month after Arkle's, you might imagine that Foinavon's presence would have been somewhat overshadowed. The future champion's calibre, though, was not immediately apparent. 'At the start Arkle was like a car with four flat tyres,' Peter McLoughlin says, while acknowledging that he was already a 'brilliant' jumper. Pat Taaffe was more explicit still, remarking, 'He moved so terribly behind, you could drive a wheelbarrow right through between his hind legs.'

A year younger than his stable companion, Foinavon was a fine-looking horse. A photograph from these early days depicts him as a big, raw four-year-old with a trace clip in the front yard with an appreciative McLoughlin. It appears, though, that he was at Greenogue for some time before acquiring his name. In the *Sporting Chronicle*'s 'Horses in Training' list for 1962, he is there, but recognisable only by his parentage. With Arkle and another future Cheltenham winner, Ben Stack, who came to the stable at the same time, named after mountains on the Duchess of Westminster's Sutherland estate, you can appreciate how she might have conceived the idea of naming her third young horse under Dreaper's tutelage after another mountain, one of the highest in Scotland not to be a Munro. And so Foinavon he became, in time for him to start the first of his more than 60 races, on 18 May 1962.

The term 'bumper race' might conjure up images of the fairground. In fact, it is a term for flat races held at jump-racing meetings. They are so called because the amateur jockeys who used to ride in them were thought so ungainly they would let their backsides 'bump' on their mount's saddle as it galloped, in contrast to the more polished, or perhaps merely fitter, professionals. In Ireland in the 1960s, these races were mainly for maidens, in other words horses that are yet to win a race. Part of the theory behind them was that they allowed young animals to gain racecourse experience without the added hazard of jumping. They are also a good test of stamina: according to Ivor Herbert, 'a horse which stays two miles on the flat, almost invariably stays three miles over fences'.

So there is nothing unusual in Foinavon's first race – the 1962 Tally-Ho Plate at Dundalk, 40 miles north of Greenogue on the road to Belfast – being on the flat. Nor, given his subsequent record, was there anything especially unusual about him finishing unplaced out of 13 runners. His first jockey, Mr Tony Cameron, reckons he came in around fourth and was 'a bit one-paced'. Though nobody realised at the time, there was the faintest precursor of what fate held in store, in that Cameron, who would go on to represent Ireland in the three-day event at the 1964 Tokyo Olympics, had come fourth in the Grand National at Aintree seven weeks before on Gay Navaree, a 100/1 rank outsider. Given his accomplishments as a horseman, there is not the slightest chance Mr Cameron let his backside bump on the young gelding's saddle.

The novice did progress over that first summer. A second 'bumper' at Galway in August brought a first visit to the winners' enclosure following a third-placed finish. In September he went one better, coming second behind a horse called Commutering in a two-mile Flat race, the Williamstown Maiden Stakes, at Phoenix Park in Dublin. To go from there to making his debut over obstacles at the citadel of English jumps racing that is Cheltenham, as Foinavon did on 16 November, would be a tall order for any horse, however. It is hard to imagine that a trainer-owner combination as knowledgeable – and patient – as Dreaper and the Duchess of Westminster would have expected too much from his tilt at the three-mile Cowley Novices Hurdle. 'Little is known of Foinavon,' proclaimed *The Times* on the morning of the race, although it added that Dreaper 'did say lately that he was hopeful that some of his young horses this season were useful'. In the event, the hurdling debutant managed a creditable third place, from 19 starters, in his first race under Taaffe. It was left to a stable companion running in his first steeplechase the following day to deliver incontrovertible evidence that the trainer's hunch was justified.

In journalist and commentator Peter O'Sullevan's words, 'Arkle … seemed almost embarrassed by his effortless 20 lengths superiority over the nearest of his 11 opponents in the 2½-mile Honeybourne Chase'.

As Arkle marched on, going through the entire 1962/63 season undefeated, however, Foinavon was consistent only in his mediocrity. He contested four more hurdle races, on each occasion partnered by Taaffe, and was unplaced every time. A second visit to Gloucestershire, for the 1963 Cheltenham Festival, saw him fail to make the frame in the Spa Hurdle. Ground as soft as dough afforded mitigating circumstances of a sort, though the conditions did not stop Arkle cruising home by more than 20 lengths in the Broadway Novices Chase. This was also the festival at which Arkle's great rival Mill House trounced Dreaper's Fortria to win the Cheltenham Gold Cup for the one and only time.

Taaffe's verdict on Foinavon was affectionate but unflattering. 'I don't think I ever met a horse with less ambition,' he said. 'With a little dedication, he could have done a lot better than this. But his attitude was quite clearly, "Why beat myself to a frazzle when there are easier and more enjoyable ways of running a race."'

Taaffe also said that nothing ever worried or scared Foinavon – an attitude that was to prove highly significant in future and for now at least made him popular with his handlers back at the yard. 'He was a Christian of a horse, the best horse to look after,' according to Vincent Slevin, then a £6-a-week stable lad, who tended to Foinavon as one of his three charges, along with the future Cheltenham Gold Cup-winner Fort Leney and Dicky May. 'He was a grand horse in front, but he had no tail-end in him. He hadn't the power behind. He had a powerful shoulder and a deep girth, but he was very slack in the hindquarters.' As part of his duties at Greenogue, Slevin remembers spending 'umpteen' nights on a made-up bed in box number 8, next door to Arkle. He used to stay there for the last three nights before the yard's new star was due to run as a precaution against would-be horse dopers. As steeple-chasing was a winter sport, this was not a job for the faint-hearted or, better said, the thin-blooded. However, nothing suspicious or dramatic ever happened on his watch.

After this disappointing sequence of results, Foinavon was packed off back to Bryanstown, where it was noted that he had been 'growing during the winter'. In August 1963, at around the time Martin Luther King delivered his 'I Have a Dream' speech on the steps of the Lincoln Memorial in Washington, he was returned to Dreaper.

With Arkle now gunning for the very top prizes in the steeplechas-ing calendar, it became quite infrequent for the two stablemates to travel to the same race meetings. This may in part explain why Foinavon started to be ridden by a wider variety of jockeys. And since, ambitious to succeed, they were often prepared to ride him in robust fashion, this may well have been a contributory factor in the marked improvement in results which became apparent once he had turned six.

His first outing over the big fences ended in familiar fashion when he was unplaced at Leopardstown under Liam McLoughlin, who won the Irish Grand National on Kerforo in 1962 and was Peter's elder brother. But he carried Taaffe to fourth place on his official sixth birthday on his first visit to Baldoyle, a nearby seaside course in north Dublin that the experienced jockey regarded as not really suitable for 'young, green' horses. In his next nine races, stretching over the 1964 calendar year, he was placed six times, winning twice. It seemed a corner had been turned.

Race-riding in those days was a tough old business, especially in Ireland. As if navigating half a tonne of horseflesh around a curving course at high-speed over hedge-like obstacles was not a perilous enough way of making a living, jockeys had appended some additional hazards of their own, courtesy of their fiercely uncompromising racing tactics. According to Bobby Beasley, a top Irish jockey of the day and prime exponent, 'It is a strange part of the Irish character that when competing against each other on horses, nearly everyone wants to "do" the other riders. They would try to ride each other off, put each other over the rails and so on.' Describing how he once deliberately pulled across rival jockey Willie Robinson when he tried to come up on his inside, in an incident that left Robinson nursing a broken collarbone, Beasley argued, 'I believed these were the right tactics in Ireland at the time … It was rough and tough but I loved it. As with everything else connected with racing, I studied the technique ruthlessly, so that soon no one dared even to poke his nose up on my inside and very few tried to "do" me for fear of reprisals.' While jump jockeys, corralled into one of sport's most precarious and demanding professions, exhibited legendary camaraderie at all other times, in sight of the winning-post it was dog eat dog. Explained Beasley, 'You wouldn't get any more rides from a trainer if you let someone get up on your inside.' Besides, he added, 'Willie didn't mind. He'd done the same to me before.'

Foinavon's first victory came in a two-mile steeplechase at Naas on 29 February 1964 – exactly 652 days after his Dundalk debut. Paddy Woods, another senior member of the Greenogue staff, who was Arkle's regular work-rider and a stalwart of the yard's Gaelic football team, remembers it well; he had to work hard for his bonus.

He had earned a reputation by this time as 'sort of a lazy type', Woods recalls. 'So I stoked him up as hard as I could … I started to hit him at the first fence and didn't stop until we had finished.' The horse responded to the hard ride and 'jumped like a buck', but Woods was so worn out by the time they passed the winning-post that he nearly collapsed and was 'hardly able to talk' when he reached the weighing-room. His efforts had not gone unnoticed: the Duchess of Westminster herself saw fit to bring him a pick-me-up in the shape of a post-race cup of tea.

A week later Arkle won his first Cheltenham Gold Cup, turning the tables on reigning champion Mill House, who had beaten him in the Hennessy, in their first 'clash of the titans' at Newbury the previous November. The yard was flying high and in April Foinavon delivered another victory.

This time his jockey was Peter McLoughlin. The two-mile Tickell Chase at Punchestown was only the young stable lad's second ride over fences. In his first, he had broken a collarbone. So he was strongly motivated to show that he had what it takes. The early pace was fast and McLoughlin soon found himself well back in the field. 'After a mile, I was probably driving,' he says. 'Foinavon would never pick up speed. He was a true, true stayer. I was going nowhere when, all of a sudden, the other horses started getting tired.

'I kept driving, pushing, kicking. Going to the last, there was one horse in front of me. I was ten lengths behind, then four lengths. He just stayed, stayed, stayed. I remember Mr Dreaper saying, "You certainly got the best out of him."'

In spite of these hard races, Foinavon was said to be looking 'awfully well' in May when returned to Bryanstown for his summer break. It was seven months before he was seen on a racecourse again, though in September he was 'up and being ridden by [Johnny] Kelly', the stud groom at Bryanstown, who had arrived there early that year. As a more seasoned chaser of proven staying ability, he was to be aimed in the 1964/65 season at three-mile races that were all the more likely to sap the strength of his opponents. This, though, was as good as it got for Foinavon at Greenogue. In January came an incident that would all but seal the now seven-year-old gelding's fate at the yard.

Baldoyle today is a sad sight for any racing enthusiast. The members' entrance is through a fine red-brick arch; the turf is springy; and the setting, just across the road from a stretch of shoreline where godwits drill for food with their elongated bills, is idyllic. But the arch is concreted up and the last race meeting was four decades ago. The death-knell? A notification from the course's insurers, received in 1968, that they would not much longer be able to insure the grandstands – now long demolished – because of rusting reinforcement rods.

On 2 January 1965, though, the course, and the entire village, would have been buzzing as the crowds poured in for the New Year's meeting that was the most important National Hunt event of the year at Baldoyle. In the parade ring, local high society in the form of men in crombie and astrakhan coats and women in furs studied the runners as they circled skittishly with their handlers. In the outside enclosure, the hoi polloi clustered around catering tents, bookmakers' pitches, or the portable Tote building, clutching racing cards, cigarettes and steaming beverages, or a drop of the hard stuff from the Dolphin Hotel marquee. As course commentator, Michael O'Hehir was probably there calling the finishes as the horses flashed by Baldoyle's star-shaped winning-post. Between races, the film-processing van's pungent diesel generator throbbed insistently. This was to be rendered useless for the last race, which went off 14 minutes late in rapidly fading light, forcing the judge to fall back on the evidence of his own eyes and declare a dead heat.

Foinavon made the short trip across from Greenogue to run in the fourth race on the card, the Claremount Handicap Steeplechase over 3 miles and 100 yards. The bald facts are that he was sent off as the 4/1 favourite only to disappoint again, succumbing to a heavy fall, his first for almost a year.

That was bad enough, but what happened immediately afterwards made matters even worse. There are various versions, which differ somewhat in their particulars. Taaffe, riding him for the tenth time and yet to win on him, described the episode quite colourfully as follows. 'On a day at Baldoyle, we fell very heavily. We parted company in mid-air and after I'd bounced, I looked round, half-expecting to see Foinavon in trouble. And there he was lying down … eating grass, cool as you please, just taking time for a snack. He was that kind of a horse.

If he had been a man, he'd have spent his days, hands in pockets, whistling through his teeth, scuffling the dust.'

Tony Cameron, Foinavon's first jockey, who was at the course that day, adds a couple of details, saying that the horse 'tipped up' at the fence and 'lay for dead'. He goes on, 'Pat took one look at him and gave him a belt on the backside. He jumped up. He was no more dead than flying to the moon.'

Peter McLoughlin was also there, having ridden in the first race. His recollection is that Taaffe at first couldn't get him up and thought that his back was broken. As the jockey walked away, however, his mount sat up on his haunches and started cropping grass. McLoughlin says that Taaffe then heard a whinny and a drumming of hooves and, as he turned around, Foinavon raced past and aimed a kick at him, which fortunately missed. 'I think Pat told Mr Dreaper he wasn't going to ride him again,' he adds. He never did.

Chapter 4

KEMPTON PARK

About 250 miles away – and several divisions below horse racing's Premier League – the only man who rode Foinavon in more races than Pat Taaffe was halfway through his sixth season as trainer-cum-jockey. John Kempton's path into this tough but exciting world was far from direct.

The son of a South London car dealer who sold used Citroëns from a showroom in East Hill, Wandsworth, Kempton was studying in the late 1950s to be a vet when his world was turned upside down by the collapse of his father's business. His father Jack – who had served an engineering apprenticeship with the Campbell racing team of Bluebird fame and spent the war inspecting damaged Wellington bombers at Brooklands – suffered a nervous breakdown as a result, spending some time in hospital. The financial consequences of this included turfing John out of vets' school to seek gainful employment.

During a childhood spent mainly in Wimbledon and Epsom, John had developed a fondness for horses, learning to ride on Wimbledon Common and in Richmond Park. At the time of his father's illness, he had acquired ownership of a horse with a club foot called Monsieur Egbert, which the family used to enter in the occasional race. Reluctant to give up the horse, he and his mother, Molly, began looking for stables to rent in the Home Counties, with the notion of starting a livery yard business.

The residents of Compton, the Berkshire village where they settled, might never have had it so good, in Prime Minister Harold Macmillan's era-defining phrase, yet recreational riding was still beyond the budgets of most families in the area, those without their own stables anyway, so this idea didn't work out. Never shy of trying things out for himself, Kempton had learnt to shoe horses. He now turned to farriering in an attempt to make ends meet. Servicing villages near the dyed-in-the-wool racing town of Newbury in a small van, under the mission statement, 'Anywhere, any time, £1 a set', this went rather better. 'I made them myself out of strip metal,' he recalls. 'I made a profit out of the £1.'

Shoeing unknown horses can be a hazardous business, however, and it wasn't long before Kempton started thinking in terms of obtaining a trainer's licence. Eventually he persuaded one of his farriering clients to buy two racehorses and he started training in 1959 with the sum total of four possible runners. He was just over 20.

In time, Jack was discharged from hospital and joined his wife and son in the bungalow across the yard from the single L-shaped stable-block they had purchased. With winners as scarce as new owners, however, it was a hand-to-mouth existence and John was obliged to keep doing the rounds of the local equine population in his little van.

The new decade brought welcome reinforcement in the shape of Colin 'Jake' Hemsley, a seven-and-a-half-stone livewire with a shock of dark hair and an Isetta bubble-car, who had previously worked in the yard of Captain Ryan Price in Sussex alongside top jockeys such as Fred Winter and Josh Gifford. Hemsley had seen at first hand the precision and discipline with which a leading racing stable operated. He slotted in as head lad with responsibility for ensuring the horses were appropriately fed and exercised. This freed Kempton to concentrate on his riding and shoeing – and to prospect for new owners. His efforts soon bore fruit, pushing up the number of horses in training at the yard towards double figures.

They rolled their own oats and installed a chaff-cutter for making the hay and grass 'chop' that was part of the lunchtime feed. On Wednesday evenings, in a small blue and white caravan equipped with a Burco boiler that also served as a tack-room, Hemsley would make up a linseed mash in a Redex tin with the top cut off. To save money, he often heated the mixture using home-made briquettes made from the tightly folded pages of old newspapers. With open country close at hand, he and his assistants regularly rode the horses several miles across the Downs to villages such as Lockinge and Harwell. When not being schooled or exercised, however, the horses remained in their stables.

If a small yard had any potential edge over the likes of Price and Dreaper it lay in the individual treatment they could accord their horses in their efforts to bring out the best in them. Indeed, given that the animals they were working with were often regarded as damaged goods in one way or another – which is what brought them into the small owners' price bracket – judicious experimentation was frequently the most rational way to try to make a difference, to turn an inveterate also-ran into a competitive racehorse. 'Psychoanalysis' (with apologies to Freud) is what Kempton called it.

When a new charge arrived, Hemsley and Kempton would spend hours observing and discussing its characteristics – particularly in Sunday morning planning-sessions – trying to work out how to turn it into a more successful racehorse. In June 1961, the Kemptons paid around £500, on behalf of an owner from one of the families behind the Peek Frean biscuit company, for a horse called Seas End. It was a giant of a horse that Kempton would later ride in two Grand Nationals, with feet so flat he couldn't be ridden along the stonier downland tracks. After performing well early in his career, the horse appeared to be in decline, running 11 times in the 1959/60 season for just one third place and being pulled up on several occasions. After taking him hunting a few times, as he often did with new horses, Kempton noticed he had a very tender mouth, so they started racing him in a rubber bit, with somewhat improved results. Then, larking around at home (while wearing his business suit) the trainer realised the huge horse was so controllable he could steer him around a field using just a flimsy hay-tie attached to his head-collar.

At this point, encouraged by Hemsley, Kempton fashioned a bridle like a padded head-collar and attached the long-necked Seas End's special long reins to it, putting nothing in the horse's mouth. 'I went to the stewards at Devon & Exeter racecourse and asked if I could run a horse without a bit,' he recalls. 'They said, "There's nothing in the rules to say you can't, but be it on your head because if you interfere with any other horse, you'll immediately be up with us." I rode him without a bit that afternoon and he won by 12 lengths.' The horse's progress continued to such effect that he once broke a course record at Cheltenham. Kempton concludes, 'It was an absolute transformation.'

Such successes simply did not come often enough, however. Without the leverage to extract adequate fees from the owners of their horses, small trainers faced a grinding battle to make ends meet in the 1960s. Speaking in 1966, after completing a hat-trick of Flat trainers' championships in England, Paddy Prendergast, the Irish-based trainer, summarised the situation as follows, 'No trainer can afford to keep a horse under 16 guineas a week. A large majority of them are forced to charge considerably less than this sum. But even if he charges 16 guineas there is no salary for him if he does not win races.'

Enthusiastic owners who paid reliably, tipped the staff regularly and were committed to the sport were a valued commodity. One man who did more than most to help the Kemptons keep the wolf from the door was Gordon Passey. A well-known figure in Newbury, Passey was from a family that had supplied knackermen to the local racecourse since 1925. His grandfather had rejoiced in the title 'licensed horse slaughterer to

Her Majesty'. As mechanised transport took over from horses even in semi-rural Berkshire, the family diversified its business. By the 1960s, Passey was also one of the leading scrap metal dealers in the area. He was once heard to observe that he had three ambitions in life: to own a Rolls-Royce, to be a millionaire and to have, as he put it, 'an 'oss' good enough to run in the Grand National. He came up short only on the third count. As well as keeping racehorses with the Kemptons, Passey was instrumental in keeping things ticking over at the yard in other ways. He supplied the unusual grey-blue-coloured paint, the sort of shade you might find on a naval vessel, with which the stable doors were coated. And when the cylinder-head of the old petrol-engined horsebox they used cracked, it was Passey who saved the day by telling them the equivalent part from a – readily obtainable – Humber Super Snipe car could be pressed into service. He also procured Hemsley's living quarters.

It must have been quite a sight, the 38-foot-long mobile home as it trundled across the Downs on a low-loader trailer all the way from the US air base at Greenham Common where Passey had bought it as scrap. It had two bedrooms, a bathroom, central heating, even air conditioning and, once it had been plonked down behind the stable-block in a field that also housed an ever-growing heap of wood shavings from the horses' discarded bedding, Hemsley lived there for years with his wife Jill and son Shane.

The Kemptons' bungalow housed a memento of family success earlier in the century in a different form of racing. This was a cut-out photograph of Mick the Miller, the famous greyhound, who had been owned by a relative called Phiddy Kempton. There were also some pieces of fine glass from the days before the war when the family owned a glass-works. Sometimes, when the horses were running poorly or unexpected expenses incurred, Molly would sell a piece of glass to make ends meet. More often they would strive to balance the books in the same way many other trainers did, including Prendergast in his early days – by placing bets.

You might see no great harm in this. And when trainers merely staked a small sum on a horse of theirs they thought was in with a particularly good chance in order to balance the books, you would probably be justified. (Jockeys were banned from betting.) But, of course, in such circumstances there would be a strong temptation both to enhance a likely horse's chances of winning and to cash in to the greatest extent possible when you found yourself with a 'sure-fire certainty' on your hands. This led to practices such as the deliberate 'stopping' by jockeys of improving horses whose trainers had their eye on a substantial pay day in a race or two's time and did not wish too promising a performance in the meantime to spoil things by getting the horse saddled with a punishing handicap. It also gave trainers a strong incentive to try to disguise whatever betting activity they were engaging in to avoid cramping the odds and reducing the amount of money they stood to make. This was all rather hard on the poor punter, who might find himself unwittingly backing a horse which had almost no chance of winning for the very good reason that its connections had no intention of allowing it to win, even if capable of doing so.

As part of his graphic account of the seedier side of racing during this period, Barry Brogan, a leading jockey active between 1962 and 1977, spelt out some of the pitfalls for ordinary racegoers. 'There is no end to the ways in which gullible, unsuspecting punters are ripped off by the professional fixers,' Brogan wrote. 'Favourite methods include deliberately running horses with sore shins, sore backs, sore withers, pulled muscles, over the wrong distance, on unsuitable ground conditions and when they simply aren't fit enough to do their best.' Brogan also reckoned that, notwithstanding the rules, 'up to 50 per cent of jockeys bet on horses every day'.

Trainers could fall foul of dishonest dealers as well, as the Kemptons had discovered before moving to Berkshire, when running the gallant Monsieur Egbert in a humdrum race at Wye, the Chatham Hurdle. The horse had recently had a couple of promising outings and the family fancied his chances, so Jack Kempton had a substantial wager on the outcome. The horse romped home at long odds with plenty to spare, but anxious to secure the highest possible payout, Jack had given his stake to a stranger who said he could place the bet in such a way as to avoid the price being shortened and Jack's winnings reduced accordingly. He never saw the stranger again and the stake was lost. The Kemptons had to make do with their comparatively meagre prize-money of £137.

On setting up in Compton, John still thought enough of that victory to want to commemorate it. The yard was renamed Chatham Stables.

Chapter 5

A HORSE TO RUN IN THE NATIONAL

One chilly morning, not long after Foinavon's Baldoyle tumble, Colin Hemsley found himself planting plastic daffodils in the circular centrepiece at Chatham Stables. It was customary (and sensible) to have the yard looking its best when new owners called. There was still snow on the ground and the head lad thought that the flowers, which were then given away with packets of washing powder, would brighten up the place for the visit of Mr and Mrs Watkins, a local Berkshire couple thinking of buying the odd racehorse for the Kemptons to train. Hemsley felt he and the stable girls had done a good job. Even so, he was surprised when Mrs Watkins asked how they got their daffodils to bloom so early.

The couple – comfortably off but far from wealthy – had the sort of profile you might expect of small-time racehorse owners in an age when rising prosperity was stoking demand for leisure activities and opening new routes to social advancement. Cyril Watkins, a cab proprietor's son in his mid-fifties, was a football pools concessionaire, responsible for the smooth processing each week of thousands of coupons collected by agents from workplaces around the pleasant market town of

Reading. The idea was to team up in the racehorse venture with another concessionaire called McIntyre 'Mac' Bennellick. Mac, who also owned a hairdressing shop in Rainham, was based in Essex.

Cyril and Iris married at the register office in Iris's home city of Nottingham on 6 December 1947. The country was still basking in the glow of another wedding, between Princess Elizabeth and Philip Mountbatten, just two weeks earlier. But this was austerity Britain with people still rationed, much to Cyril's frustration, to two ounces of butter per week. Cyril was 39, a divorcee and a Didcot-based stores foreman for the Air Ministry. Iris Nixon was the 30-year-old daughter of a deceased brewery clerk. She was also a dressmaker and would draw on these skills in years to come to make silks for the jockeys who rode their horses.

By the early 1960s, the couple was living in a small Edwardian semi on Craig Avenue in the Norcot area of Reading. Part of the house was pressed into service as an office for Cyril's football pools concession. Around the middle of the decade, however, they upgraded to a new bungalow, set in acres of land, on leafy Nine Mile Ride in well-heeled Berkshire suburbia. Cyril traded in his Ford Zephyr estate for a pillar-box red Inspector Morse-style Jaguar.

Cyril and Iris had no children, but several animals. These included Shoes and Socks, two boisterous Airedale terriers, a couple of escapologist bullocks, called Mr Wart and Mr Bossy, and a goat. The property was initially heavily wooded and was traversed by a stream frequented by frogs and adders. Once the land had been prepared, however, the couple acquired two thoroughbred brood-mares called Betty – short for 'Betting Control' – and Peggy. By this time, Cyril also owned a pet-shop in Tilehurst, a village just outside Reading. Around the back of the shop was a small office building which became the focus of the football pools business, with Cyril's agents delivering completed Littlewoods coupons there on Friday nights for despatch to the company's head-quarters in Liverpool.

At this time, the football pools were as much a part of the fabric of British life as the Grand National. They had also become very big business. In the 1950s, when cash betting on horse races was still technically illegal except on the racecourse, as many as 7¾ million people were said to be sending in pools coupons on a weekly basis during the football season, staking upwards of £50 million a year. By the 1960s, the sums gambled in this way had comfortably exceeded £100 million. 'The pools are an interest which no government can ignore,' observed Northampton MP Reginald Paget in May 1960. 'They have become a power in the land because they represent an awful lot of money.' The pools were also an efficient source of tax revenue, described by one MP as 'the cheapest tax in the world'. Finally, they were a significant source of employment, especially on Merseyside. In 1968, there were said to be 2,000 people in Glasgow, 1,000 in Cardiff and 14,759 on Merseyside whose jobs depended on the pools. Nearly 1,800 of these were in Prime Minister Harold Wilson's Huyton constituency.

As the plastic daffodil story suggests, Iris Watkins was scrupulously polite and perhaps at times a little naïve. Another story has her struggling to pull out of a tight parking-spot before finally accepting an offer of help from a man. The good Samaritan duly parked her vehicle perfectly for her, upon which Iris thanked him without daring to point out that she was now back to square one.

Cyril could be generous to a fault, but he also had a more roguish streak and more than his share of eccentricities. Taking his turn on the tea-run during the war on a ship in heavy seas, he is said to have been sick over the tray of drinks he was carrying. Thinking himself unobserved, he wiped away the evidence and continued on his way back to his cabin-mates, rather than disposing of the contaminated beverages and collecting another round. Unfortunately for him, this indiscretion was witnessed. It earned him a beating.

He had a gambler's interest in horse racing, spending Saturday afternoons in front of a large television set while phoning in bets. On

Sunday mornings, he would walk the Airedales up to the paper shop in his pyjama jacket. He smoked heavily, ate his beef very rare and his bread brown, thinly sliced and with butter covering every single millimetre of the surface.

Mac Bennellick was the son of a Boer war veteran, who endured the siege of Ladysmith and spent much of his later life as a Devonshire postman. Born in Holsworthy, Mac moved to Rainham, where he met his wife Peggy, as a young man. In 1949 they had a son, Colin. Though initially a hairdresser, he had stopped wielding the scissors by the time the idea of a horse-racing partnership with Watkins came up, spending his days instead in his office below the hairdressing business. Like Watkins, Mac did very well from his Littlewoods pools concession.

Hemsley's daffodils did the trick. A few months later, the Watkins–Bennellick partnership bought a four-year-old hurdler called McCrimmon out of the Duke of Norfolk's Arundel stables for 800 guineas and started keeping him at Compton. Within five weeks of the start of their first season as racehorse owners in 1965, the young gelding had won a race for them – a novices' hurdle at Devon & Exeter worth all of £136. Before the end of September, he won again, at Folkestone.

After that, he was obliged to run in better races, against other horses who knew what it was like to visit the winners' enclosure. What is more, the handicaps in such races were often not wide enough to truly reflect the relative merit of all the runners. Like many other racehorses before and after him, McCrimmon turned out to be not quite good enough to excel in such circumstances and his form fell away. His novice owners' appetites had been whetted, however. As John Kempton recalls, 'They got more enthusiastic and said they would love to have a horse to run in the National.'

Chapter 6

MA TOPHAM AND THE BATTLE FOR AINTREE

It was one thing to have a horse to run in the Grand National, but would there be a Grand National for that horse to run in?

On 1 July 1964, the world of horse racing was stunned by a 255-word statement, issued from the racecourse offices at Aintree, which appeared to bring down the curtain on a 128-year-old sporting institution. Authored by Mirabel Topham, the domineering ex-actress who, as chairman of Tophams Limited, had managed the property since before the war, the statement disclosed that the company proposed applying for planning permission to develop the land. As a result it had been decided 'with the greatest regret' that the 1965 Grand National 'must be the last to be run at Aintree'.

At 72, and with no children of her own to take over, Mrs Topham was on the face of it only doing what owner-managers of other family businesses have done unremarked since the dawn of capitalism: cashing in on a lifetime's hard work and preparing to take things a bit easier. Not many family businesses are founded on events as popular as the Grand National, however. And a negotiator as dogged as Mrs Topham would undoubtedly have realised that securing clearance to build on the racecourse was key to obtaining an attractive valuation for the property, while also guaranteeing that the transaction would be big news. She had worked hard for her windfall though.

In 1946, she performed wonders to enable the first post-war Grand National to be staged within weeks of the US evacuation and was rewarded with a bumper crowd, estimated at up to 200,000. She brought motor-racing, including the British Grand Prix, to Aintree, overseeing construction of a £100,000 circuit that opened in 1954. She had a new horse-racing course with easier fences – intended to serve as an introduction to Aintree for young animals – built inside the Grand National circuit. She did all she could to augment the National's international appeal, through initiatives such as the Soviet horses and jockeys who took part in the race in 1961. And she strove to ensure that the race made appropriate allowance for changing public attitudes towards animal welfare while remaining steeplechasing's sternest test.

From her base at Paddock Lodge, a compact house on the Aintree property, she adopted a particularly hands-on management style, using an old-fashioned bell-pull to summon different members of staff. 'Nothing on the racecourse was ever done unless she said "Yes"', recalls Ossie Dale, who worked there for three decades, beginning in 1953, for the most part as stable manager. There is no doubt that her reputation for forcefulness was richly deserved and she kept a tight grasp on the company's purse-strings, but she was loyal to her core workforce and well capable of recognising when a more indulgent approach was warranted. For example, when Steve Westhead, Aintree's chief jump builder and, as such, an absolutely key member of staff, was faced with 'domestic trouble', she advised that the company 'stand by this man who had always been an extremely good and reliable worker.' She also made arrangements for him to have 'a hot meal cooked for him each day right through the winter.'

'We used to call her Ma Topham,' says Ossie Dale, recalling how much she appreciated his regular offerings of chrysanthemums grown in his greenhouse. She also seems to have had a genuine fondness for animals, raising pigs and cattle at Aintree, and coming out to give apples to the workhorses Dale used to mow the lawn in front of Paddock Lodge.

Not all Ma Topham's innovations worked out, however, and, try as she might, she just could not arrest the relentless slide in revenues which set in quickly once the euphoria that greeted the end of the war had ebbed away. In 1946, the year of that big post-war Grand National crowd, Tophams Limited enjoyed income of nearly a quarter of a million pounds (£241,760). By 1950, this had dipped below £200,000 and by 1956 – the year of the Devon Loch incident when the Queen Mother's horse inexplicably collapsed when about to win the National – below £120,000. Even after the race had started to be televised in 1960, income struggled to rise far beyond £130,000. These figures were generally enough to produce a profit – even after the payment of dividends to shareholders, of whom Mrs Topham was, of course, one – and to enable the family to live in some style. In addition to Paddock Lodge, Mrs Topham had a London house in a Nash terrace in Regent's Park and a holiday house on the Isle of Wight. Just five months before the bombshell announcement, the board of which she was part agreed to give her a 50 per cent increase in her salary and expenses.

The problem was, though, that the stands and other racecourse buildings were falling into poorer and poorer repair. No matter how brilliantly, or abstemiously, Mrs Topham had managed Aintree's day-to-day affairs, it was impossible to see how the property, as then configured, could generate the income-stream necessary to upgrade facilities to a level worthy of the world's best-known steeplechase. Yes, intervention by some outside agency, such as the newly established Horserace Betting Levy Board, charged with using money from betting to improve the sport, could conceivably have identified a way to fund the improvements. But the sums involved would have been huge and Aintree's autocratic boss was never likely to stand for the levels of interference such a scheme would entail, even supposing that the sport's notoriously fractious politics didn't themselves form an insuperable barrier.

By 1963, then, it seems Mrs Topham had had enough. She embarked on negotiations with a view to selling the property. As the individual responsible for every decision of note taken at Aintree for more than two decades, the Tophams chairman must plainly have realised that paving over the Grand National course would be controversial. But she seems genuinely to have imagined that the race could be staged elsewhere. She may even have felt that a commitment to do so would mitigate the outcry.

In early 1964, therefore, a subsidiary company of Tophams was formed for the purpose of acquiring 'the goodwill and title and all other rights of whatsoever nature attaching to the Grand National Steeple-chase.' By distancing the race from Aintree in this way, at least on paper, Mrs Topham was ensuring that a steeplechase called the Grand National could in theory be staged by another racecourse, while also creating a structure which ought to enable Tophams Limited shareholders such as herself to collect royalties wherever it was run. When the statement was released, on 1 July, it emphasised that efforts were being made to arrange for the Grand National to be 'transferred to a new locality and continue as one of the country's greatest sporting events.'

The choice of the property development company which would buy the 270-acre Aintree site for £900,000 once planning permission had been obtained was also interesting. Capital and Counties Property Company Limited was headed by Leslie Marler, a man well known in racing, as well as property, circles, who for a time owned O'Malley Point, the horse which finished third in the 1961 Grand National. The 1960 Hennessy Gold Cup, another of jump-racing's biggest prizes, adorned his family's dining-room table. He would go on to build a stud near his Buckinghamshire home.

Marler, who had been a classical scholar at St Paul's School, seems in some respects to have been cut from a similar cloth to Mrs Topham and the two are said to have hit it off. For one thing, he was just as inclined to grasp the bull by the horns as she was. In the First World War, he joined the mounted artillery at the ripe old age of 16 and ended up fighting with the White Russians. At one point in the Aintree talks, meanwhile, he is said to have been flying back from the Isle of Wight with Mrs Topham in a private aircraft when he took over the controls for a short period, in spite of having never piloted before. 'It's quite easy,' he remarked subsequently. 'It's just like riding a horse.'

Following announcement of the deal, he too sought to emphasise that the Grand National would go on. 'It's not a question of destroying the Grand National,' he said. 'You cannot destroy a great thing like the Grand National. I'm sure it will go on, but homes come first ... Once we start, there will be houses in six months.' A 1:2,500 scale, three-dimensional model, now in the possession of Aintree, gives a striking impression of what the Aintree Paddocks development, providing housing for 15,000 people and other amenities, would have looked like. A chain of geometrical white shapes, like a row of teeth, stretches the better part of a mile from the site of the old grandstands to Becher's Brook, the course's most famous fence. Look closely and you see a scattering of hexagonal towers, of varying heights. Somewhere near the location of fence number 12 is a cog-shaped school.

Marler sailed off with members of his family within hours of the announcement on a 22-day cruise along the Norwegian coast aboard the Royal Mail liner *Andes*. His daughter remembers the crew throwing oranges to children in small rowing boats who had never seen them before. 'They were munching them skin and all,' she says.

Immediate reaction to the deal was by no means universally negative. A chronic land shortage and the need to replace tens of thousands of slum dwellings meant that housing was always high on the political agenda in Liverpool. Even those who valued the National often felt that new homes had to take precedence. 'Let's have the houses not the horses,' said Norman Pannell, a Conservative MP with an ear for a soundbite. 'I wish they could still jump and race round the houses,' said Labour MP Sir Arthur Irvine less succinctly. 'But the housing situation in Liverpool is so serious and the need for housing so intense that one welcomes news that land on a large scale is becoming available for a major social purpose.'

Liverpool was not the only city where land was in high demand, clouding the future of other urban racecourses. Manchester racecourse had been closed in November 1963 and Birmingham would follow, making room for accommodation for 7,500 people, in June 1965. Just a week after the Aintree announcement, Home Secretary Henry Brooke told MPs that Bogside racecourse at Irvine in Scotland was one of four to have been informed by turf authorities that they would be allocated no fixtures after the following year. This forced the removal, from 1966, of the Scottish Grand National to Ayr.

The stock market welcomed Capital and Counties' prospective Aintree takeover, with the shares climbing 4½d on the day, adding over £740,000 to the company's market value. By the time of an emergency Tophams board meeting on 15 July 1964, Mrs Topham had received many letters 'and only a few begging and abusive ones.' Even the Aintree staff were said to have taken the news in an understanding way. By mid-October, however, three key members of staff had handed in their notice and left the company.

The most important reaction to Mrs Topham's announcement, though, was negative. It came from the seventh Earl of Sefton, whose family had owned Aintree for 750 years until he sold it to Tophams in 1949 for £275,000, under a mortgage paid off in March 1963. Lord Sefton said he hated the prospect of no racing at Aintree and thought it an 'appalling loss' to Liverpool. He then promptly went to the High Court and obtained a temporary order restraining Tophams from selling the land for any purpose other than horse racing and agriculture.

The court hearing proper, before Mr Justice Stamp, began on 2 October, in the midst of a general election campaign that was to see

Labour returned to power after 13 years in opposition, but with a majority of only four. The legal battle would not be resolved until the eve of the next general election, at which pipe-smoking Prime Minister Harold Wilson cemented his hold on 10 Downing Street, in March 1966. Throughout this period – and, as it turned out, for several years thereafter – the future of the Grand National was in doubt.

It was – and is – tempting to see this battle for Aintree through the prism of class conflict: hereditary peer and former Lord-in-Waiting to Edward VIII challenges self-made entrepreneur over a modest but irreplaceable piece of the national heritage. And the century-old National Hunt Committee and 200-year old Jockey Club – and hence the aristocrats and military types who populated them – were indeed about to see their power over the sport diluted.

The main threat to their pre-eminence, however, was not Mrs Topham – who, as head of a family which had managed Liverpool racecourse for more than a century was, in her way, as much of a dynast as some of them. She was in any case seeking a golden goodbye from the sport rather than more control. No, the emerging power in racing's land was the Levy Board and the trump-card in its possession was oodles of cold, hard cash, collected from punters who, since 1961, had been pouring into betting-shops as well as through turnstiles. According to Martin Crawshay, who spent 28 years with the body until 1991, the Levy Board 'could, if it wished, control the sport absolutely'. It was not until the Labour appointee George Wigg replaced Lord Harding as chairman in 1967 that this became most strikingly apparent. In the body's early years, in Crawshay's words, the 'grandees of the Jockey Club ... while much welcoming the establishment of the Levy were reluctant to see the power of expenditure ... in hands other than their own.'

The case hinged on interpretation of a covenant in the 1949 agreement under which Lord Sefton had sold Aintree to Tophams. Lord Sefton argued that the Capital and Counties deal was in breach of this since it restricted use of the land, in his lifetime, to horse racing or agriculture.

In his evidence, the peer talked about a meeting in December 1963, when Mrs Topham 'with tears in her eyes' told him that expenditure was such that she could not carry on and asked to be released from the covenant. She had breathed 'not a word' about negotiations with Capital and Counties.

He suggested that £2 million might be needed to bring course facilities up to scratch, an assessment with which Mrs Topham later concurred. 'The stands are getting older and older and it is looking very disreputable, despite all the money we have spent,' she told the court.

On 30 October, Mr Justice Stamp ruled in favour of Lord Sefton. Tophams' arrangement with Capital and Counties was concluded, he said, 'without regard to Tophams' legal or moral obligations to Lord Sefton. Tardily, Mrs Topham asserted to Lord Sefton that the covenants were no longer reasonable, but did not tell him that her company had concluded an agreement for sale.' Tophams, he went on, had 'failed to satisfy me that racing cannot profitably be carried on at Aintree.'

Round one, then, to Lord Sefton, but Mrs Topham and her old flying partner Leslie Marler retained a right of appeal. Would they choose to exercise it? Reporters inquiring on the day of the judgement were told the Tophams chairman was not available to comment. A three-hour board meeting at Paddock Lodge on 28 November left the question unresolved, with pressing matters including the death of a staff member called W. Taylor, crushed against a wall by a lorry when loading grain. Attitudes in the racing industry seemed to be hardening, however, with Major W. D. Gibson, acting senior steward of the National Hunt Committee, stating that no 'substitute Grand National' would be allowed.

It was not until 9 January 1965 – at a meeting at which they also received the unwelcome news that the AA was proposing to charge 13 guineas for the erection of 84 route-signs for Aintree's spring meeting – that Mrs Topham and her fellow directors agreed 'unanimously' to appeal.

By this time, owners had flocked to enter eligible horses in the race, set for 27 March, which many expected would indeed be the last Grand National at Aintree and conceivably the last anywhere. A bumper 112 entries had been received by the deadline on 5 January. 'Owners were buying horses just to run in the last National,' says John Leech, a jockey who rode in the race.

At their meeting, the Tophams directors decided against incorporating the phrase 'last chance' into that year's Grand National posters. Better, they thought, that the posters be 'fly-stuck' nearer the time.

Chapter 7

THE ROAD TO DONCASTER

The uncertainty over the Grand National was also colouring Foinavon's future. Part of the importance of that Baldoyle race which he had crashed out of so disappointingly was that it offered the winner a ticket to the great Aintree spectacular. On the morning of the race, indeed, Foinavon was described in the press as 'Tom Dreaper's Grand National hope'.

Under normal circumstances, there would have been other opportunities for the horse to redeem himself. The closing date for the 1965 Grand National, however, fell just three days after the Baldoyle meeting on 5 January. So he had blown his chance of lining up that year in the world's most famous steeplechase. And with Mrs Topham still intent on selling Aintree for housing, that opportunity might never come again. That fall at Baldoyle, in other words, had cost the horse his one and only chance of running in a Liverpool Grand National – or so it would have seemed at the time.

Given this and the questionable attitude that Foinavon's subsequent grass-cropping antics had made manifest, it would have been surprising if Tom Dreaper – though still sick with an infection that had kept him away from Arkle's victory in the 1964 Hennessy Gold Cup at Newbury in December – had not started reviewing Foinavon's future at Greenogue. This is even though the great trainer had 'always said', according to jockey Peter McLoughlin, that the horse 'could win an English Grand National', one of the few races to elude him throughout his glittering career.

For the time being, though, there was still a heavy Irish racing schedule to negotiate. On 9 January, McLoughlin had a good crack at maintaining his 100 per cent winning record on the horse in another three-mile chase at Naas. Running on heavy ground, at a meeting where the Dreaper team notched two other winners, Foinavon fell for the second week in a row. The *Irish Field*, though, put a favourable gloss on events, noting, 'There might have been a third success for our top National Hunt trainer if Foinavon had not tumbled at the last in the Boyne Handicap Chase when he was coming storming along to challenge the ultimate winner Cavendish.' McLoughlin concurs with this account. 'If he had landed running, I think he would have won,' he says.

A week later, on the day that Pat Taaffe collected his fifth consecutive Irish jockeys' title, the pair were in action again, this time at Leopardstown. For the third time in four races, Foinavon started as favourite (at 5/2 on this occasion). However, once again, he disappointed, with the *Irish Field* recording that he was 'well beaten when he was brought down at the last fence.' McLoughlin remembers seeing a loose horse on the ground, presumably Snow Trix, the only faller. 'I decided I wanted him to go left; he decided right,' he says succinctly. 'I would have said "unseated rider".'

Expectations were commensurately lower three weeks later when, after a period of snow and ice in Ireland, Foinavon next ventured on to a racecourse. The Foxrock Cup on 6 February would be his sixth race at Leopardstown and he had yet to finish in the first three. He was up against Cavendish, the victor when he fell at Naas in January. What is more, he would be partnered by another new jockey, Sean Barker, who had yet to win a steeplechase. The portents, then, did not look good. This, though, was another of those races that would have a pivotal influence on Foinavon's eccentric path through life.

Jockey Barker, who would go on to finish second in the 1970 Grand National and third in 1972, received much of the credit as Foinavon, an 8/1 shot, got up to overhaul Quintin Bay in the last few strides of the course's stiff uphill finishing stretch to win by a neck. This after hot favourite Cavendish had fallen at the second fence. 'The winner … was magnificently ridden by 29-year-old Sean Barker,' wrote 'Burnaby' in the *Irish Field*. 'He displayed tremendous dash and strength all the way through the race. In spite of the fact that Foinavon was slightly outjumped by Quintin Bay at many of the fences, Barker gave his mount plenty of encouragement and set his mount at his fences with the utmost bravery.' The third horse, Zonda, trailed in 15 lengths behind.

The win completed a memorable week for stable lad Vincent Slevin, whose other two horses, Fort Leney and Dicky May, had both won at Gowran Park two days' before. 'When he paid me, my boss said, "My gosh, you had a bloody good week",' Slevin still remembered 46 years later. More significantly as it turned out, the victory did qualify Foinavon to run in a future Grand National. The credential would only count for anything, however, if the race continued beyond 1965 – and at that stage, 49 days before that year's field was due to gather in Liverpool, it still looked like it might not.

Exactly a month later – and a week after Foinavon had reverted to type by falling in another Leopardstown chase, albeit under a lot more weight than in his winning run – Mrs Topham gave a firm indication that she was considering bowing to pressure by allowing racing to continue at Aintree for one more year. Meeting at Paddock Lodge on 6 March, the Tophams' board was informed by the chairman of various exchanges on the subject between herself and the turf authorities. These followed advice to Mrs Topham to the effect that 'it might be unwise to leave the course derelict for a long time pending planning permission.' It was agreed that a further board meeting would be called in due course to make a decision.

Grand National day dawned on 27 March with the future of the race still uncertain. But racing fans would have been able to reflect that evening that if this was to be the last Grand National, or the last to be run at Aintree, then at least this great national institution had gone out with some style.

For one thing, there was a royal presence, with noted racing enthusiast the Queen Mother arriving to see her horse, The Rip, perform. She was accompanied by Princess Margaret, resplendent in a mohair tweed coat in what the local paper described as 'overchecked aquamarine'. There was a good crowd, with an estimated 75,000 people on the course by 3pm. This in spite of the absence of 20,000 Liverpool fans, on a day trip to Birmingham to watch their team play Chelsea in the semi-final of the FA Cup. Aer Lingus were said to have operated five extra services. Even the railways behaved, with Princess Margaret's train – 'one of the five Aintree Specials from Euston' – pulling into platform three of nearby Sefton Arms station a mere two minutes late. There was record prize money of more than £22,000. Finally, the race was an absolute corker, with Jay Trump from the United States just getting the better of the popular Scottish horse Freddie, his nostrils 'inflamed like the inside of anemones', after a hard-fought duel along Aintree's excruciating run-in. The Rip was far from disgraced in seventh place. Once the bean-counters had done their work, it was discovered that takings were similar to 1958 levels, though expenses were, of course, higher.

By the week after the race, with Tophams' appeal against Mr Justice Stamp's judgement in favour of Lord Sefton soon to be heard, word of a possible temporary reprieve for the racecourse was spreading, with Mrs Topham acting as conduit. The Tophams' chairman showed little originality in pinning the blame for the imminent U-turn on the slow pace of English justice. 'Court proceedings inevitably take a long time,' she told the *Illustrated London News*. 'If there are enough delays, we may well see another Grand National at Aintree next year.'

In fact, Lord Justices Sellers, Harman and Russell reached their conclusions with commendable speed and on 28 May the appeal was dismissed. By this time Foinavon had been sold to a well-known horse dealer who lived near Clonsilla, west of Dublin, called Jack White.

With his trilby, his friendly demeanour and his raconteur's gift, White was an Irish horseman out of central casting. He dealt in showjumpers as well as racehorses, maintained a network of contacts from Scandinavia to Italy and had a reputation for making sure that his friends struck good bargains as opposed to grasping every penny of profit for himself. He lived, slept and breathed horses. 'When I married him, my only holiday would be to Cheltenham races or Doncaster sales,' says Aline, his widow. 'He was not a wealthy man, but very generous.'

White would have been one of the first men in Ireland to know that the 1966 Grand National would probably be run at Aintree after all. What is more, he would have recognised the consequences for the marketability of horses, such as Foinavon, with a qualification to run in the race – even if they had no chance of winning. Some time in April he paid the Duchess of Westminster £1,800, by no means a trifling sum, for her one-paced, seven-year-old gelding. On 20 April, the day after Tom Dreaper had saddled his sixth consecutive Irish Grand National winner, Foinavon ran in White's name, for the one and only time, at Fairyhouse. He finished unplaced.

White was not the only man who had tried to buy Foinavon. His first jockey, Tony Cameron, had approached the duchess after witnessing a particularly unfruitful visit to Leopardstown. 'I distinctly remember him coming up to the last fence and refusing,' Cameron says. 'He put his shoulder to the fence and just rolled over gently. I swear he did it on purpose. I have never seen another horse fall on purpose.' Cameron put it to the duchess that, while he was clearly not enjoying his racing, he was a very clever horse and might make a three-day eventer. He never heard back from her.

By the time of the Doncaster bloodstock sales in October 1965, the future of the Grand National was settled – for one more year. On 5 June, the Tophams board decided to press ahead and apply for four fixtures in 1965/66, culminating with a Grand National meeting in March. News of the move broke two and a half weeks later on 22 June. 'Grand National is on next year,' announced the *Liverpool Daily Post* the following morning. 'But Mrs Topham warns: it will be the last.'

Within a month, the Mistress of Aintree had underlined her determination to pursue her legal battle with Lord Sefton to the bitter end, as Tophams decided to take the case to the House of Lords. With costs to date estimated at £20,000, this was a brave, or a foolhardy, move. The company also felt duty-bound to put in finally for planning permission.

Nonetheless, as John Kempton set off for South Yorkshire on a fine autumn day, with a remit to find his new owners their Grand National horse, he knew that they would get at least one opportunity – but perhaps only one – to fulfil their dream. By the time he came home, he had handed over the largest sum he would pay for a horse in his career as a trainer.

Chapter 8

HELLO SUSIE

It was Lot 59 in the catalogue that had caught John Kempton's attention. At seven, the dark brown gelding was still young for a steeplechaser and might be expected to have plenty of races left in him. His sire was Vulgan, whose reputation as a stallion was by then firmly established. And for most of his life, he had had just one considerate owner, Anne, Duchess of Westminster, known for the sensitive handling of her racehorses. Think of the sales ring as a used-car dealership, with many potential pitfalls awaiting the buyer; the duchess's prominence on Foinavon's curriculum vitae was like seeing an AA stamp of approval on the vehicle Kempton had his eye on.

The key phrase that jumped out at him, though, was 'qualified for the Grand National'. With just five months to go before the 1966 race, which was again potentially the last Grand National, he needed an eligible horse if his enthusiastic new owners, Cyril Watkins and Mac Bennellick, were to have the best chance possible of fulfilling their Aintree ambition. That battling Leopardstown victory in February 1965 had conferred this eligibility on Foinavon.

'He was very clean on the legs,' Kempton recalls, a big plus-point in a steeplechaser, whose limbs come in for fearful punishment during the course of a long career. The young trainer also noted that the horse 'had a lovely big heavy shoulder to him'. He saw at once, however, that he was 'a bit herring-gutted', an evocative term used to describe horses whose belly has a pronounced upward slope from front to back. The shape of such animals could make them prone to slipping saddles, not a problem any jockey would wish to contend with while negotiating steeplechase fences.

There was also the question of price, which the 'Grand National-qualified' tag was bound to inflate. 'We only really had about £2,000 to spend,' says Kempton. So it came as a relief when he was able to snap up the horse for 2,000 guineas (£2,100). This was many times less than the sums for which proven Grand National horses such as Anglo and Rutherfords would be sold in subsequent years, but still at least double what Kempton and his owners were in the habit of paying for their racehorses.

The long journey back to the Berkshire Downs transported Foinavon from the Manchester United of the horse-racing world, where he had resided up to that point, to the equivalent of local club Reading, then a fair-to-middling side in the old English Third Division. He immediately found himself expected to work a lot harder than under Tom Dreaper's minimalist regime. Regular downland hacks were a feature of life for all the Kemptons' horses, but Foinavon clocked up more miles than his stablemates, as head lad Colin Hemsley and his staff tried to build up his stamina with Aintree in mind. There were hours and hours of monotonous schooling on the end of a rope over practice fences, with a view to correcting any vices in his jumping technique that might explain why he had fallen so much in his final months in Ireland. Kempton took him out hunting too, as he endeavoured as quickly as possible to get to know the horse he now expected to ride in his third Grand National. 'I didn't just toddle around,' Kempton says. 'I'd pop him over everything that was available.'

Joy Douglas, the £5-a-week stable girl who rode Foinavon out most days in his first year at the yard, often wearing a pink woolly hat and old-fashioned jodhpurs, remembers him as a good-natured and happy horse. 'We used to tickle him behind the saddle and he would try to buck you off,' she says. 'I think we all gave them far too many peppermints and Polos.'

There was one problem, however: the newcomer was at first reluctant to eat up his regular feed. Fortunately, a solution was close to hand.

Susie was a ruthlessly single-minded white nanny goat which the Kemptons had bought from a roadside verge near Crewkerne in Somerset on the way back from one of their summer sorties to the racecourses at Newton Abbot and Devon & Exeter where the season traditionally got under way. There was a school of thought in racing to the effect that goats made good companions for horses. Irish jockey Bobby Beasley's first Grand National mount, Sandy Jane II, was 'inseparable' from her cloven-hoofed friend. After the race, he recalls seeing her lying flat out in her box while the goat licked her stomach scratched 'red raw' by the Aintree fences. The Fossa, a Worcestershire-based racehorse whom Foinavon would run against at Liverpool and elsewhere, was another who travelled with a nanny goat. Her name was Amelia.

Susie, whose obsession was eating, was bought initially to accompany Seas End, the Kemptons' first Grand National horse. This worked well enough for a time, until the horse – who otherwise was so good-natured he used to stroll up to the side-door of the Kemptons' bungalow to ask for tea and biscuits from them – started chasing her away. When Foinavon arrived in Berkshire without his appetite, it was decided to switch Susie to this new partner to encourage him to eat up. Thereafter they went everywhere together. 'He was quite possessive over having her,' Kempton says. 'It wasn't just a little gimmick; it did seem to work.'

The relationship had its ups and downs, however – particularly at feeding times, which in a way was the whole point. 'That was the dangerous time,' says Clifford Booth, who worked as a stable lad at Compton. He describes how the two animals would stand in different corners of the stable eyeing each other as he put the feed in the manger, the horse with its ears flat against its skull in a classic posture of aggression. Very soon, the goat would run out of patience and race for the manger, whereupon Foinavon would charge across, grab her by the neck and throw her out of the way. Woe betide anyone who hadn't exited the stable by the time this happened.

The odd couple also caused Booth the occasional difficulty at race-meetings. The pair had to be unloaded together from the horsebox, he recalls, otherwise the goat would panic. Yet they would often be fighting as they got off. If, as sometimes happened, the upshot of this was that they tore off in opposite directions, Booth would have to let one of them go. 'The thing is,' he says, 'if you let the goat go, she was harder to catch, so I used to let Foinavon go. I let Foinavon go at Liverpool.'

There was one other element in this farmyard soap opera: the horses were all greedy for the goat's milk, even though Booth thinks it tended to make their legs swell up. 'We used to milk the goat into a bucket and take it around and they would all drink it,' he says. The horses' craving was particularly useful after their six-week summer break, for which they were turned out unshod. When the time came to recapture them and put them back into training, a bucket of goat's milk would bring them all tearing obediently over to be caught.

About ten weeks after Foinavon's arrival at Chatham Stables, on New Year's Day 1966, Kempton rode him in a race for the first time. It was a three-mile chase at Newbury, their local course, and a horse called Rondetto, who had run well in the 1965 Grand National, was the red-hot favourite. Predictably enough, in his first race for more than eight months, Foinavon was in the rear from beginning to end and plodded past the post fourth and last. But he had stayed on his feet, as he did again the following month over some of the stiffest fences outside Aintree – at Kempton Park, in Sunbury-on-Thames near London.

Foinavon, though, wasn't the only member of the partnership who had work to do if he was to be ready for the Grand National at Liverpool on 26 March. As a six-footer, Kempton was unusually tall for a jockey. Though rake-thin, this meant that when riding in handicaps against rival horses with better records, he might exceed the weight that his mount had been allotted, hence reducing their chances of a good result. In his first two outings with Foinavon, he was able to carry over 11 stone, which was not a problem for him. At Aintree, he would need to get down to as close to 10 stone as he could manage. This presented a major challenge.

Chapter 9

WASTED

The 1960s was the decade when Twiggy launched a million diets. But not even the most devoted mimic of the waif-like teenage model could have monitored her own weight more meticulously than Britain's 500 or so jockeys.

First thing in the morning – and often last thing at night too – these skinny men would stumble across their landings to consult an item of equipment that regulated their lives as rigidly as a factory clock: their bathroom scales. On race-days, what the dial told them would often determine how they spent the balance of the morning so as to be able to ride at the correct weight that afternoon. Since, unlike most Twiggy lookalikes, jockeys had to retain enough strength to control a skittish half-tonne animal galloping at high speed, many of them would eat a relatively hearty evening meal. This meant it was common practice for jockeys to wake two or three pounds heavier than their lightest comfortable riding weight. Hence, too, the first thing most of them would do on arriving at the racecourse was stand on the main scales. 'The scales become everything to you,' says Brough Scott, the jockey-turned-journalist. There is a reason why the place jockeys go to get ready is called the weighing-room.

These spare, flinty individuals had, in essence, four options for shedding excess pounds. They could exercise, they could starve, they could sweat or they could resort to pharmacological assistance. In practice, many jockeys would work a combination of these methods into their daily routines.

Josh Gifford, the talented and determined Sussex-based rider who was champion jump jockey four times in the 1960s, favoured exercise. 'I did a lot of running and sweating,' he told me. 'We had to put a plastic sweatsuit on go running and running and running and come back and jump in a hot bath.' Gifford only turned to so-called 'pee-pills' once – 'I nearly fell off.' Then again, he had a couple of important things going for him. First, as one of the many National Hunt jockeys who started their careers on the flat, he was relatively light to begin with. Second, he was working for a trainer – Captain Ryan Price – who, in this respect at least, was prepared to be accommodating. 'I used to say, "I can do 10st 3lb" and the old man used to say, "If they can't win with 10st 3lb they are not going to win with 10st,"' Gifford recalled. 'Nine times out of ten' he wouldn't mind putting up 3lb overweight.

Gifford's great friend and rival Terry Biddlecombe, however, battled hard with weight throughout his career. Such a well-known figure did the blond West Countryman become in the Turkish baths which could still be found in many British cities at this time that when television's *This is Your Life!* decided to feature him, host Eamonn Andrews conducted the obligatory ambush at the Savoy Baths in London's Jermyn Street. According to Biddlecombe, who as the clock ticked down towards the 1966 Grand National was well set to retain the jockeys' title he first won in 1964/65, another Turkish baths in Gloucester 'almost became my second home'. After a cup of tea, he would get to the baths at 7am and promptly weigh himself. He reckoned to be able to lose up to 6 or 7lb in a couple of hours. 'If I had not stuck rigidly to my routine at the baths I would never have been able to carry on riding,' he said.

The Savoy Baths, equipped with cubicles with bunk beds inside, were even sometimes used by jockeys as a *de facto* guest house. '£1.50 – cheapest bed in London,' recalls Richard Pitman, the jockey-turned-broadcaster. Pat Buckley, another jockey, once spent from Thursday evening until Saturday morning in the baths, losing 12lb in the process. He then went to Sandown Park in suburban Esher and got the better of the great Mill House in the big race on a horse carrying a minuscule 9st 7lb. 'So severely had he been forced to fast,' according to Reg Green, best known as a Grand National historian, that Buckley 'could hardly stand to receive his trophy from the Queen Mother.'

These unorthodox sleeping arrangements did lead to the occasional tense moment between the bristlingly heterosexual jockeys and the Savoy's many gay customers. Mostly, however, the two groups contrived to ignore each other.

Biddlecombe has commented on the 'quite awful' smell if you were late getting into the hot rooms in the morning. 'So many people congregated down there during the night that the aroma of stale sweat went up your nose and into your mouth so that you could taste it,' he added. Dave Dick, the rider who won the sensational 1956 Grand National, taking advantage of Devon Loch's collapse, used to take matters into his own hands, scrubbing out the affected rooms with Dettol – no doubt getting rid of another unwanted pound or two in the process.

Biddlecombe also had his own personal sweatbox, heated by 150-watt bulbs with bamboo filaments, that had been sold to him by Dick for £25. He used to sit in the box in a deckchair wearing goggles, suede shoes and a sweatsuit. 'I had an old carpet on the floor to absorb some of the sweat,' he recalled. 'I had a little bowl in the box that I used to step into at intervals, pull the leg of my sweatsuit away from my leg and let the water pour out. It was just like turning on a tap.' Other jockeys even sweated in their sleep, retiring to bed clad in pyjamas and plastic Stephanie Bowman sweatsuits with a tracksuit as the top layer. When they woke in the middle of the night, perspiration would bucket off them.

Part of the attraction of the baths, as opposed to other weight-loss methods, was their social side. This was often accentuated by the presence of alcohol, which was in turn justified by the highly questionable notion that consumption of champagne in particular helped you sweat. Biddlecombe recounts how at 9.30am in the Gloucester baths he would order 'the usual'. This consisted of a Worthington E beer and a port and Babycham. 'I would drink exactly half the beer before going back into the baths. Then I would come out and finish it.' He would sip the port and Babycham driving to the races in his car. If drinking did serve a genuinely useful function in all of this, it was probably to keep up morale during what could be a tedious and uncomfortable process, as well as providing an incentive to do another stint in the hot room. Jockey Barry Brogan acknowledges regularly attending the Warrender Turkish Baths in Edinburgh with champagne and a quart bottle of brandy. 'The champagne helped me sweat and the brandy was for [a tiny masseur called] Jimmy. I would get him so utterly drunk that he couldn't stand on his feet, and I would laugh myself silly just watching him swaying and swerving, then falling flat across the naked customers he was supposed to be massaging. Jimmy's performances certainly made the baths a lot more tolerable for me.'

Brogan talks of regularly not eating 'a crumb' for up to five days, but Biddlecombe generally preferred to avoid fasting. 'I tried special diets and low-calorie programmes but I used to get so depressed that I preferred the rigours of wasting,' he remembered. There were times, though, when even the champion jockey had no choice but to starve himself. 'If I was really going light, I'd have a steak and a bit of salad. I'd chew the steak and spit it out.'

The so-called 'pee pills' alluded to by Gifford were another weapon in jockeys' weight-reduction armoury at the time. The diuretic of choice was called Lasix, better known in more recent years in racing circles as a means of preventing horses from bleeding through the nose during racing. The drug, whose generic name is furosemide, prevents the body from absorbing too much salt and is used in the treatment of high blood pressure and abnormal fluid retention, or edema.

Unpredictability is and was the norm in jumps racing. So there would have been moments in many jockeys' careers when these pills would have come in extremely useful. A last-minute call to ride at light weight at a course several hours' drive away might be one of them. A jockey in this position would have no time to sweat, starve or run an excess pound or two away. But he could pop a pill, though it would mean more than the ideal number of stops en route.

A few jockeys resorted to pee pills much more regularly than this. Barry Brogan, a heavy drinker, was 'gulping Lasix pills by the handful' to try to keep his weight down. 'They left me limp and weak,' he remembered. 'I had to follow up with bottles and bottles of potassium tablets to restore the salt balance.' Richard Pitman's first venture with Lasix forced him to make seven stops in 60 miles 'some of them in a state of panic'. He lost 11lb, felt like 'death warmed up,' but rode two winners. Side-effects included being able to hear his own voice inside his head 'as if it were a cave' and cramp, an affliction unpleasant enough at any time, but, you would think, potentially disastrous if it struck on the approach to a steeplechase fence. 'I tried to keep Lasix as a last resort,' he concludes. 'But, like all other medicines, in the end one pill would not even make my eyes water.'

Laxatives were also very much part of the weighing-room scene in 1966, whether swallowed as 'physic pills' or in chocolate form, sometimes as a chocolate sandwich. According to Pitman, both were taken a day ahead of the race, necessitated many nocturnal toilet visits and were 'unpleasant but effective'.

Still more drastic remedies were available for occasions when the target weight was abnormally low, or the pounds proved impossible to shift. Brogan's 'favourite trick' was to weigh out without the pad that rests under the saddle. In June 1965, meanwhile, Biddlecombe slimmed down to a svelte 9st 12lb after enduring an 'irrigation' – a process involving a funnel, a nurse with a cigarette in her mouth and a quantity of soapy water. 'I said, "It's going to come out of my throat in a minute", Biddlecombe recalls. 'That was hard, very hard.' In spite of his ordeal, he could only finish sixth.

Cursed with a sweet tooth, John Kempton had taken his fair share of tablets and pounded the Berkshire lanes extensively over the years, donning his plastic suit, getting dropped off a dozen miles from the family bungalow and running back. It was typical of his maverick approach to racing though that, with the Grand National approaching, he alighted upon a novel way of attempting to take the drudgery out of wasting.

Kempton had recently taken up with his future wife, Patricia, and her mother had turned to a hypnotist to try to wean her off smoking. He now decided to ask the hypnotist, a Gloucester-based practitioner called Henry Blythe, if he could help him to control his weight. Blythe duly set the jockey/trainer a target of shedding 10lb before the big race at Aintree on 26 March. This would have enabled him to clamber aboard Foinavon at 10st 2lb, around the weight he regularly attained in the summer. Unfortunately, Blythe had a business trip planned and could manage only two consultations before departing for Scotland. In his absence, he left his client a record of his voice, with instructions to play it whenever his craving for sweets came back, while concentrating on his picture. 'It may not work,' a sceptical Kempton told a newspaper reporter at the time. 'I don't know if I am a good subject for this sort of thing, but I'm willing to give it a try.'

The treatment may have had some effect, with Kempton riding as light as 10st 7lb that spring. But Foinavon didn't make it to Liverpool. With his preparations disrupted by wet weather and performances far from breathtaking when he did run, the horse was eventually withdrawn from another huge National field. In the event, 47 runners lined up and hared away towards the Melling Road. The race was won by a striking chestnut outsider called Anglo, with the unfortunate Freddie again second. The going was so soft it was described to me by the winning jockey Tim Norman as 'up to your eyebrows'.

The gold trophy was duly presented to Stuart Levy, the winning owner, whose company, Anglo-Amalgamated, produced the Carry On films, and whose business partner, Nat Cohen, had won the 1962 National with Kilmore. The race came less than a week after the theft of football's World Cup, making security of what might have been the last Grand National trophy a concern as the big day approached. The *Liverpool Daily Post* reported that a guard from a national security firm and 12 'hand-picked heavyweight shop assistants' were making sure that it didn't disappear. One member of staff at the city centre jeweller's where it was on display was said to be a weightlifter and another a ju-jitsu expert.

Chapter 10

1966 AND ALL THAT

A striking black-and-white photograph captures the brooding atmosphere that hung over Liverpool that frigid, grey spring meeting. It is taken at The Chair, the biggest fence on the Grand National course. But it could be the scene after a mortar has landed. Three figures in white riding breeches catch the eye. Two are slumped, dazed, on the ground among dislodged spruce boughs. The other is balanced hopelessly on one leg while clinging with his left hand to one rein of the black horse he has just toppled from – and which he now has his back to. Industrial buildings populate the background. Though, in reality, 50,000 people and 46 more horses are not far out of camera-shot, these might be the last four creatures on earth.

A second or two earlier, as Jeremy Speid-Soote, the man on one leg, told me, his mount – a 100/1 outsider called Black Spot – had landed on top of the fence which, at 5ft 2in high and 3ft 9in wide, and guarded on the take-off side by a 6-foot wide open ditch, was as forbidding an obstacle as you could encounter on an English racecourse. This had happened, he said, because, on approaching the fence, Black Spot had seen another horse stuck in the ditch and had consequently taken off from too far away. This marooned animal was Game Purston, the mount of Paddy Cowley, the jockey sprawled in the foreground of the photograph. Game Purston had breasted the fence, but it had stopped him dead and he crumpled back into the ditch, leaving Cowley to soar over the barrier without him and crash to earth. Another jockey, Ken White – who had ridden Game Purston to victory in a big race at Haydock the previous year, but was out of action recovering from a fractured skull – had brought his wife of four days to Liverpool to round off a short Lake District honeymoon. By chance, they had decided to watch the race from a vantage-point beside the fence. It was White who ended up catching the trapped horse and leading him out of the side of the ditch in his jacket and tie.

Just after the camera-shutter clicked, more drama: Speid-Soote heard 'this clatter and this crash, and I saw this poor bloody horse … It had got the ring of its bit stuck over one of these bloody great stakes that stick up in the middle of the fence.' This was Fujino-O, the mount of top rider Jeff King, and the first Japanese horse to run in the Grand National, his bridle festooned with good-luck charms. 'He was left hanging there,' King remembers. 'His feet didn't even touch the ground because it was such a deep ditch in those days. I leaned up his neck and pulled the ring off and he fell down into the ditch.' He too was eventually led out and ran another race at Folkestone just 11 days later.

Aintree's fate at that time was hanging in the balance every bit as much as Fujino-O's in those moments before King freed him. There was a sense about the place that something was about to happen. But what? One experienced local reporter described the atmosphere throughout the three-day meeting as 'that of a spy story', with knots of newsmen huddled in hopeful expectation at strategic points. The fact that these were also the final days of a general election campaign called early by Prime Minister Harold Wilson in a bid to strengthen his hold on power might have added to the intrigue. Not even the presence of Paul McCartney, awarded the MBE with his fellow Beatles by Wilson the previous summer, could significantly change the mood. McCartney did, though, have cause to twist and shout before the afternoon was over: his father's horse Drake's Drum won the race before the National in a tight finish.

Four days after the crowds had squelched their way home, and on the eve of polling day, something did happen: the Law Lords ruled in favour of Mirabel Topham. 'Aintree Can Be Sold For Housing', announced the *Liverpool Echo*. 'Earl of Sefton faces £30,000 bill for costs.'

If you had walked past that headline on a news-vendor's stand, you would probably have assumed that the game was up; that Aintree had staged its last Grand National and that, if the 1967 race was held at all, it would be at Ascot or Doncaster. In fact, that particular caravan had moved on. Over the 21 months that Liverpool racecourse's future had been officially in question, it had become clear to those with some insight into the matter that the planning authorities almost certainly would not allow housing to be built there. Now the talk was of the need to preserve Aintree as a public space and, in particular, of a scheme for a £4 million sports centre to provide local people with a year-round amenity without condemning the race. Sports minister Denis Howell, campaigning in Birmingham, reacted to the judgement by proclaiming that 'the future of Aintree is more a planning matter than a legal question' and described plans submitted to him as 'extremely imaginative and realistic'. Even Mrs Topham referred to the Law Lords' decision, much in the manner of a cricket captain thwarted by stout resistance from the opposition's tail-end charlies, only as 'a moral victory'. That did not prevent a fellow director from stating, at an April Fools' day meeting of the Tophams board, held as the sweeping extent of Mr Wilson's election victory was becoming clear, that 'thanks and congratulations should go to Mrs Topham for the hard work she had put in on the legal matter which had resulted in our triumph.' The tone of this reminds me irresistibly of the portrayal of another Mrs T and her Cabinet in the *Spitting Image* satirical puppet show of the 1980s and 1990s.

There was just one small problem: the lack of £4 million – a detail that ensured the future of the racecourse remained as much a matter for conjecture after the Law Lords' pronouncement as it was before.

By late May, it was confirmed that planning permission for the original scheme had indeed been refused. Relations between Mrs Topham and Leslie Marler had in any case been subjected to strain by a letter to *The Times* in which the Capital and Counties boss appeared to be trying to position the company for a role in whatever new scheme took shape. 'I think it quite possible that a first-class racecourse could be restored and the area generally developed, both as a centre of recreation and for housing and its various ancillary usages,' Marler wrote. 'I believe that private enterprise is much more likely to give a lead in bringing this about than any amount of government talk.' The letter was branded 'extraordinary' by Mrs Topham and her fellow directors, meeting at Paddock Lodge on May Day afternoon (a Sunday). Mrs Topham 'had expressed disapproval when he had read it to her over the telephone before sending it to the paper,' the minutes expostulate. What was more, 'his press conference had been given without reference to us or our lawyers and was in fact insulting to the racecourse.'

This left Mrs Topham to negotiate with Lancashire County Council over the sale of the property, a task she set about with customary gusto in an attempt to compensate for what had now been exposed as a decidedly weak hand. By late July, she had sent them a new proposition, while erecting posters inscribed with huge question-marks outside Aintree in a futile attempt to chivvy councillors along by keeping the impasse in the public eye. By October, she had come up with a new ruse: advertising the course for sale the following spring in 'an American paper'. She had even composed the sales pitch: 'Grand National course for sale with copyright of the world famous Grand National Steeplechase – £2,000,000.' For all this, the long-term future of Aintree remained as much of an enigma as ever.

One important question had been resolved over the summer, however: Mrs Topham had consented to put on the race once again in 1967. She had even agreed to have the stands repainted – and received a 'very, very reasonable estimate'. A particularly late date – 8 April – had been selected, and the Tophams chairman expressed the hope that this would 'help to give us better weather and so encourage more spectators to come along'. The rain and cold that affected the 1966 race had hit takings, which were down around £10,000 from the successful 1965 meeting. Catering alone had produced a £1,000 loss. While the Grand National was again saved, it was considered too late to organise the usual autumn and Christmas meetings at Aintree in another symptom of decline.

September brought fresh disappointment in the shape of a letter from the prime minister's office declining Mrs Topham's invitation to attend the Grand National 'owing to a prior engagement'. In the event, Wilson, a Liverpool MP, spent the eve of the race visiting a frozen-food factory in nearby Kirkby. One can imagine the reaction of Aintree's *grande dame* to this snub by an upstart politician who could find time to stare at fish-fingers, but not attend the national institution over which she presided. Then again, Liverpool's decaying racecourse scarcely squared with the image Wilson was cultivating as a resourceful young leader, in tune with youth culture and alive to the excitement of new technology and its transformational potential for stuffy old Britain.

After missing that 1966 Grand National, Foinavon plodded unspectacularly through the last two months of the season, staying on his feet in a succession of middling races, but rarely threatening the leaders. However, he was starting once again to make up ground on rivals in the final furlongs of his races, as his fitness-oriented training regime took effect. This was most notably the case when he ran into third place – his best result in England for three and a half years – in a three-mile steeplechase at the picturesque Northamptonshire course of Towcester, noted, then as now, for its stiff uphill finishing stretch. He also showed every sign of appreciating Kempton's employment with him of the same sort of bit-less bridle that had rejuvenated Seas End. But there was nothing as yet to suggest that his pools concessionaire owners would recoup their investment in him – no matter how many races he ran in.

That freezing spring did bring one brief, but significant, encounter. On 16 April, Foinavon was due to return to Cheltenham to run in the *Sunday Express* Handicap Chase, which, at four miles, was a long-distance contest only about half a mile shorter than the Grand National itself. The meeting was due to be televised by the BBC's *Grandstand* programme – a detail which would have appealed to Cyril Watkins and Mac Bennellick, his owners, who were keen for their horse to run in big races, even if he stood little chance of winning. The weather, though, was atrocious. Two days earlier, the worst spring blizzard for 16 years had swept across 33 counties in southern Britain, cutting off villages and forcing snowploughs to be taken out of storage. London experienced its coldest April day since 1911: 20 people were stranded on Lundy Island in the Bristol Channel, and British featherweight champion Howard Winstone slipped over in Merthyr Tydfil and broke a small bone in his leg. Most importantly from Foinavon's point of view, the first of what was scheduled to be two days of quality racing at Cheltenham was abandoned. In the event, the elements eased up just enough for the second day to go ahead, with an extended card of ten races, prompting a cavalcade of horseboxes to slither their way towards Prestbury Park, on the edge of the Cotswold escarpment.

From his base outside Banbury, John Buckingham had an easier journey than some. Even so, it was a hard way to earn one solitary riding fee. Especially as the horse was an outsider he had never ridden before. Buckingham was unusual among jockeys in that he had not been near a horse, much less sat on one, until attaining the ripe old age of 15, when he followed his mother to work for Edward Courage, a member of the brewing family, on his extensive Edgcote estate. That was in 1955. Now, after a decade of schooling and riding Courage's renowned string of largely home-bred racehorses, he was an able jockey who, while always popular, lacked the pushiness required to snare rides and force his way to the very top of his unforgiving profession. More importantly for John Kempton, Buckingham was a lightweight, who, unlike him, could easily make the sub-ten-stone riding weight Foinavon had been allotted that day.

It was not a fairy-tale start. After jumping off with the leaders, Foinavon soon dropped back and came home sixth of the seven runners, just behind Vulcano, the old adversary who had won the Grand National qualifier at Baldoyle when Foinavon blotted his copybook so badly. Even so, Buckingham remembers that he gave him a good ride in his bit-less bridle and that the owners seemed pleased. The race was won by a horse called Jim's Tavern, who had battled to fifth place in the Grand National three weeks before.

The big race of the day, the *Daily Express* Triumph Hurdle, worth more than £3,500, was won, appropriately enough, by Black Ice ridden by Bobby Beasley. In wintry conditions such as those prevailing that afternoon, the Irish jockey's riding equipment would certainly have included his 'angora finger'. This was a device, knitted for him by his wife Shirley, to combat a complaint brought on by frigid weather. This, he used to find, cut through the thin material of his racing breeches and left him 'suffering from freezing cold in a most embarrassing place.'

Fifteen weeks later, on a typical English summer's day of sunshine and showers, 92 racehorses, their handlers and jockeys assembled in the quiet Devon market town of Newton Abbot for perhaps the most neglected season-opening fixture in the history of sport. The lack of interest in the first meeting of the new National Hunt racing season in England was attributable partly to the shortage of quality on display. With the seven races on the card offering aggregate prize money of less than £2,000 and the going classified as 'firm', this was not an occasion for the big equine stars of steeplechasing. But the same could have been said of the sport's traditional West Country curtain-raiser in any other year. What made 1966 different was the meeting's coincidence with an unseasonal football match 200 miles away in north London.

By the time the ten runners in the last race of the day, the Lustleigh Handicap Chase, had cantered to the start, Geoff Hurst had blasted home the sixth and final goal of the World Cup final, inspiring one of the most famous commentating one-liners in history, and the England football team were world champions. Foinavon proceeded to run as if determined not to upstage Bobby Moore as he climbed the Wembley steps to collect the Jules Rimet trophy. Ridden by Kempton, he was at one point labouring in last place, though he did rally characteristically towards the end to cross the line a distant sixth.

The jumps-racing schedule invariably started with a clutch of West Country fixtures. It was the Kemptons' practice to travel down with a string of horses and base themselves there for this period, lodging in Newton Abbot at a popular stopping-off point for jockeys called the Rendezvous Café.

A mere four days after his seasonal debut – and barely 48 hours after Mrs Topham had confirmed that the 1967 Grand National was on – Foinavon was in action again, in another three-mile chase, this time in an evening meeting at nearby Devon & Exeter. He performed much better, leading for much of the race, before the odds-on favourite got on terms at the second-last and ran on to win by one-and-a-half lengths. This winner, steered home by the former champion jockey Josh Gifford, was Honey End.

This began a spell of much-improved consistency for Foinavon. Starting with that runner-up spot, he finished in the first four in seven races out of eight over a six-month period, without ever finding the speed to register a victory.

On 7 October, he ran at Ascot for the first time, in a mixed National Hunt and Flat racing meeting of sufficient note to attract the television cameras once again. In a field studded with Grand National horses, BBC *Grandstand* viewers saw him perform honestly enough in the hands of another lightweight jockey Joe Guest, without ever getting close to the trio in front. These were led home by Bassnet, a promising seven-year-old steeplechaser, who had finished second in a race over the big Aintree fences that March.

It was at about this time that Mac Bennellick ran out of patience with his supposed Grand National horse and tried to offload his half-share to whoever would buy it. He could find no takers, though, for an animal that had gone 17 races since tasting victory. So he ended up simply giving his stake – and responsibility for the horse's livery, training and racing fees – to his partner Cyril Watkins.

Two days after Christmas, following a grim autumn in Britain dominated by the Aberfan colliery disaster, Foinavon was back at Kempton Park, nestled among the reservoirs south of London airport, for the biggest race of his life so far. The King George VI Chase was, and remains, one of the highlights of the English racing calendar, a colourful alternative to football or department store sales for Londoners intent on a Boxing Day outing. In 1966, though a Christmas-night freeze forced the race's postponement by 24 hours, a bumper attendance of 16,000 braved the traffic jams and a grey, misty day. Numbers were boosted by two factors in particular. The first was what trainer-cum-author Ivor Herbert calls the course's flirtation with 'a very restricted pay-TV experiment' with 'only a few homes in some London boroughs … connected to the system'. The second was the presence of Arkle. Everyone there expected to witness another serene exhibition by Tom Dreaper's wonder horse, Foinavon's former stable companion. What they got was high drama of an unimagined kind.

Approaching the second last, the race was still there for Arkle to win, but anxiety in the big crowd, which had sent him off at prohibitive odds of 2/9, was mounting. He had clouted one of the black birch fences on the far side of the course, was not moving with his habitual lissom power and now the rangy Woodland Venture, ridden by champion jockey Terry Biddlecombe, was hovering at his shoulder. Biddlecombe, still going easily, thought he had the race in his pocket. But Woodland Venture overjumped at the vital moment, leaving Arkle clear and his floored jockey ready to weep with frustration. Rather than capitalise on this reprieve, however, Arkle's stride shortened and he clambered over the last hanging painfully to his left. By this time, the Irish horse's many backers in the stands had noticed with disbelief that another challenger was gaining ground.

Dormant had not won a race for two-and-a-half years. He had finished a remote second to Arkle in the King George VI the previous year – a race marred by the fate of Dunkirk, a bold, front-running two-mile specialist, who crashed through the 15th fence, his lungs congested with blood, and landed dead on the other side, pinning jockey Bill Rees under his hot corpse with a broken right thigh. Subsequently, trainer Roy Pettitt claimed he had given Dormant sugar lumps coated with a tonic called Collovet, which contains caffeine, ahead of the race. This was one of a number of disclosures made by Pettitt and published by the *Sun* over the first week of its appearance in radically revamped format in 1969. Even with caffeine in his system though, Dormant could not – in 1965 – get close to Arkle. Jeff King, his jockey, not a man known for mincing words, has described him uncharitably as 'an ignorant old shit of a horse' who used to gallop through fences. Yet, in those final agonising seconds at Sunbury, this was the animal closing with every stride on the most dominant steeplechaser who ever drew breath. Dormant did have 21lb less on his back, but this was the sort of handicap that Anne, Duchess of Westminster's horse was accustomed to overcoming with ease.

Inexorably, King and Dormant ground down Arkle's lead and hit the front coming up to the line to win by a length. It was only then, as Foinavon neared the winning-post with John Kempton in a distant but secure fourth place, that the full significance of what had happened became clear. Arkle was lame, very lame. Already, as Pat Taaffe, his disconsolate jockey, removed the weight-cloth from his back in the unsaddling enclosure, the realisation was starting to dawn that an era of horse-racing history had probably ended. An unnatural hush hovered over the scene.

This was at 2.15pm. By 3.45pm, X-rays had been taken and by next morning news of the injury was on the front page of *The Times*. Arkle had fractured his pedal (pronounced 'pea-dal') bone, the bottom-most bone in a horse's leg and, as such, one of the most critical parts of a race-horse's anatomy. In footballers' parlance, you might say he had 'done' his metatarsal. Except that the potential consequences of the injury were much more severe: a broken pedal bone could be career- or even life-ending. In the event, Arkle was lucky. Blessed with a calm disposition, a patient owner and the best veterinary attention then available, he survived. But he never raced again.

This – the only occasion on which the two former stable companions, named after neighbouring Scottish peaks, lined up together for the same race – was not quite the last time their paths converged. On 4 February, Foinavon was back at Kempton Park for another three-mile chase, though this one was endowed with little more than a tenth of the prize money at stake on Boxing Day. Arkle, unfit to be moved, was still in residence in the racecourse stable-block, his injured foot encased in a 5lb plaster cast, his stable-wall adorned with a plywood hoarding covered with over a hundred 'Get Well Soon' cards. During the champion's enforced stay in the London suburbs, he was attended by a rota of trusted lads, sent over from the Dreapers' Greenogue base for about a week at a time. This February meeting was on Peter McLoughlin's watch. Clifford Booth, a strapping 16-year-old stable lad who had recently started working at Compton, was with Foinavon. He remembers McLoughlin coming up and asking to see his old partner who had carried him to his first win over fences. Only the enterprising – and lucky – got on in the racing industry in those days. And Booth was a young man imbued with both those qualities. He proposed a 'swap' whereby, while McLoughlin was with Foinavon, he kept an eye on Arkle. 'That's what we did,' he says. 'I went in with Arkle.'

As it transpired, McLoughlin would have to wait less than six weeks before seeing Foinavon again. This time the circumstances were different: they were milling around on the start-line for the Cheltenham Gold Cup, the most prestigious prize in British steeplechasing.

Chapter 11

500/1

Foinavon's winless streak had now stretched to 19 races. Yet his schedule for the remaining months of the 1966/67 season included Britain's two most prestigious steeplechases – the Cheltenham Gold Cup and the Grand National.

It was part of the ethos of National Hunt racing at this time that bad horses could run in good races. Cyril Watkins was not the only owner of relatively modest means enthused to keep putting money into the sport by the realisation that he could take an active role in its grandest occasions for an outlay comparable to the price of a good car. Others bought a thrill of a different kind by, in effect, paying to actually ride in the Grand National, one of the world's great sporting spectacles. Probably the best-known of these swashbuckling amateurs was the 18th Duke of Albuquerque. Seven times he rode in the race with frequently hair-raising results. It was by no means obligatory to have a Spanish nobleman's treasure-chest to make it to the start-line, however.

At about the time Clifford Booth was enjoying his tête-à-tête with Arkle, Nobby Howard, a 36-year-old steeplechasing romantic with hard blue eyes, was selling off his livestock, a herd of two cattle and 22 steers. He had just lost possession of his farm – a smallholding where he had been a sub-tenant, a status which meant he would be due no compensation. Having liquidated his assets in this way, Howard did what anyone in a similar situation might do: he started looking around for a Grand National horse on which to spend the money. 'It looked like it would be the last Grand National,' he says, as if this explains everything. 'I always loved it from when I was a kid.'

On 24 February, two Grand National-qualified horses were to be sold at the Ballsbridge spring sale in Dublin. Howard flew over – 'I had never been on a plane before' – but the horses fetched more than his £1,000 budget, so it looked like a wasted journey. It was then that Providence, in the shape of Toby Balding, a gregarious and impeccably well-connected English trainer who happened to have been standing next to Howard, took a hand. 'Do you want a horse to ride in the Grand National?' the trainer asked. 'I took an option on one this morning.'

They flew back to England together – Howard remembers people being excited because it was their first time on one of the new three-engined Tridents – and next day Balding asked him if he could collect the horse from an address in Sussex. It was a foul day with driving rain and trees being blown down by gusting winds. The only vehicle Howard had at his disposal was a borrowed horsebox with no roof. 'I covered the horse with macs and a New Zealand rug and set off for Toby's,' Howard recalls. It was a filthy journey, undertaken largely in darkness, but eventually they arrived, with the help of a police officer asked by Balding to keep an eye out for them. Howard was able to buy the horse, a ten-year-old chestnut gelding called Scottish Final, for a more than reasonable £680. They managed one race together before Aintree, at Wye, finishing second. The scarlet and yellow colours Howard chose for his jockey's silks were the same as those sported by Elizabeth Taylor in the 1944 film *National Velvet*, whose plot line focuses on the race and helped sow the seeds of the Grand National dream Howard finally fulfilled 23 years later.

One of the horses sold for more than Howard could afford at Ballsbridge – Ronald's Boy – was bought on behalf of a London stockbroker called Paul Irby. His Grand National dream had taken root much later than the ex-tenant farmer's. Irby started riding in the early 1950s, but visited Aintree with a horse-dealing friend for the first time only in 1966. The atmosphere in the run-down stands appealed to him at once. 'I liked the smell of it really,' he recalls. He said to his friend that they would return the following year – but this time he would be riding.

He was initially unsure how to finance the purchase of a suitable horse. Towards the end of 1966, however, he made a handsome profit on the stock market for a client, a New York carpet-dealer based on Third Avenue. Over dinner at the Connaught, topped up with 'the best part of a bottle' of Hine brandy, the client, Frank Robins, consented to buy a horse that Irby could ride in the race. Ronald's Boy fitted the bill and was duly acquired for 1,500 guineas. The vendor was Gay Kindersley, Old Etonian grandson of the 1st Lord Kindersley, and a noted socialite. Kindersley, a former champion amateur jockey, had ridden the hard-pulling Ronald's Boy in the 1965 Grand National, but come down at the third fence.

The fact that a former tenant farmer and a well-to-do stockbroker, let alone a seemingly indestructible Spanish nobleman, could line up together on equal terms before Liverpool's teeming stands was a good illustration of how jumps racing – and the Grand National in particular – playfully subverted the class system. This was then being challenged far more brazenly by the new breed of decadent millionaire pop star that television and increased post-war prosperity had combined to propagate. But steeplechasing had for years offered intoxicating glimpses of a world where the established social order no longer applied.

The Masters of the Universe out there among Aintree's dark, forbidding fences were skilled, professional horsemen like Josh Gifford, a Huntingdonshire farm boy who had left school aged ten. The likes of Gifford cheerfully accommodated accomplished gentleman amateur jockeys like John Lawrence, the noted journalist. But there was no doubting who was in charge. Beginners and no-hopers were tolerated, provided they didn't get ideas above their station and stayed out of the way. The equation was complicated because young apprentices aspiring to carve out careers as jockeys would often start off as amateur riders. This could spark a degree of friction with the old pros, whose rides they were, in some cases, taking and whom the best apprentices were destined eventually to supplant.

This is not to pretend there was any shortage of sports in 1960s' Britain whose most accomplished performers were working-class heroes. But steeplechasing was unusual in that toffs and farm-boys were out there, shoulder to shoulder, battling first for survival then against each other, jammed into the same cramped weighing-rooms and even exchanging occasional jokes.

Of course, this scrambling of social stations lasted only as long as the race itself. Once they had passed the winning-post, jockeys were back under their trainers' thumbs, being held accountable for their every action in the race by men who, in those days, very often held military rank and were intolerant of insubordination. The trainers, in turn, were answerable to their horses' owners, many of whom, starting with the Queen Mother, inhabited society's uppermost echelons and traditionally governed the sport. The command structure of the racing industry, in other words, was establishment through and through. The Grand National, though, could be seen as a rollicking nine-and-a-half-minute parody of the classless society.

While both Howard and Irby made it to the Aintree start-line in 1967, John Kempton didn't. He was still pursuing his riding devotedly enough to have piloted Foinavon to fourth place at Lingfield on 20 January – the day before he married Patricia. He had by now recognised, however, that the horse had little prospect of running well at Liverpool unless he carried the weight actually allotted to him by the handicapper. This would be 10 stone – simply too light for the tall trainer no matter how diligent or imaginative he was with his wasting methods. This meant though that he and Watkins would need to find and retain a lightweight jockey for the Grand National. This explains why, in the weeks leading up to the big race, the gelding was asked to carry a succession of new partners.

At Kempton Park on 4 February, his jockey was Ron Atkins, a Londoner whose father had a shoe-shop opposite Wembley Stadium. Atkins was several inches shorter than Kempton, but had powerful shoulders befitting the flyweight boxer he nearly became. Like Foinavon's trainer, he was a man who liked to think things through for himself. His strong inclination was to speak his mind. With his long brown hair, he probably came as close to embracing the 'groovy' new Carnaby Street chic as any professional jockey in that period. He also showed a precocious appreciation of the power of branding, riding in a skullcap emblazoned with his initials, though he says this was partly to stop his helmet being purloined. This all resulted in him acquiring a reputation as a non-conformist who, as safety officer for the Jockeys' Association, would play a big part in years to come in driving up the sport's woeful safety standards. As the crocuses poked through in 1967, however, Atkins was an up-and-coming rider who had yet to try his hand at a Grand National.

In a competitive field, he conjured one of Foinavon's best performances to date in England, though he still feels he could have won. Since the King George VI Chase on Boxing Day, Kempton had been using blinkers on the horse to restrict his peripheral vision and 'keep his concentration on the jumping'. The new jockey was still expected to operate with a bit-less bridle, however. Turning for home, Foinavon was up with the leaders, but starting to tire. 'He was tending to duck the issue a little bit, hiding behind the other horses,' Atkins recalls. 'I was trying to get him out. If I could get him away from the backsides of the horses in front of me, I was pretty sure that I would get up.' Atkins, who served his apprenticeship on the flat under the tutelage of top jockeys such as Joe Mercer and Scobie Breasley, was accustomed, however, to the more reliable control over his mount that an orthodox metal bit, pressing against the horse's sensitive mouth, can provide. 'Scobie used to say to me, "Treat your reins like cotton; if you pull too hard they'll break and then you have no control." Joe used to say it was like fly-fishing for trout. "You can catch a 10lb trout on a 3lb line. How? Because you play with it. When you've got a horse with a bit-less bridle on, it takes you two or three rides to sort him out."'

Atkins did manoeuvre the horse into position to mount a challenge, but he was up against the experienced Josh Gifford on a horse called Loyal Fort, the 6/4 favourite. He pushed them all the way, but passed the winning-post a length in arrears. An objection, lodged against the winner for crossing, was overruled. 'I got off the horse and said, "With a rubber bit I'm pretty sure he would have won because I would have had a bit more control",' Atkins says. 'That upset the owner; I know it did.' Given the length of time Watkins had now been waiting for his horse to win, his frustration was perhaps understandable.

Atkins does not remember any mention of Aintree being made on that occasion. Though when he was asked to ride Foinavon again a month later at Newbury, the horse's local course, the subject was very much a live issue. 'I thought, "Is he the ride for me? Hmmm, I don't know. I'll have to think about it",' he says.

It was the norm at this time for jockeys to receive an additional fee for riding in the Grand National. A payment of £200 – the amount Atkins got for riding a horse called Some Slipper to 13th place in the race the following year – was commonplace. If successful, the rider stood to make a lot more: Bobby Beasley bought a small farm with the £2,000 'present' he received in 1961 after winning the race on Nicolaus Silver, the last grey victor until Neptune Collonges in 2012. This was unwelcome news for Cyril Watkins who had not exactly been inundated with prize money during his brief tenure as a racehorse owner, at least not since his winning start with McCrimmon. Since erstwhile partner Mac Bennellick had got cold feet in the autumn, moreover, Watkins had been left to pay the bills for stabling and training their horses alone. He had no intention whatsoever of shelling out a sum that was more than the value of many small races to some jockey who, in his view, should be grateful for the ride.

According to Atkins, the crunch came after the Newbury race. 'I just said, "OK – what's the deal? All jockeys get extra for riding in the National." Watkins said, "I'm not giving you any extra, you should be lucky to ride in the National." I thought, "On your bike." So I had a falling-out with them. I said, "If there's nothing up front, I'm out of here."'

Watkins's mood would not have been improved by his horse's lacklustre performance in a race, staged in the presence of the Queen Mother, the day before the League Cup final was played for the first time at Atkins's dad's local stadium. Up against some good younger horses, Foinavon quickly lost touch and trailed in a remote sixth.

Nine days before this, at Ascot, the horse had been teamed with another new jockey, Bruce Gregory, who was even lighter than Atkins and had once been attached to the mighty Fairlawne operation in Kent, presided over by Major Peter Cazalet. The Queen Mother and Hollywood star Gregory Peck both kept horses in training at Fairlawne. The Queen Mother's horse Devon Loch, deprived of the 1956 Grand National when mysteriously spreadeagling within yards of the winning-post, was trained by Cazalet. Gregory's best day in racing had come almost exactly three years before, on 29 February 1964, when he partnered a horse called Out and About to victory in a big race at Newbury, the Mandarin Chase. A lively character, he was also known for his car, a souped-up Volkswagen which, according to fellow jockey Terry Biddlecombe, 'had a Porsche engine in it'.

Given that jump jockeys at that time thought nothing of clocking up 50,000 miles a year on wintry roads, this was a real asset. He later moved to France, started dealing in horses and, more recently, was said to have become involved in a motorbike accessories business.

The rain had been sluicing down on Ascot – an inch and a quarter in five days. Racing was cleared, nonetheless, to go ahead with one fence omitted. Foinavon appeared to relish the very soft conditions and was disputing the lead with a horse called Cornucopia when he came down at the 11th fence in a fall that left his new partner nursing a dislocated shoulder. 'Nothing was going better,' observed *Sporting Life*'s man on the spot. When stable lad Clifford Booth went down to catch the horse, he came across a man who had been scouring the ground for Foinavon's bit. 'I've been looking everywhere,' the man said apologetically. Booth explained that the horse ran without one.

Three weeks later, Cheltenham was bathed in sunshine for the first Gold Cup without Arkle since 1963. His absence, along with that of other equine stars, was keenly felt. 'Cheltenham without Arkle, Flyingbolt and Salmon Spray,' bemoaned *The Times*'s racing correspondent, 'is rather like England at Wembley without Charlton and Moore or the West Indies without Sobers.' A competitive field of eight horses had been assembled nonetheless. This consisted of seven of the best steeplechasers around (excluding Tom Dreaper's two absent superstars) plus Foinavon. His seven rivals had won 12 races between them already that season; his winless streak was now up to 23. In boxing terms, it was like putting a punch-drunk veteran in the ring with Henry Cooper, a verdict reflected in a starting price of no less than 500/1.

Foinavon would not even have a weight advantage to help bridge the class chasm. Each of the entrants would carry 12 stone, a generous enough imposition to enable John Kempton to ride the horse, in his usual bit-less bridle, without resorting to sweatsuits, pee-pills or even hypnotism.

Milling around at the start as they waited for one runner – the grey, Stalbridge Colonist – to be reshod, Kempton chatted amiably with Peter McLoughlin, the Irish jockey Foinavon had carried to his first victory over fences at Punchestown nearly three years before. It was a token of the quality of Dreaper's string that even with his best two horses sidelined, McLoughlin's mount, Fort Leney, was favourite to win the race. Dormant, the crippled Arkle's conqueror at Kempton Park, was also there. So was the broad-backed Mill House, winner of the last Gold Cup before Arkle's hat-trick, pacing the turf like a bull. To Mill House's left circled the white-fronted What a Myth, a racehorse with great stamina but questionable jumping skills, ridden by Paul Kelleway, one of the characters of the weighing-room, wearing a distinctive spotted cap. Kelleway once gave fellow jockey Bobby Beasley the shock of his life by snaking his hand through between Beasley's backside and saddle as they approached the second hurdle at Warwick and catching hold of his crotch. 'How are you going, matey?' Kelleway grinned. He did let go before they jumped, however. Woodland Venture, the youngest horse in the race, was sweating up, his right shoulder traced with white foam as he walked around briskly. His jockey Terry Biddlecombe might have been forgiven for getting himself into a similar lather given the week he had had thus far. Two days earlier, a brand-new stirrup-leather had broken precipitating one fall and he had come unstuck again on the eve of Gold Cup day, with his mount, Glenn, kicking him hard above one knee, 'ripping my breeches and almost castrating me'. That afternoon, before racing began, he had had a painkilling injection. Even then, he had managed to get unshipped once more just 40 minutes before the Gold Cup.

They were running late, so no sooner had Stalbridge Colonist joined his rivals than a roll call of jockeys' last names was barked out and the bowler-hatted starter urged them to, 'Come on jockeys, make a line!' With that, at 12 minutes past four, the flag shot up and the 42nd Cheltenham Gold Cup was under way. And who should burst into the lead over the first of 22 testing fences, but Foinavon, one of the biggest outsiders in the race's history.

Running downhill around the first left-handed bend away from the crowd, the Berkshire-based no-hoper surged ten lengths clear in his distinctive pale hood. John Kempton, looking like a jockey sculpted by Giacometti so elongated were his limbs, urged him on sporting Cyril Watkins's unmistakable racing colours: light green and light blue with cross-belts and cap of Mackintosh tartan. Just as Kempton was shaped differently from the other jockeys, so the proportions of Foinavon's body stood out: not even Mill House had a more powerful shoulder, but his haunches seemed underdeveloped compared with the likes of Woodland Venture and the small but powerful Stalbridge Colonist. He was also jumping with inordinate care, which while no bad policy at Cheltenham, meant that after the water, his rivals were taking a couple of lengths out of his lead with every fence. A poor jump at the 11th, when he hung to his right, enabled Mill House and Woodland Venture to overhaul him. While he regained momentum on the flat, he promptly lost it again going over the water-jump for the second time and was never in touch with the leaders after that.

Mill House, the 1963 winner, whose surge of power as a youngster was once memorably described by Pat Taaffe as 'oceanic', was looking well capable of book-ending the Arkle years until, out in the country, he succumbed, almost in slow motion, to his first fall since he was a novice. This left the long-striding Woodland Venture in the lead with five to jump. It was never easy and he was pushed every yard of the way by a typically frenzied finishing burst by Stan Mellor aboard Stalbridge Colonist, but an overjoyed Biddlecombe, bad leg and all, held on to win. The fast-finishing What a Myth was third.

In a surreal moment as he left the unsaddling enclosure, Biddlecombe was confronted by an over-excited and triumphant doctor waving around the hypodermic needle that had allowed him a pain-free ride.

Cheltenham was a reassuringly unostentatious place in those days. Soon after they flashed past the winning-post, the numbers of the first four finishers in the 'fourth race' were displayed on a hoisted result-board that a village cricket club would not have been overly proud of. Harry Collins, the victorious owner who had taken an old cow to market so as to be able to wager an extra £100 on his horse, was presented with the trophy by Lady Willoughby de Broke from a glorified kitchen table.

John Kempton, meanwhile, was left to make his way back across the Cotswolds knowing that he only had three weeks left to find a jockey for the Grand National.

Chapter 12

A JOCKEY TO RIDE IN THE NATIONAL

Easter Monday is traditionally one of the busiest days in the British horse-racing calendar – and 1967 was no exception. A dozen meetings were scheduled from Carlisle to Chepstow, Wetherby to Wincanton. At Huntingdon seven races, none worth more than £700 to the winner, were to be contested by around 60 horses. One of these was Foinavon who, rather than travel to Sussex for a race at Plumpton where he was also entered, was driven up the A1 to Oliver Cromwell's birthplace to see how he got on with yet another new jockey.

Dave Patrick had previously lived in Compton and so already knew John Kempton. He remembers Foinavon running a 'half-tidy race' to finish fourth in the Fitzwilliam Chase, the fourth contest of the day. The race has also lodged in the memory of stable lad Clifford Booth because of an accident that befell another runner who crashed through the wooden rails, sustaining a grisly shoulder wound. 'The amount of blood that was running down ... That has always stuck in my mind,' Booth says. The unfortunate animal was patched up, nonetheless, by a course vet and driven off in a trailer.

Patrick says that he was offered the Grand National ride on Foinavon after this race, but politely turned it down on the grounds that he had already got a ride. This was on a horse called Bob-a-Job, who, coincidentally, had just come fourth at Plumpton in the race Foinavon would have run in if he had not gone to Huntingdon. Unbeknown to Patrick, he would shortly lose the Grand National ride he thought he had and would never get another chance to take part in the Aintree showpiece. 'It's just one of those things,' he concludes, scoring top marks for stoicism.

The start of the Grand National meeting was now just ten days away and, while Kempton still hadn't found his jockey, Mirabel Topham was about to be confronted with some unexpected last-ditch problems of her own. On Easter Monday night, vandals struck at Aintree. The damage was concentrated at the far end of the course, site of the main signature fences. The *Daily Mirror* published a litany of the havoc wreaked. The Canal Turn fence, located right on a corner and hence enabling the bold to gain ground by jumping diagonally across it or seemingly changing direction in mid-air, had been destroyed and would have to be completely rebuilt. The turnstile doors at Becher's Brook, the most famous fence of all, had been broken open. A wooden bar counter at the Canal Turn stand, adjacent to that part of the course, had been knocked over and broken. Washbasins and toilets had been smashed with bricks. Hurdles had been uprooted and thrown across the racecourse. Sections of posts, railings and link fencing had been pulled out. A pavilion on the Aintree property had been burnt down.

Mrs Topham, already contemplating, no doubt, the unbidden bill that would eventually run well into four figures, proclaimed the situation 'a tragedy'. The Aintree staff, obliged because of the meeting's unusually late timing to work through the Easter holiday to get ready for it, were understandably 'nearly in tears'. Police officers with dogs were detailed to patrol the course round-the-clock in the run-up to the National. 'We have talked to many boys in the area,' a police spokesman said sternly later in the week, 'but so far no arrests have been made.'

Foinavon was not exactly being wrapped in cotton wool ahead of the big race. On 1 April – just five days after his Huntingdon outing and exactly a week before the National – he was scheduled to run yet again, in the aptly named April Fools Handicap Chase. Bruce Gregory, the jockey who had ridden Foinavon for the first time at Ascot in February, had recovered from his dislocated shoulder and it was to him that Kempton now turned in his pursuit of a rider for both Leicester and Liverpool.

There are two explanations as to why Gregory eventually missed out on that date at Aintree, even though he was identified more than once in the press as Foinavon's expected partner. Money is usually the reason given. The jockey is said, like Ron Atkins before him, to have asked for a special one-off Grand National payment. There is nothing to indicate that Cyril Watkins – who was receiving treatment at the Royal Berkshire Hospital at this time – would have looked any more favourably on Gregory's demands than those of Atkins. However, Colin Hemsley, the head lad at Foinavon's stable, traces the decision, at least in part, to a different cause. This was a freak mishap that befell the partnership in that April Fools Day race at Leicester.

Entering the final stages, a storming finish was in prospect, with the top-weight Loyal Fort, who had edged out Foinavon two months before, battling to keep the lead, but being overhauled by Praepostor, a horse five years his junior carrying a lot less weight. Foinavon was on their heels and looking enviably placed with four fences to go when, out of the blue, one of Gregory's stirrup-leathers snapped. With no support for his foot and the horse wearing his habitual bit-less bridle, this left the jockey high and dry, like a driver whose car loses power, steering and brakes all at the same time. They quickly dropped out of contention and trailed in sixth, nearly 30 lengths behind the winner. *Sporting Life* reporter Len Thomas was appreciative, nonetheless, of Gregory's efforts. The jockey, he wrote, 'must be congratulated on completing the course on Foinavon, who would surely have gone close but for the mishap'. This was not though, it seems, a view universally shared. According to Hemsley, Jack

Kempton, the young trainer's father, felt aggrieved that his jockey had not kept going well enough to finish in the top three and, hence, earn some prize money. It was this, the head lad believes – perhaps allied to whatever payment demands Gregory had made – that triggered a change of heart regarding Aintree. There was now only a week to go and Foinavon was once again without a rider for the severest test in British steeplechasing.

It was some 90 hours after seeing Praepostor home to his comfortable victory in what was his 801st ride as a jockey that John Buckingham picked up the phone. It was ten o'clock on a cloudy Northamptonshire morning and the young horseman was readying himself to attend his uncle's funeral. The telephone had rung as he was knotting his black tie. The caller was John Kempton and, given the circumstances, he got straight to the point. Would Buckingham be willing to ride Foinavon in the Grand National in three days' time? Would he ever! At 26, he had still not ridden in the race and, in his unassuming way, had 'more or less resigned myself to the fact that I never would'. He had once tackled the big Aintree fences in bitter cold the previous year, two days before Anglo's National victory, but had failed to complete the course. He did also know Foinavon, having ridden him around Cheltenham's testing circuit about three weeks after that Liverpool disappointment.

Whether it was that solid performance in Gloucestershire or his winning ride at Leicester that prompted Kempton to pick up the phone to Buckingham that morning is impossible to say. His options were, of course, narrowing by the minute, with upwards of 40 jockeys already booked for the Aintree race and many others either injured or supremely unlikely to agree to Cyril Watkins's terms for embarking on the ride. In any case, the trainer invited him down to Taunton the next day to talk about Liverpool and ride a horse called Sailaway Sailor against 20 rival hurdlers on the leafy Somerset course.

As Buckingham recalls, Kempton told him that Atkins and Gregory had turned down the ride over money and explained that the owner 'did not want to pay an extra £200 or so just to see the horse pulled up after only a few fences'. Later, he says, Watkins told him that he would pay 'according to how the horse ran'. This time, however, they had come to the right man – a jockey who so coveted a place on the Grand National start-line that 'I would have done it for nothing if necessary'. As Sailaway Sailor hit the front three from home, it looked for a moment as though the rider's euphoria would yield immediate dividends. In the event, it wasn't to be, with the horse fading on the run-in to finish a close-up fifth.

Next morning, on the eve of the National, a brief interview with Kempton was published by the *Daily Mirror*, as part of journalist Ron Wills's regular Spotlight column. In an assessment that must have had many readers tittering over their breakfasts, given that the horse had now not won for more than two years, the young trainer was defiantly upbeat about his gelding's chances. 'It's true Foinavon hasn't yet turned out as well as we thought he would, but he's improving,' Kempton insisted. 'Foinavon is a funny horse and you want a funny horse at Aintree … Foinavon can do it. He's a Grand National type. Three miles is always too short for him.'

Wildly optimistic it might have been, but Kempton's description of Foinavon was not so very different from his most regular Irish jockey Pat Taaffe's. For Taaffe, Foinavon was eccentric and 'droll' and he admitted to 'quite a soft spot' for him. The fact remained, though, that the two men had by this time ridden him in a grand total of 26 races without once tasting victory. The earth would surely need to tilt on its axis to put him in with a chance at Aintree against horses like What a Myth, who had beaten him by half the length of Gloucestershire in the Cheltenham Gold Cup; like Freddie, the popular Scottish chaser who had been runner-up the previous two years; and like Honey End, another horse trained in Sussex by the plain-speaking Captain Ryan Price, who was being tipped as a leading contender and whose disposition was so gentle he was nicknamed 'George' by his stable lad.

Chapter 13

AN IRON BUNK-BED AND TWO ARMCHAIRS PUSHED TOGETHER

As early-rising *Mirror*-readers were smiling at John Kempton's rose-tinted view of Foinavon, two men were flipping a coin. Tony Hutt and Geoff Stocker were the drivers who took the gelding to most of his races. As you might expect in Grand National week, the purpose of the coin-toss was to decide which one of them would transport him to the world's most famous steeplechase. As you might not expect, it was the loser – Hutt – who got the job.

There are two reasons why this superficially glamorous journey did not appeal to either man. First, it would take a long time, probably upwards of five hours. Second, as soon as Foinavon was unloaded at Aintree, the driver would have to turn around and come straight back. This was because the Kemptons had another horse running on Grand National day – at Worcester, beside the River Severn. This horse, a chestnut colt called Three Dons, of whom the Kemptons had high hopes, would need to be driven to his race the following morning. Hutt's plan was to ask another local horse transport firm to bring Foinavon back. The 16-year-old stable lad, Clifford Booth, would stay overnight in Liverpool and tend to the horse on race-day.

And so at around ten o'clock on Friday morning, it was the tall figure of Hutt, a Woodbine on his lip, who turned down the lane by the Red Lion pub in his cream-coloured Newbury Racehorse Transport horsebox. After executing a precise three-point turn, so as to be facing the right way when his cargo embarked, he pulled up outside the gateway into Chatham Stables. Hutt, the son of a stud groom, was an ideal driver, as he had been among horses all his life and knew instinctively how to handle his highly strung passengers in any situation. Like many others in racing at this time, he had also tasted military action, in his case in Korea with the Gloucestershire Regiment, the so-called 'Glorious Glosters'. The vehicle's arrival would have been heralded from some distance away in the quiet Berkshire countryside by the insistent putter of its two-stroke diesel engine. 'You could hear it coming,' recalls Colin Hemsley, the Kemptons' head lad. 'It was a Commer with a big exhaust.'

The process of loading up was brisk and well choreographed from frequent practice – and also because a strong north wind and gunmetal grey clouds had brought a wintry edge to the day. An old laundry-basket with a padlocked top was already out at the side of the lane where the horsebox had pulled in. This contained rugs, quarter-sheets, spare lead-reins, spare bridle, sponges, the first-aid kit – everything the horse might need at Liverpool. The contents had been checked and double-checked to ensure nothing was forgotten. Extra travelling garments were loaded loose into the box, so as to be easily accessible if Foinavon got hot or cold in transit. Waiting on a wheelbarrow to be carted up the driveway and stowed onboard were Hemsley's carefully prepared batches of feed for the three days away: quantities of chaff, corn, hay and bran, some glucose for his eve-of-race feed in Liverpool that evening and pure oats for his pre-Grand National breakfast – the equivalent of the Apollo astronauts' launch-day steak and eggs.

Most important of all was the racing tack, minus the saddle, which was the jockey's responsibility. Much of this was with the jockey's silks in the trainer's colour bag, which looked like a briefcase with a special brass name-plate affixed. Even more thought than usual had gone into this. For one thing, Foinavon was to run with a rubber bit fitted to his bridle. Kempton and Hemsley felt this was only fair on jockey John Buckingham, given the sheer size of the fences, the inevitable hurly-burly of a race with 44 runners and the fact he had only ridden the horse once before.

And then there were the blinkers. Foinavon had been running regularly in orthodox closed-cup blinkers since the King George VI Chase in December. The trainer and head lad were worried, though, that with such a large field clustered around him, it might be counterproductive to restrict their horse's field of vision quite so severely. There was also the risk that clods of mud might become lodged in the eye-pieces. In the days leading up to the race, Kempton had therefore arranged to have a special set of blinkers with huge, open eye-pieces made up. Fashioned in his mother Molly's yellow-and-black racing colours, these would prevent the horse seeing what was going on behind, but not around, him. That week, after their Leicester debacle, they put them on him and practised jumping him over a fence, camouflaged with dark-green spruce to resemble Aintree. He seemed as imperturbable as ever.

Once everything else was loaded, Booth strode across the yard to fetch the horse, wrapped up in a Witney blanket and travelling bandages, along with Susie the goat. Since Kempton and Hemsley would be going to Worcester not Aintree, Foinavon already had his racing plates fitted. These lightweight racing shoes had been fashioned, as usual, by Kempton himself at his small open-air forge beside the bungalow. In a typically Heath Robinson-esque touch, the trainer had rigged up a vacuum-cleaner, set permanently on blow and operated with a string like a bathroom light-switch, to heat up the coke to the point where the metal became pliable. The plates were affixed cold in the horse's box.

The trainer had a portable anvil for final adjustments, but was such a good judge that these were generally very minor.

Hemsley and Kempton were off exercising two of the other horses on the nearby Ridgeway, while the trainer's father was to join Booth at Liverpool the next day. At last the teenager jumped up into the passenger seat in his flat cap, half-length jacket and smart race-day trousers and, in a cloud of diesel fumes, they were on their way.

An excited John Buckingham was setting off at about the same time from Chipping Warden, his Northamptonshire village, with brother Tom. He too had been due to spend Saturday at Worcester before receiving Kempton's last-gasp invitation to ride Foinavon, but had managed to extricate himself from this commitment. What had proved harder was finding a bed for the night on Merseyside at such short notice. After several phone calls, some acquaintances who lived in a small house just across the road from the racecourse said he and Tom could kip there, though it wouldn't be very comfortable. This turned out to be an understatement. In the circumstances, his wife Ann decided not to make the journey. She would watch the race with her grandmother in Leamington Spa.

The day's showpiece sporting occasion, a solemn one, was taking place 200 miles south of Liverpool. At Westminster Abbey, a memorial service was being held for Sir Frank Worrell, the first black man appointed West Indies cricket captain, who had died in Jamaica the previous month, aged just 42. With the prime minister expected in Kirkby for his frozen-food factory visit; he was represented at the service by the ever-dependable Denis Howell.

It was also, however, the second day of Aintree's spring meeting – the sole event at the course that season. And as Buckingham and Hutt ploughed their separate furrows along the unlovely trunk roads of the English Midlands, at a little after 2pm, an event of some significance occurred in the first race of the day, the Thursby Selling Plate. This was a distinctly unpromising five-furlong sprint for two-year-olds, worth all of £300. As it turned out, though, the nine runners contrived a thrilling spectacle for their shivering audience, with the result eventually called a dead heat between Curlicue and a little-fancied 5/1 shot whose jockey, Paul Cook, was wearing the black-and-pink quartered colours of Maurice Kingsley, a Manchester manufacturer. Eight years later this horse was sent off at significantly shorter odds for a Grand National. What the sparse audience had just witnessed was the first Aintree victory, albeit a shared one, by Red Rum.

These were conspicuously good times for the port city of Liverpool. A wave of big-company investment had made it less dependent on its famous docks, with manufacturing – as it turned out, briefly – taking over as the largest sector in the local economy for the first time. In addition to the sort of food-industry plants being visited that day by Harold Wilson, carmakers were largely responsible for the good times, with three new factories creating 30,000 jobs between 1962 and 1967. The boom had a cultural dimension too, with the staggering worldwide success of the Beatles attracting talent scouts to the city and sending its 'cool' quotient through the roof. As Red Rum and Curlicue flashed past the winning-post together, the Fab Four were actually nearing completion of *Sgt. Pepper's Lonely Hearts Club Band*, their masterpiece, in a London studio.

The city had become rampant on the football field too. In the four seasons culminating with 1965/66, one or other of its two big clubs – Liverpool and Everton – had won the league championship three times and the FA Cup twice. Tens of thousands of local sports fans, indeed, would be spending Grand National day, not at Aintree but in Nottingham watching Everton take on a classy Forest side in an FA Cup quarter-final.

Everton players Alan Ball and Alex Young had been among what the man from *The Times* described as 'the thimbleful of spectators' present for the start of the three-day meeting on Thursday afternoon.

Not even these local heroes or the welcome sight of a fresh coat of paint on the stands had been able to distract attention from other problems, however. As a 23-strong field lined up for the Topham Trophy, a popular race run over the Grand National fences, part of the starting mechanism came away in starter Alec Marsh's hand. He ended up resorting to the old-fashioned flag method to send the runners on their way some eight minutes late. There was a false start in one of the Flat races on the card when half the starting-gate failed to rise. Shortcomings were also noted with the loudspeaker system. As it later transpired, even the paint job left Mrs Topham and her colleagues dissatisfied. Meeting three weeks after Grand National day, the Tophams board regretted that the contractor had been forced to 'withdraw their best labour and institute local'. This had been 'extremely careless'. There were, Tophams said, 'many faults to rectify before the final payment was made'.

Given the thrills and spills endemic to jumps racing, it was inevitable that accidents over the first two days of the meeting would affect jockeys booked to ride in the big race on Saturday afternoon. Within a couple of minutes of that delayed start to the Topham Trophy, a quartet of National jockeys were splayed across a patch of Aintree's famously springy turf, victims of the formidable 5ft 2in Chair, probably the second-most intimidating fence on the course after Becher's Brook. On this occasion, no serious damage was done, although one of the four – the Irish rider Johnny Lehane – was later said to be nursing sore ribs. The Aintree jockeys' book notes that a crepe bandage was applied. Macer Gifford, due to ride a horse called Popham Down in the National, was another to suffer a fall, though his came on the meeting's second day, while John Buckingham, Tony Hutt and Foinavon were heading north.

By far the most serious incident, though, was the one that befell Eddie Harty and a four-year-old hurdler called Spearhead in the very first jumps race of the meeting, the Lancashire Hurdle. Harty, a versatile enough horseman to have worked as a cowboy in the United

States for two years as well as representing Ireland in the three-day event at the 1960 Rome Olympics, had just taken up the running two from home and was going well. At the second-last flight, however, his mount put his feet through the top of the hurdle and came crashing down. Harty was left with a broken collarbone and thumb; Spearhead a broken neck. On the morning of the National, the *Irish Independent* – besides publishing a third instalment of *Populorum Progressio,* Pope Paul VI's recent encyclical – found room to mention that Harty would ride with 'a heavily bandaged hand'. This was to prove a handicap of some significance.

It was a relieved Clifford Booth who jumped down from the passenger seat when the cream-coloured horsebox pulled up beside the bustling Aintree stable-yards. The young man found that time crawled by on the way to the races and the trek to Liverpool had been his longest confinement yet in Foinavon's ponderous conveyance. With many of that day's runners heading home and other National entrants arriving, the scene was as busy as a railway station forecourt, as short men with stout shoes and weatherbeaten faces strode purposefully about in different directions, some with skittish young racehorses in tow. With Tony Hutt facing a long drive home in gathering gloom, the teenage stable lad was going to have to learn the ropes on his own, a gelding in one hand, a goat in the other.

There was, though, a presiding authority in the shape of stable manager Ossie Dale, who had clocked up nearly a decade and a half with the Tophams by this time and had seen it all before. Such was Dale's devotion to duty that in Grand National week, he always slept in the loft above his busy office in Paddock Yard. He had catered for plenty of travelling goats in his time. True, they had once had an escapee, but it was found next morning at the station across the road from the racecourse, grazing contentedly on the morning newspapers that had been dumped on the platform.

Soon enough, Foinavon (and Susie) had been assigned box number 98 in New Yard, Aintree's biggest stable-complex. Many of the horse's National rivals were already in residence. Some of the Irish contingent, including Leedsy, whom some fancied as a capable outsider, had arrived on Wednesday night after enduring a rough flight from Dublin. Freddie's owner Reg Tweedie, a Kelso livestock farmer who had ridden in the 1940 National, ending up with blood-splashed breeches after his mount broke a blood vessel, had decided, by contrast, to bring his star chaser to Aintree only at the last moment. Scotland's big hope was accordingly spending the night before his third and final tilt at steeple-chasing's greatest prize in a box at nearby Haydock Park.

Booth was found an iron bunk-bed in a large dormitory for stable-lads at the Sefton Arms Hotel beside the racecourse. At about 4am, he remembers hearing a rustling of nearby bedclothes and assuming it was time to get up. In fact, this was the sound of his neighbour, one of the most experienced lads on the circuit, returning from a night out. The Buckingham brothers, meanwhile, had got to their lodgings just after nine – and found them all that they had been promised. After sandwiches and coffee, they were in 'bed' – which in John's case meant two armchairs pushed together – by 10.15pm. 'Funnily enough, I slept,' he says.

Another Friday evening arrival in the city was Gregory Peck, the Hollywood film-star, whose horse, Different Class, was among the favourites for the big race. It is safe to say that Peck did not spend the night on two armchairs pushed together. He and his wife Veronique were among the great and good of the racing establishment ensconced in the splendour of Liverpool's very own palace hotel – the Adelphi. Built more than fifty years before for the launch of the *Titanic*, this marble-lined edifice still took the breath away with its opulence and scale, from its wood-panelled bedrooms to its gargantuan Grand Lounge. The 51-year-old actor had never seen Different Class race before and was hoping his presence at Aintree would not bring the horse bad luck. 'It's a chance I have to take,' he told a local reporter. 'The Grand National I felt I just had to see. I had to be here for this … I have loved this race since I first came here in 1950. I think it's the greatest sporting event in the world.' It was four years since the couple had made their last trip to the National. On that occasion Peck's horse, Owen's Sedge, a striking grey, could manage no better than seventh place. Just nine days after this disappointment, and 6,000 miles away, Peck had had a different kind of triumph to savour, capturing the Oscar for best actor for his role as lawyer Atticus Finch in *To Kill a Mockingbird*.

That evening, as Clifford Booth slept in his iron bunk-bed and the Buckingham brothers tucked into their sandwiches, the Pecks were dancing in the Adelphi when John Gaines, a US horseman who had recently bought the 1966 Grand National winner Anglo, approached them. 'What about a $500 side-bet, horse against horse?' Gaines, who was later to be credited with founding the Breeders' Cup, the richest North American race meeting, proposed. Peck smiled and extended his hand, 'You're on,' he said.

Chapter 14

THE ECSTASY
OF AINTREE

The race regarded by Gregory Peck as the greatest sporting event in the world is not quite as old as steeplechasing itself. This is believed to have originated in 18th-century Ireland in the form of match races between two riders, usually hunters, across open country from point A to point B, often a church steeple. The Grand National is, though, among the more venerable contests in British sport, pre-dating the Football League, cricket's County Championship and even, by one year, the Victorian era.

It does not, however, pre-date the classic races of the Flat-racing calendar, the Oaks, the Derby and, oldest of all, the St Leger, first run in 1776. Indeed, the sport of steeplechasing might not have developed in its modern form had it not been obliged to co-exist with Flat racing and its many influential patrons.

By the start of the 19th century, it had become the custom for the cards of regular – Flat – race meetings to include flat races for hunting horses. This, though, posed a problem: how to ensure that speedy, light-weight Flat racing horses were excluded? Organisers of a race meeting at Bedford in 1811 had the idea of erecting a number of artificial barriers to be cleared by the participants – an effective deterrent since regular racehorses would not have been taught how to jump. In the event, there were only two runners, though the occasion proved popular enough to attract a crowd then estimated at 40,000. According to the writer, Elizabeth Eliot, this was 'the first example of the development of steeplechasing through a line – Flat racing – a race for hunters, and the revolt of the hunters against the race horses.'

In the 1830s, a St Albans hotel proprietor called Tom Coleman, often referred to as the 'father of steeplechasing', oversaw the next big step in the sport's development: the institution of a regular, annual, steeplechasing fixture. Writes Eliot, 'Up to this date, 1830/31, steeplechases had been run spasmodically when one gentleman took it into his head to challenge another gentleman.' Coleman began this move away from impulse races towards properly organised, pre-arranged meetings.

It was in 1834, at the height of the St Albans Chase's success, that the first jumps races, over hurdles, were staged at Aintree. This was a new venture for William Lynn, landlord of Liverpool's Waterloo Hotel, the man who, five years earlier, had established the new course. In those early years, Lynn had faced competition from another Flat course at nearby Maghull, which staged its first races in 1827. It was the closure of Maghull – and the monopoly of Flat racing in the local area bequeathed to Lynn as a result – that appears to have persuaded him to attempt to broaden Aintree's range of attractions.

This was an initiative not without risks. South-west Lancashire was starting to acquire a reputation for hare-coursing, due largely to support from the Earls of Sefton, whose name would come to be linked just as readily with the Grand National. The main steeplechasing centres, however, were located well to the south in the foxhunting country of the English Home Counties and the rural Midlands. Word of Lynn's latest venture had, though, reached the redoubtable Captain Martin Becher, a rider as dominant in that age as A. P. McCoy is in this. He duly won the first race in impressive style on a horse called

Milliner and the meeting, held on 24 October, was judged enough of a success to be repeated and expanded the following year.

Emboldened by the favourable reception greeting this experiment and a degree of financial pressure to drum up revenues, Lynn went a step further and decided to stage a steeplechase at Aintree. This 'Liverpool Grand Steeple-Chase' was run on 29 February 1836 – 128 years to the day before Foinavon's maiden victory at Naas. The victor, once again, in a ten-horse race was Captain Becher riding a sturdy chestnut with one white sock called The Duke. In an innovation essential to the sport's development as a spectator attraction, moreover, the race started and finished in the same place and not by some distant church steeple.

It is the 1839 contest, won by Lottery, the Arkle of his day, which has come to be seen as the first Grand National – not least because this was the race to which the phrase 'Grand National' was first applied by a correspondent for *Bell's Life* writing under the name of 'Sam Slick'. But John Pinfold, an Oxford historian who has made extensive scrutiny of contemporary documentation, is convinced that the 1836 race should properly be accorded this honour. 'This race was run over what to all intents and purposes was the same course as that used today,' he says. What Lottery's race did achieve was to establish Aintree as the most popular and prestigious steeplechase in England. This was in part because of the demise of the St Albans Chase, whose timing had clashed with the Liverpool race in 1837, preventing Lynn from building on the success of the 1836 event. It was, furthermore, not until 1839 that Liverpool could be reached by train from both London and steeplechasing's Midlands heartland. This facilitated both more runners and a bigger crowd.

Then, as now, the Grand National was run over two circuits of the Aintree course – a distance equating throughout the 20th century to four miles and 856 yards. Thirty fences up to 5ft 2in in height are jumped. There are 16 obstacles on each circuit and all must be cleared twice, except for the biggest fence of all, The Chair, and the water-jump. In 1967, the fences were built of thorn, with many dressed with distinctive dark green spruce. Materials, which also included fir and gorse, were gathered from North Wales and Cumberland. From a hunter's viewpoint, running in a Grand National is the rough equivalent of galloping across 31 250-yard wide fields and clearing a hedge at the end of all but the last.

In terms of both distance and fence size, it is the most gruelling event on the British horse-racing calendar. True, four-and-a-half miles would be far from ultra-long-distance for a human athlete – even with 30 strenuous jumping efforts appended. But a thoroughbred racehorse weighs half a tonne – not far off ten times the weight of Haile Gebrselassie, the great Ethiopian long-distance runner. Horses are also flight animals – they flee danger – and, so far as one can tell, have little if any concept of pacing themselves, though they stick with the herd. In a Grand National, as in other races, they gallop as fast as they can, or as their jockey will allow, completing the course in 9–10 minutes at an average speed of some 30mph. To cap it all, they are humping around an extra 10–12 stone on their backs above their bodyweight.

To be able to do this, any racehorse, be it Arkle or a 100/1 outsider, needs to be able to deliver enormous quantities of oxygen to the 25kg or so of muscle crammed into each of its haunches. One key component of the remarkable biological engine that drives this process is the thoroughbred's huge lung capacity. A galloping racehorse breathes up to 40 litres of air per *second*. That adds up to around 20,000 litres of air ventilated while running a Grand National – or about what you or I might breathe in two *days*. A racehorse's heart – the pump that circulates the blood – is similarly impressive at several times the size of a cow's. The spleen also plays a vital role. This organ contains 30 per cent of the animal's oxygen-carrying red blood cells. When it starts to exercise hard, these cells go into the circulation, in a process that has been referred to by researcher Alberto Minetti as 'internal blood doping'.

Several of the Aintree fences that Grand National runners are called upon to jump have been endowed with names that are part of British sporting folklore. The most famous of all is Becher's Brook. First encountered as the sixth fence, about a mile from the start, this is named after the same Captain Becher who won Liverpool's Grand Steeple-Chase in 1836. Three years later, the good captain got a taste of Aintree's less hospitable side, when his mount, Conrad, fell and pitched him into the six-foot-wide waterway that was then to be found on the landing side of the fence. Having a keen sense of self-preservation, Becher stayed in the ditch until the other runners had galloped by, muttering, according to one version which, it must be said, has an apocryphal ring, that he never knew water tasted so filthy without brandy.

It is not the brook, which by 2011 was much reduced, that is the source of the fence's latter-day notoriety, however. It is the big drop on the landing side. This encouraged jockeys to lean far back in their saddles to prevent their mounts from overbalancing and was capable of making riders feel like they were jumping off the edge of the world. Dick Francis, the jockey-turned-thriller writer who was there reporting on the 1967 race for a national newspaper, once recalled that going over Becher's he found he had 'an extensive view of Liverpool for what seemed a very long time'. To add to the challenge posed by the obstacle facing Foinavon and the other 1967 runners, there was a steep upward slope on the landing side that seemed to claw the more hesitant jumpers back towards the brook. The drop was most severe for jockeys seeking to navigate the shortest way around the course on the inner.

Two fences further on is the Canal Turn, the five-foot barrier that bore the brunt of the vandalism ahead of the 1967 meeting. This takes its name from the nearby Leeds and Liverpool Canal and from the 90-degree left-hand turn that runners must execute as quickly as possible after clearing the obstacle. No sooner have horses veered around to the west, to run parallel with the canal, than they are confronted by Valentine's, another five-foot-high fence, sited beside the same brook that Captain Becher fell into. This was named after a horse in the 1840 National who appeared intent on pulling himself up at the obstacle only to execute an extraordinary pirouetting leap that ultimately carried him clear. Lord Sefton's stand used to be located adjacent to the landing side of Valentine's.

The Chair is in front of the Aintree grandstands near where a judge's chair used to be situated. At 5ft 2in, it is the biggest fence on the course and, like the water-jump, must be cleared only once. Guarded on the take-off side by a ditch as wide as a man is tall, the fence can appear even bigger than it actually is because it is much narrower than many of the obstacles that precede it. The solidity of its appearance tends to bring to mind a building as much as a hedge. Amateur rider John Hislop once said it seemed 'impenetrable as a prison wall'.

For some, particularly at the time of the 1967 National, the first open ditch had a reputation nearly as forbidding as that of The Chair. This was partly because it came so early in the race (the third fence in all), but also because of its size (5ft with a 6ft-wide ditch on the take-off side) and the fact that it was first negotiated when most of the field was still on its feet and bunched. John Lawrence (later Oaksey), the prominent amateur rider, racing journalist and peer of the realm, booked to ride Norther in the 1967 event, wrote that one year, 'I was not the only participant … who thought it resembled the Grand Canyon.' It was the favourite fence of Steve Westhead, Aintree's master fence-builder of the 1960s and 1970s, and was to have been named the Westhead Ditch in his memory, but this hasn't really caught on.

For all the daunting reputations of the more famous obstacles, however, it is a fence that has never warranted a name that traditionally claims the most fallers. In 2004, it was calculated that the first fence was almost seven times more likely to result in a fall than other plain fences. This is in part because it is the only fence jumped by every horse. There are other factors at play, however. It is, for example, located an unusually long way from the start-line, giving runners plenty of scope to build up speed as they jockey for race position and release the tension that builds up during extensive pre-race formalities. The fence's most absurd casualty toll came in 1951, when 11 of the 36 runners came to grief there after a botched start. First fence fallers often include some of the more fancied horses in the race – and 1967 was no exception.

Though the broad outline of the course has been unaltered since 1836, there have been many changes to fences and other details. In the early years, for example, one of the obstacles consisted of a stone wall. This was removed for good in 1844. It was not until 1885 that the National was run over a course consisting almost entirely of turf for the first time. Prior to that, horses had contended with all manner of agricultural surfaces, including ploughed terrain. From 1888, all the barriers in the race became proper fences with the elimination of three hurdles that used to be encountered on the home straight.

Much the most significant change of the 1960s came in 1961, when plain fences were sloped on the take-off side to make them more inviting to jump. According to Bobby Beasley, who won the race that year aboard the grey Nicolaus Silver, 'In the past many horses had fallen as a result of getting too close to the big upright obstacles. Now ... a horse had another yard in which to see the fence and time for take off.' By 1963, *The Times*'s racing correspondent was asserting that the change in the shaping of the fences had 'reduced by more than half the number of falls in all races over them'. The number of mistakes being made, he added, had 'diminished remarkably'.

No matter how the course has been modified over the years, the sheer life-affirming, thrill of racing around the big Liverpool fences on a bold-jumping thoroughbred has remained intact – even for professional jockeys who ride steeplechases most days of their lives. Brough Scott, who as both an ex-Grand National jockey and a fine writer is one of the few capable of capturing and conveying this magic, comments on the look in riders' eyes after the race. 'Forget about the winning jockey, all the jockeys who got round will have their eyes ablaze with the experience,' he says. Dick Francis, equally well qualified, resorted to an image that might be appreciated by yachtsman Chay Blyth, who also attended the 1967 race, to evoke his first experience of riding at Liverpool. It was, he said, 'like crossing the equator'. He went on, 'I find I cannot properly describe the ecstasy of Aintree; no one who has not ridden there can understand it.'

*

For all the residual doubts over the Grand National's future, the race that Blyth, Francis, Gregory and Veronique Peck and tens of thousands of others were converging on Liverpool to see in 1967 had an exciting look about it – in spite of a string of noteworthy absentees, equine and human. Arkle would not, of course, be there, nor would he grace any race meeting again. And his old rival Mill House had been scratched from the National field on 28 March. But it was the withdrawal three days later of another horse, Highland Wedding, which created the biggest stir, with the story making the front page of *The Times*. This was largely because the horse had been installed as favourite for the race and his withdrawal was unexpected, coming after he had hit himself on a foreleg in training. Absent jockeys included Foinavon's old partner (and Arkle's) Pat Taaffe; Jeff King, deprived by a fractured skull of the thrill of riding the hard-pulling Rondetto at Aintree; and, for the first time in 16 years, Michael Scudamore, who had won the race on Oxo eight years previously.

With the very biggest chasing stars missing, an open race looked all the more likely. There was, moreover, enough quality in the 44 runners who would go to post for John Lawrence to adjudge this 'the best Grand National field for years'.

Fifteen or more horses, including Peck's classy young chaser Different Class, were thought to have a chance. Captain Ryan Price's What a Myth was the highest-rated performer after his impressive Cheltenham Gold Cup run, and would carry top weight. A number of canny observers, however, were coming out in favour of another Price horse, the gentlemanly Honey End, who appeared well handicapped, had never fallen and would be ridden by the stylish and determined Josh Gifford. The previous year's first and second, chalk and cheese as they were, were back. Anglo, flash as a show-pony, with his blond tail and prominent white socks, had his backers. So did Freddie, the stocky, if irascible, Scottish trier who never gave in and who tended to run with glycerine-coated tongue hanging out of his mouth like a crofter's dog. Runner-up for the past two years, he was the people's choice.

Tim Norman, the jockey who had ridden Anglo to victory 12 months before, had this time chosen a different mount, Kilburn. A winner of three races already that season, in two of which he had beaten Anglo and one Highland Wedding, Kilburn was owned by Madame Borel de Bitche, the English-born widow of a Belgian ambassador who had served in that country's wartime government-in-exile in London. Unusually for a successful steeplechaser, the horse had been bought as a showjumper but switched to racing after refusing to jump tiny practice fences called *cavalletti*.

The speedy Solbina was given a squeak of a chance of outperforming stable-companion Anglo and delivering trainer Fred Winter his third consecutive Grand National victory. A few felt similarly that Kapeno might outdo his stablemate Different Class – if only he could get over his aversion to Becher's Brook. The Fossa, Foinavon's fellow goat-lover, had run well twice before at Aintree, while both Rondetto and the massive Limeking had their supporters. So did both representatives from Denys Smith's yard at Bishop Auckland in County Durham. Greek Scholar, a chestnut horse with a perfect white diamond on his forehead, was the mount of Terry Biddlecombe, the champion jockey who still, like his friend and rival Josh Gifford, was striving to win his first Grand National. Red Alligator, a lively outsider, would be ridden by a little-known local teenager called Brian Fletcher.

Another young American-owned horse called Rutherfords appeared to be coming into form at the right moment. It transpired subsequently that his trainer had been so keen to run him that he had kept the horse in the race even though he had slivers of glass in one foot. Finally, there was Bassnet, second in the previous year's Topham Trophy over the National fences, who had taken over for a time as favourite after Highland Wedding's withdrawal.

If there was much dispute over the identity of the likeliest winner of the next day's big race, however, pundits were unanimous on one point: you could rule out Foinavon.

Chapter 15

A TYPICAL DAY FOR SOMETHING TERRIBLE TO HAPPEN

By 7am the ground in front of Aintree's empty, white stands was reverberating with drumming hooves, as John Buckingham and others cantered the horses they hoped would soon be carrying them to Grand National glory. Early morning exercise sessions could be an exhilarating experience at Liverpool, the air fresh, the turf glistening with dew, the mind alive with the challenge of converting a lifetime's dreams into reality. Saturday 8 April 1967, though, had dawned very grey and very wet. Says Pat Buckley, who won the 1963 National on Ayala and this time around would be riding Limeking for mining magnate Alfred Chester Beatty, 'It was a typical day for something terrible to happen.'

Peter O'Sullevan was there at 7am too, surveying the scene, on the lookout for distinguishing marks on the horses that might inform his comments later in the day. Race-time would find the BBC's number one commentator in position on top of the main stand, keeping the broadcaster's millions-strong international audience apprised of the story unfolding, with the help of his hand-annotated racecard and a small black and white monitor screen.

This would be the eighth televised Grand National. The BBC had finally overcome Mrs Topham's misgivings about the impact of live television coverage on attendance figures at the course in late 1959. The first Grand National of the 1960s thus became the first to be broadcast in this way, ending a 17-month hiatus that had followed another landmark: the live screening of a less prestigious Aintree steeplechase after *Watch With Mother*, on 6 November 1958. Such wariness about embracing the medium on the part of sports rights-holders might seem antiquated today, but Mrs Topham was far from alone in fearing the consequences of letting the television cameras in. Only that week, as Foinavon was being drilled in Berkshire over John Kempton's spruce-clad practice-fence, Football League chairmen had taken less than half an hour to turn down a BBC live television proposal worth £781,000. In the event, Mrs Topham and her colleagues found that, while gate receipts in 1960 were indeed down, profit was up – by £2,000. Their still tentative conclusion? 'So far, television had generally paid us.'

By 1967, the great majority of people who watched the race in real time did so on television. Against perhaps 50,000 on the course, the BBC estimated that there would be 50 million television viewers getting coverage in a range of European countries. Marshal Tito's Yugoslavia was to have been included until technical difficulties intervened. Canadians would see the race live for the first time, as a signal was bounced across the Atlantic by satellite 'by way of Fucine in Italy'. This made it even more of a pity that the former favourite, the Canadian-owned Highland Wedding, would not after all be running, although the horse's owner, Charles Burns, had come to Liverpool regardless.

The drama and spectacle of the Grand National was, as became immediately apparent, just made for television – even in the black-and-white era. Forty or more handsome thoroughbreds poured at high-speed over towering fences, their jockeys striving manfully to exercise even a modicum of control. The wonders of technology brought viewers far closer to the action than they could ever hope to be at the course – and kept them in the thick of things throughout. The story of the race, meanwhile, was narrated by an expert commentary team, spearheaded by the incomparable O'Sullevan, whose voice somehow combined velocity with utter clarity and whose snap judgements and observations were rarely wide of the mark. A taste of the race's dramatic character had been available before television via newsreels shown to cinema audiences. But live coverage, combined with the rapid spread of betting-shops in the 1960s, enabled people to indulge themselves in an extra frisson of excitement not available in their local Gaumont: they could back a horse and then follow its progress in every detail while baying it on in the privacy and comfort of their own sitting rooms.

And it has to be said that the BBC did an exceptional job. One example of how the broadcaster made every effort to bring viewers the most dramatic pictures possible was its so-called 'roving-eye'. This was a camera mounted on a vehicle – initially a standard BBC van, later an adapted station wagon – that kept pace with the horses while they were racing. As Ray Lakeland, the BBC man who produced all the early Grand National broadcasts, recalls, the idea was conceived with the Lincolnshire Handicap, a Flat race run over a straight mile, in mind – and was not without its teething problems. Lincoln racecourse, as he explains, was beside a road which used to be closed on race-days. 'I had this bright idea, because the road was parallel to the track, that we might use a sort of mobile camera,' Lakeland says. 'I persuaded our engineers to put a camera on top of their camera van … I thought I had better give it a bit of a start so I placed it half a furlong along from the start and set it off at the same time as the horses set off. Within about four strides, they overtook it. I didn't realise that a horse can go from nought to 30mph in about three strides.' Once they had got the logistics right, however, the idea worked.

One of the few similarities between Lincoln and Aintree was that the Liverpool venue also had a tarmac road beside the racecourse – in this case the Grand Prix racing circuit opened in 1954. If this was good enough for Jack Brabham and Stirling Moss, it would certainly enable the 'roving eye' to operate. Indeed, this key ingredient of the BBC's Grand National coverage is a rare example of something beneficial to horse racing coming as a direct result of the introduction of motor racing at Aintree. (Another came when stable manager Ossie Dale was able to offer the head lad of Nicolaus Silver, the 1961 Grand National winner, a can of Castrol engine-oil to substitute for the horse's regular hoof-oil which had been mislaid. As Dale observed, 'It proved as effective with the horse as for its true purpose.')

The first use of the 'roving eye' at a National earned Lakeland a summons from the stewards for positioning it too close to the horses. 'There was Lord Derby in the middle, Lord Sefton to his left and Lord Cadogan to his right,' the BBC man recalls. Thereafter, the standard instruction was for the device, which was equipped with a zoom lens, to keep half a fence ahead of the leaders. The mobility that the 'eye' afforded was a particularly valuable asset in grey, rainswept conditions like those pertaining in 1967, which made the images obtained from camera positions further removed from the action indistinct. The tool's value was also greatly enhanced by the skills of Don 'Mac' Mackay, its regular operator, a short man whose working garb included a skull-hugging pre-war flying helmet. This was necessary to hold his earphones in position as he was keeping pace with the fastest horses in the field.

Come showtime, while his main man O'Sullevan was as high up as you could get at Aintree, Lakeland was hunkered down in the telegraph office under the County Stand, sitting, poised as a concert pianist, at his control panel, with 20 monitors – one for each camera-position – glowing in front of him. The sheer size of the racecourse made technical arrangements all the more complicated. Each camera was limited to about 400 yards of cable, after which picture quality would deteriorate. This meant that at least two further mobile control units had to be stationed at strategic points. Similarly, while O'Sullevan was perfectly positioned to describe the finish of the race, his contribution was supplemented by a team of commentators at other vantage-points. In 1967, for example, the key commentary position adjacent to Becher's Brook at the far end of the course was to be manned by Michael O'Hehir, the course commentator from Baldoyle.

Having done his wartime service in a tank regiment in North Africa and Italy, Lakeland, a self-confessed 'seat of the pants guy', could handle pressure. Even so, the period of transmission was a time of unremitting tension, with the story-line impossible to predict and infinite scope for something to go wrong. On one occasion, a commentator stationed in a position overlooking the course some 40 feet up was struck by vertigo and dropped his microphone just as he was being cued to go on air. 'You would come out of the control room and you would twang you were so tense,' Lakeland says. Cigarette consumption was off the scale.

Cyril Watkins was up early on Grand National morning too. Whereas other owners like Gregory Peck and Charles Burns had come thousands of miles to be at Aintree, Foinavon's owner would emulate millions of once-a-year punters with no special connection to that year's race by watching it at home on television. There were a number of reasons for this.

First, the long wait for Foinavon's first win in England was starting to tell even on him. In the run-up to Liverpool, he had concluded that his light green and Mackintosh tartan colours must be bringing the horse bad luck and so had decided to change them. In the big race, Buckingham would be sporting decidedly sombre new black silks, enlivened, like a Wall Street trader of the Ivan Boesky era, by bright red and yellow 'braces', or vertical stripes. Had he known about it, the switch would certainly have met with the approval of Sidney Spofforth, *chef patissier* at the Liverpool Adelphi. Among Spofforth's duties on one of the busiest evenings of his year would be to adorn chocolate horses, earmarked for the hotel's traditional post-Grand National banquet, with the colours of the leading finishers. 'We will just have to pray that the winner does not carry tartan colours,' Spofforth joked to a local newspaper reporter as the big day approached. 'Anything else we can cope with.'

Watkins's second reason for staying at home was that, as his recent hospital visits indicated, he was not in the best of health. Most significant of all, however, was the fact that it was FA Cup quarter-finals day. This meant a busy weekend for the football pools industry from which he made his living. The previous evening would have been spent, like most Fridays during the season, in the office behind his Tilehurst pet-shop, just up the road from an imposing red brick United Reformed Church. There he awaited the arrival of the Littlewoods agents who worked the area he held the concession for, with their bundles of completed coupons and weekly takings garnered from local homes and workplaces. The process of ensuring all was in order – with coupons dispatched, ironically, to Liverpool, where the company was headquartered – was long and finicky and would not be completed until well into Saturday morning. Only then could he get into his pillar-box red Jag, make his way back home to Finchampstead and allow his mind to drift off to Aintree and the bets he had placed, more in hope than expectation, on his recalcitrant chaser.

A bleary-eyed Tony Hutt, meanwhile, had made it back from Merseyside in his cream-coloured horsebox and was setting out for Worcester with the Kemptons' big hope for the weekend, Three Dons, on board. The chestnut colt had won a hurdle race at Huntingdon on Easter Monday – just half an hour after Foinavon's one and only outing with Dave Patrick – and now, like McCrimmon before him, was in the brief transition period during which he was still eligible for novice races. That Huntingdon result had been the yard's first victory of the entire

1966/67 season. That, together with the imminent loss of Three Dons's novice status, plus the fact that he could make the weight the colt had been allotted to carry, explains why John Kempton chose to go to Worcester not Aintree, delegating the long and probably fruitless trek to Liverpool to his father Jack.

Three Dons, then, was at that moment the star of the yard, a status he underlined by exhibiting a star's temperament. Head lad Colin Hemsley, the apple of whose eye he was, was the only member of the stable's entourage who could venture anywhere near him without risk of getting bitten or kicked. 'When I went away, the others used to drop his food over his stable-door because they wouldn't go in with him,' Hemsley says. By way of mitigation, the colt had a star's looks too. 'He absolutely glowed,' according to Hemsley. Owner Frank Reynolds, who lived at Balsall Common near Coventry and was managing director of a company called the Commando Group, thought so much of him he bought a car with the registration mark DON333.

Clearly, when Three Dons ran, it had to be Hemsley who accompanied him to the races – which ruled the head lad out of going to Liverpool that day too. For one horrible moment, though, when he and Hutt reached the Cotswolds, Hemsley feared that their carefully laid plans were in jeopardy. There was snow on the ground: what if the Worcester meeting was called off? Fortunately, the snow turned out to be confined to high ground. Long before they turned into the narrow road that led to the stable entrance on the opposite side of the racecourse from the old Grand Stand Hotel, Hemsley's fears had evaporated.

After morning exercise, Buckingham went to walk the course with his brother Tom before heading back to his digs, while other jockeys drove back to Southport where they were staying in close proximity to the local Turkish baths. According to champion jockey Terry Biddlecombe, who had won two of the three National Hunt races the previous day and was due to ride the moderately fancied Greek Scholar in the National, there would be 'at least ten or twelve jockeys in there who really had to get the weight off.' At about 9.30am, a bustling old masseur would go out and bring back champagne or fresh orange juice, 'which refreshed everybody'. At 11am, they would all pile out, in order to check out of their seaside hotels before the noon deadline.

Buckingham kept being told by his landlady that he was going to win. He didn't take it too seriously, thinking, 'Oh yes, you know, she's just saying that'. Two Irishmen staying at the house had the same confidence in him; they backed Foinavon.

Back in the marble-lined luxury of the Liverpool Adelphi, guests were whiling away the morning beneath an avalanche of newspapers. Along with a wide assortment of tips for one or other of the more fancied runners, they might have noticed a small item about Tim Durant, a 67-year-old American whose colourful past included spells as a stockbroker and a rider in cowboy movies. For his latest adventure, Durant was aiming to become the oldest man to finish a Grand National, aboard a 100/1 shot called Aerial III. This was in spite of undergoing an operation to remove a cancerous lump from his ankle. His attempt had become one of the talking-points of the race. Now came news that the 'Galloping Grandad', as Durant had become known, had sent a telegram to Ladbrokes, the London bookmaker, asking, 'Will you lay me £60 at 15/1 against Aerial III finishing in Grand National?' The sporting reply, from the company's chairman, was also published. 'We lay you £60 at 15/1 against Aerial III finishing,' it read. 'Will throw in case of champagne if you survive Becher's twice.'

Those who took the trouble to scrutinise Charles Benson's Horse-by-Horse Guide in the *Daily Express* – headlined 'Mug or maestro ... this page is on your side!' – might, meanwhile, have noticed, perhaps with a wry smile, how curtly he dismissed another outsider. 'Foinavon has no chance,' he advised sagaciously. 'Not the boldest of jumpers, he can be safely ignored even in a race noted for shocks.'

Chapter 16

'JOHNNY, WHAT'S THIS YOU'RE RIDING?'

The atmosphere was building as John Buckingham crossed the Ormskirk Road and re-entered the racecourse. A succession of special trains, including one, from Grimsby and Cleethorpes, that was steam-hauled, had pulled into the nearby railway station and disgorged groups of Scots, Geordies, Londoners and Brummies who joined local race-goers milling around the sodden facilities. Trilby-hatted bookies under large umbrellas vied for bets on the first race of the day, the Liverpool Hurdle. Though it was hardly the weather for high fashion, trouser-suits were numerous among the more traditional headscarves and sheepskin coats. Colours were as varied as the Grand National parade itself: citron-yellow to navy blue, lime-green to orange.

It was lunchtime for any normal human being, but there are sound, practical reasons why jump jockeys don't really do lunch. As Bucking-ham explained some time later, 'I never have lunch when I'm riding. I don't think anybody does ... If you have an accident, you see, you have probably got to have some sort of an operation – and anyway, you couldn't ride on a full stomach.' Ten of the 44 Grand National jockeys, including most of the big names, had mounts in the curtain-raising hurdle race, but Buckingham was not one of them. So he waited.

Up at the far end of the course, John Pinfold, the future historian, then a teenager from Woolton, was attending his first Grand National accompanied by his father, who worked for Whitbread, the brewer. Regular viewers of the annual BBC broadcasts, they had decided this time to drive the five miles to see the race in the flesh for fear that it might be discontinued. They had paid the princely sum of 14 shillings for parking and right of admittance to the small, recently vandalised concrete stand adjacent to the Canal Turn fence. The crowd in this area, far from the main grandstand, was a mixed bunch, combining local Scousers, the county set with their shooting-sticks and car-boot picnics, and a smattering of moralistic stump orators, standing on soapboxes inveighing against gambling and the wages of sin.

Pinfold remembers that one of these characters, more eloquent than most, had attracted 'quite a little crowd' of young men around him. All, it seemed, was going swimmingly until he disclosed, as it turned out injudiciously, that before finding God he had been a Liverpool policeman. At this revelation, the preacher's audience moved as one, as if impelled by some invisible force, carried their haranguer to the fence at the edge of the racecourse and deposited him with a splash into the canal on the other side.

Another member of the sizeable crowd gathering at this end of the course was Michael Daley, also a Liverpool teenager. He and his two friends, wearing fashionable dark blue 'mod macs', were trying to secure a vantage-point next to Becher's Brook from which to watch the race. So slippery and muddy were the conditions, however, that they gave up, opting to stand instead by the small unnamed fence between Becher's and the Canal Turn. In the Fazackerley railway yard behind and above them, meanwhile, another train had by this time pulled into a berth usually reserved for the loading of flat-bed wagons with sections of track required to carry out repairs. This was the so-called 'officers' special', for retired railway employees, which trundled the six miles from Liverpool Exchange station on Grand National day every year and trundled back after the race. It was no good, of course, if you wanted to see the finish, which would be fought out a good mile away. But the carriages were excellently placed to watch the National's most spectacular sight: the field streaming over Becher's Brook. Some passengers, moreover, were sitting warm and dry barely 20 yards from the fence where Michael Daley and his friends had taken up station, the fence usually referred to as the 'one after Becher's'.

At eight minutes past two, with more than an hour still to go before the Grand National was due to start, the bold-jumping Jupiter Boy flashed past the winning-post leaving blond-haired Terry Biddlecombe to celebrate his third Aintree winner in two days. A hundred miles south of there at Worcester's pancake-flat racecourse beside the River Severn at the same instant, 18-year-old Graham Goode – later to become a household name with Channel 4 – was preparing to deliver his first solo live commentary at a race-meeting. Fittingly, it was a novices' hurdle. Among the nine runners and riders heading to post were a blinkered Three Dons and John Kempton, carrying a distinctive whip with a large leather flap on the end. It was an important moment for the small yard, with the trainer's mother Molly – who had also come to Worcester – betting a significant sum on the outcome, on the strength of the colt's victory at Huntingdon on Easter Monday. Sadly, there was only a small crowd to witness Goode's maiden commentary, with the biting wind and rain keeping many away.

The unusual whip – known in the trade as a 'bull's pizzle stick' – was a calculated move to bring out the best in a temperamental animal. Three Dons, like many racehorses, needed encouragement to move into overdrive. Yet he stopped running when hit with an ortho- dox racing whip. The idea of the big flap was to produce an implement that would yield a resounding crack when brought down on the horse's rump without hurting him. That afternoon, it worked like a charm. Sent off at 5/1 third-favourite, Three Dons overhauled the favourite, a horse called Threadbare, approaching the last and cruised home four lengths clear. Delighted head lad Colin Hemsley proceeded to lead his favourite horse into the winners' enclosure, a sweat-rug neatly rolled under one arm, a yellow bucket in his left hand. After making sure Three Dons was comfortable, Kempton and Hemsley made for the single-storey green-and-white building that housed the jockeys' room. There, a small television set in the corner, away from the wall-mounted wooden saddle-racks, would enable them to watch the big race from Liverpool.

Buckingham was spending the final tense minutes before the race formalities began collecting autographs on behalf of a female race-goer. He went around all 43 of his fellow Grand National jockeys – no easy task when conditions were so cramped that, according to Richard Pitman who, like Buckingham, was about to ride in the great race for the first time, 'you only had enough room for one buttock on the bench.' Like others before and since, Buckingham was struck by the unaccustomed quiet. 'The lads were all sitting down,' he recalled, 'whereas they'd normally be larking about.' Pitman, though 'not very religious', says he always went to church on the way to the course. 'I don't know why really,' he adds – although, 'no end of jockeys, even the blasphemers, will ask for the good Lord's help at some stage in a race. "Just let me get over the next and I'll be good for the rest of my life."' The air in the confined space was heady with the mingled aromas of sweat and leather, cigarette smoke and embrocation. John Lawrence may have been indulging in his pre-race regimen of glucose and orange quarters. Demand for the toilet would undoubtedly have been heavy. According to Biddlecombe, 'I have never seen so many trying to have a last "go" – if you had held a tablespoon under them they could not have filled it.' How the valets tending the jockeys managed to ensure that everyone was equipped with the correct colours and gear in such circumstances is a mystery, one suspects, known only to them.

Finally, it was time to weigh out and the 44, in full racing attire, trooped over to await their turn on the scales. It was at this point that Michael O'Hehir, the Irish commentator assigned by the BBC to Becher's Brook and the other fences at the far end of the course, caught sight of a set of racing colours that, for all his exhaustive preparations, he did not recognise. As he later recalled, 'I have a habit that through the years I go into the weigh-room at Aintree, with permission of the stewards there, and I stand for about an hour before the National checking off each jockey's colours as that jockey gets into the weighing scales. I've been working for two months beforehand on paper ... but to actually see these colours, you know, the shade of blue, the tinge of red. It can make all the difference.

'I saw this man standing in a line of jockeys with a black jacket and the yellow-and-red braces effect on him and I went down my list and I went to the racecard and I couldn't make out what [it was]. I said, "Oh to hell with it, I'll go over." And I went over and I said, "Johnny, what's this you're riding?" "Oh I'm riding Foinavon," he said ... "The owner thought that green was unlucky and they decided that today they'd use these new colours."'

The length and breadth of the British Isles – and beyond – people were now settling in for the race. At Mullingar, a small racecourse-town in the Irish Republic, students at a local college were assembling at an old gymnasium, where a 22-inch television-set had been positioned in pride of place in the middle of a stage. At the Oatridge point-to-point near Edinburgh, George Pottinger had told his son Piers that he intended to have a bet on Foinavon 'because I fish there'. He walked across to the bookies, from the car where they were sheltering from the rain, saw that the horse was listed at 750/1 and decided not to bother. On a coach taking Everton fans to Nottingham to watch the FA Cup match against Forest, Michael Walters paid £1 10s (£1.50) to take part in an impromptu sweepstake organised by a stranger. He picked out Foinavon. With kick-off at 3pm, he was in the City Ground engrossed in the football by the time the race got under way. On the Orion oil rig in the North Sea, Eric Brown, a member of the catering staff, whose duties included fishing for cod off the rig on Thursday nights, organised his own £1-a-go sweepstake for fellow workers. He had sold all the tickets when a senior colleague approached him in a temper because he hadn't been offered the chance to take part. Brown was reluctant to sacrifice his own ticket, which was for one of the favourites, yet this colleague was too important to risk alienating. So he decided to pretend he had one ticket left – for a horse that had no chance of winning. 'You can have the last one,' he told him. 'It's Foinavon.'

In Berkshire, Cyril Watkins, Foinavon's long-suffering but persistent owner, had phoned in a final £2 bet on his horse to the Tote before sitting down with wife Iris in front of their large television. Watkins had placed most of his bets on the race around four weeks earlier, securing odds of 500/1 with two bookmakers. Mac Bennellick, Watkins's former co-owner, was preparing to watch the race in his office in Rainham, but had not backed the horse, although his son Colin had risked £1. Watkins's pet-shop in Tilehurst, where items on sale included sacks of 'racehorse manure', was being staffed that afternoon by Sheila Nixon, Iris's sister-in-law, and her daughter Lyn. They had to make do with a radio in the storeroom. Bennellick's future daughter-in-law, Chris, by contrast, had wandered into a Romford electrical shop and had a selection of televisions to choose from.

It was still a few minutes before three o'clock, but already the Aintree parade-ring was filling up with National horses, walking clockwise around the perimeter. They were labelled for the benefit of the huddled spectators, their names on the paddock-sheets strapped to their backs and their numbers on the left arms of the handlers leading them.

Gregory Peck's horse Different Class, a striking chestnut, gazed alertly into the crowd to his left, while Bassnet looked a picture as befitted a horse sired by Manet. The Scottish challenger Freddie, safely arrived from Haydock, had already started sticking out his tongue. The long-legged Honey End looked as calm as Forecastle, the only grey in the race, looked agitated, appearing quite unperturbed when the frisky Anglo, the 1966 winner, bowled into the ring in front of him. The eyes of spectators flicked from racecard to horse, horse to mud-flecked race-card, their shield-shaped badges tied prominently to their coats.

There had been a false start in the six-furlong Flat race that preceded the National, with one of the runners haring down the entire length of the course before his rider could pull him up. The resultant 16-minute delay looked like prolonging the agony of the steeplechase jockeys now itching to get under way. At 3pm, as the day's four FA Cup ties kicked off in Nottingham, Birmingham, Leeds and London, the 44 men were released from their purgatory. Into the paddock they strode, eyes darting from group to group in search of their horse's connections, some tipping the peak of their brightly coloured caps with due deference as they approached. Biddlecombe, dazzling as a tropical bird in the blue, yellow and cerise colours of Greek Scholar's owner, was one of the first to mount. Soon, clumps of discarded sheets and rugs were littering the middle of the paddock as, one by one, the jockeys climbed aboard their conveyances. It was at this point that the BBC camera, which had been flitting from horse to horse as commentator Clive Graham outlined each runner's form and prospects with a few deft phrases, alighted on Buckingham and Foinavon. 'Thirty-eight in the blinkers Foinavon,' Graham began. 'His chance must be considered remote. He's not won from 14 starts this season and it seems unlikely he will make an exception here.'

It was as the jockeys rode out in single file towards the racecourse, where they would parade in front of the grandstand before cantering down to the start, that their expressions and posture conveyed most poignantly the tensions raging inside them. For one of them, in all probability, these formalities would be the prelude to the most important race of his career. For many more, the day would end in disappointment; for one or two, more than likely, in disaster.

Freddie's jockey Pat McCarron, in blue and red, mindful no doubt of the near misses of the previous two years, looked particularly tense. Andy Turnell, at 18 the youngest rider in the race, lips pursed, seemed grimly determined. Nick Gaselee, a leading amateur rider, held his head high and his back ramrod straight like a Roman centurion in chocolate and yellow. Roy Edwards, riding Princeful, appeared almost avuncular beneath his black and yellow spotted cap. Tommy Carberry, one of the Irish contingent, bore a resemblance to the young Bob Dylan on Packed Home, a horse owned by Raymond Guest, the US Ambassador to Ireland. Brian Fletcher, another teenager, aboard Red Alligator, a horse many expected to run well, looks in retrospect a bit like a young Ryan Giggs, albeit in colours – purple and green – more readily associated with Wimbledon than Manchester United. Pat Buckley, his left hand on his hip, his colours recalling the Irish tricolour, was at least smiling, though it is hard to tell if this was a manifestation of confidence or tension. Much the happiest-looking jockey, his stick tucked under his left arm, was the oldest man in the race, the 67-year-old American, Tim Durant. Perhaps he was the one who felt he had least to lose.

It was coming up to 3.15pm as the top-weight What a Myth, at the head of the parade, led his 43 rivals past the winning-post, moving in the opposite direction to the one in which the winner would later gallop up to it. This was a moment of pure pageantry, like medieval knights saluting their patrons before some joust or tournament. But it could also be particularly nerve-racking for both horse and rider. What a Myth's jockey Paul Kelleway, in the Eton blue-and-black colours of his patron, Lady Weir, the horse's owner, assiduously stroked the horse along the base of his neck, aware that the rain would have improved his chances. At around this time, news was breaking that a half-share in another of Captain Ryan Price's Sussex-trained horses, the placid Honey End, was in the process of changing hands. This appeared to change the tone of what had been an indecisive betting market. In the minutes remaining before the off, the odds offered on Josh Gifford's already well-fancied mount tumbled, making him clear favourite.

Sitting in the grandstand as a guest of the executive was Marie Christine Ridgway, whose husband John had spent the previous summer accomplishing a feat which made even riding the Grand National course appear mundane: he had rowed across the Atlantic with a companion, Sergeant Chay Blyth. Blyth, who was also at Aintree that afternoon, had called his Scottish house Foinaven, after the mountain near where it stood. When he noticed that a horse of that name was running, it was hardly surprising that he could not resist having a small flutter.

Someone else on the course that day who was keen to have a bet on Foinavon was stable lad Clifford Booth. No sooner had he let go of the horse, leaving it to wheel away with Buckingham at the end of the parade, than he made his way to the Tote windows. 'I had ten bob in my pocket,' he says. 'I was going to have four bob each-way on him which would have left me two bob to get home for food.' Sadly, when the National got under way a few minutes later – the signal for betting on the race to halt – Booth was still waiting in line to be served. 'I couldn't get a bet on,' he says.

Chapter 17

OVER THE MELLING ROAD AND FAR AWAY

Every serious athlete knows it. The moment when you step into the arena and the rest of your life is put on hold until the match, fight or race in which you are about to take part is over. For most of the 44 Grand National jockeys, this threshold would have been crossed during the six or seven nerve-jangling minutes that they milled around in the starting-area, against the backdrop of a poster advertising Vernons football pools, waiting for the commanding, bowler-hatted figure of starter Alec Marsh to send them on their way. For the unlucky ones, this state of grace would last no more than a minute or two; for the finishers, considerably longer. But whatever banana-skins the racing gods were about to strew in their path, the 1967 Grand National was now for all of these men, in Brough Scott's phrase, 'the capsule of their existence'.

The hands of the square-faced clock surmounting the frame where the names of all 44 jockeys were displayed were creeping towards 3.25pm when the horses began coming into line, signalling that the start was imminent. In such a large field, the position assumed by each jockey on the start-line can be a good indication of the type of race he intends to run. At Aintree, a great deal of ground can be saved by riders prepared to hug the inside rail. There is, however, a *quid pro quo*: the drops on the landing side of the daunting drop-fences, particularly Becher's, are at their most severe on the inside. It is a route for the bold, best avoided by beginners. It was not surprising, then, to see Fred Winter's jockeys Eddie Harty (Solbina) and Bobby Beasley (Anglo), on whose shoulders rested the trainer's hopes of securing a hat-trick of Grand National victories, lining up on the inner. Alongside them was the experienced Stan Mellor, perhaps the weighing-room's foremost tactician, riding The Fossa. At the last moment, they were joined by David Nicholson on the well-backed Bassnet, runner-up in the previous season's Topham Trophy, run over the Grand National fences. Nicholson had been quoted in one of the papers that morning saying, 'I have never had a better chance of winning.'

At four miles and 856 yards, the National, though, is a very long race. In those days, a less aggressive approach whereby riders 'hunted' around the first circuit, assessed the situation and then set about getting into the race, was deemed perfectly respectable. For jockeys adopting this race-plan, a central or outside line was preferable, since it would afford them the best chance of avoiding trouble in the chaotic early stages, when bad luck could strike at any moment. On this occasion, those lining up on the outer consisted mainly of long-shots, such as the Galloping Grandad's mount Aerial III, Harry Black, Ross Sea and Foinavon's old rival from Ireland, Quintin Bay, who had finished sixth the previous year. Josh Gifford was plainly intent on allowing Honey End to acclimatise to conditions in his own time and had lined the favourite up slightly behind most of the others. John Buckingham, almost certainly not alone in thinking that the preliminaries 'seemed to take ages', had positioned Foinavon 'between the inner and the middle'.

Finally, the imposing, long-legged figure of Marsh strode deliberately across the line of horses, removing his raincoat as he approached the rostrum, and expertly started his 15th Grand National. Considering he was operating without a tape, the big field got away remarkably evenly.

In spite of its marathon length, the National nearly always begins at a blistering gallop. The pent-up tension affecting rider and horse, the temptation to jockey immediately for position given the large number of runners and the knowledge that the first fence is far, far away over the cinder-cushioned Melling Road all help to explain this phenomenon. With the rain making the going slippery but far from soft, the 1967 race was certainly no exception. And for a few strides, Buckingham and Foinavon were among those leading the herd as they sped away from the stands in a north-easterly direction, hooves drumming like a stampede of 44 buffalo.

It was all of 470 yards to that deceptively alluring first fence – and National debutant Richard Pitman had encountered an unforeseen hazard even before he got there. Galloping across the Melling Road aboard Dorimont who, at 13, shared with fellow outsider Bob-a-Job the distinction of being the oldest horse in the race, Pitman was 'so heavily showered with dust that I could not see the first fence'. The old chaser, though, jumped it 'with ease'.

Not everyone was so lucky. Indeed, while the first-fence casualty toll was nowhere near as heavy as in the 'Crashionals' of 1951 and 1952, the 4ft 6in thorn obstacle can never have exercised a greater influence over the destiny of the race.

Stockbroker Paul Irby, riding Ronald's Boy, survived by the skin of his teeth. 'I bloody nearly fell off,' he says. 'I lined up on the outside … After what seemed an interminable journey we crossed whatever road that is and came a bit close to the fence. I thought, "Oh this is it!" There was an appalling bang when the horse hit the fence and I was thrown all over [its] head. But I managed to avoid coming off.'

By the time the leaders – Princeful, Rutherfords, Penvulgo and Castle Falls – were back into their stride and streaking towards the second, three jockeys had crumpled to the wet Aintree turf. One of them was Nicholson. Bassnet had, in the words of *The Bloodstock Breeders' Annual Review*, 'completely over-jumped' the fence. A photograph, published the next week by *The Field*, captures the startled gelding lying on his right flank preparing to get up while, a couple of yards in front of his nose, the jettisoned jockey kneels on the grass as if before some deity, the peak of his yellow and green spotted cap still touching the ground. A thin scattering of spectators on the embankment beyond the outside rail surveys the scene seemingly dispassionately.

At 10/1, Bassnet was second-favourite behind Honey End. So his early demise dismayed many punters. In the jockeys' room at Worcester racecourse, however, dismay was not the emotion felt by Peter Jones as BBC commentator Bob Haines identified the first-fence fallers. Jones, who had just ridden a horse called Prince of Ormonde to victory in the 2.45pm, had partnered Bassnet in 12 of his 16 races since the start of the 1965/66 season, winning five times, with three of these victories at Cheltenham. However, after coming only fifth on the horse in Newbury's Mandarin Chase in January 1967 in a field so strong it included two of the first three horses home in that year's Cheltenham Gold Cup, Jones lost the ride. Instead, it was Nicholson who rode him to victory in the National Trial at Haydock Park on 1 February and in his three remaining races that season, including the National. It was a textbook illustration of the unforgiving nature of a sport whose competitive pressures often conspired against the journeyman jockey. 'If he could have got the milk out of your tea, he would have done,' says Jones of Nicholson, who was nicknamed 'The Duke', adding, 'He was all right, but very keen to get decent horses off you.' As Jones recalls, a cheer went up around the jockeys' room television in Worcester when Bassnet came down. 'They knew what he was like, The Duke,' he says.

Above Bassnet's withers in the photograph, in the semi-distance, lies Andy Turnell, whose debut Grand National has lasted less than 500 yards. The teenager is curled in the foetal position adopted by fallen jockeys trying to minimise the risk of injury from flying hooves while they are on the ground and directly in the path of the horses behind them. Frankly, if a half-tonne animal travelling at 35mph happens to tread on you, there is no position on earth that is going to protect you. On this occasion, though, Turnell was OK if supremely gutted. 'I was fine … just very disappointed,' he says. His mount, Meon Valley, jumped the fence 'very big, came down a bit steep and bowled straight over. So that was the end of it.'

There was one other victim, who can be seen just ahead of the cowed, crouching form of Meon Valley, caught in the act of hauling himself laboriously back to his feet. This was a ten-year-old bay gelding called Popham Down who, following the late withdrawal of Mill House, was the only representative in the field prepared by Fulke Walwyn, the five-times champion National Hunt trainer. As Meon Valley is rising, Popham Down's jockey Macer Gifford is beginning his terminal descent, feet first, over his mount's left shoulder. From the positions of those involved, it looks as though Meon Valley may somehow have interfered with his rival as he galloped past, prompting Gifford to lose his balance and topple from the saddle.

Watching in horror from the grandstand, her Zeiss binoculars trained unflaggingly on Gifford's royal-blue-and-gold check cap, was Mrs Charles Turriff, Popham Down's owner. At 27, the former Georgina Lewis was one of the youngest owners on the jump-racing circuit. This was by no means her sole accomplishment. She knew how to fly a helicopter, owned a stud farm near Wantage and competed in point-to-points, having been taught to race-ride by Fred Winter. She had attended finishing school in Gstaad, was dressed by Norman Hartnell and was acquainted with everyone from the Queen Mother to the senior stable lads at Walwyn's Lambourn yard. Her husband, Charles, was the man behind the Turriff construction and engineering company. The couple travelled widely, visiting industrial centres from the United States to the Middle East and also Sudan, where Turriff had a huge contract to build a town and 26 villages for people displaced by the Aswan Dam. The company also built office blocks, such as the Turriff Building, a skyscraper on London's Great West Road.

Mrs Turriff's – and Popham Down's – most memorable day in racing had come three years before, on 18 April 1964, when the seven-year-old had won the Scottish Grand National. The victory was obtained at the expense of Freddie in a thrilling race that saw the pair of them locked in combat over a long distance. Together over the last, Popham Down finally made his sizeable weight advantage tell on the run-in to win by half a length. It was said that the Bogside crowd's uninhibited roar was audible in Arran. Mrs Turriff remembers flying to Bogside in a private plane and staying with a member of the Shanks family of Armitage Shanks fame. By the end of the race, she was paralysed with excitement and had to be lifted down from the stand in her elegant blue-grey suit by Walwyn and another spectator.

That was as good as it got for this horse who was foaled at a farm on the Marlborough Downs and spotted by his owner at the well-known Manton yard then run by George Todd, where her husband used to keep a string of Flat racers. He continued, nonetheless, to win decent races, including Warwick's Crudwell Cup in both 1964 and 1965. Nearly five months after the second of these victories, he was a quietly fancied 22/1 shot for the 1966 Grand National, only to come down at Becher's Brook, sending regular jockey Willie Robinson somersaulting. This was, of course, a big let-down for the Turriffs, looking on from the box of Alex Bird, the well-known punter at whose moated Alderley Edge house they had spent the previous night.

Robinson says he had hoped to win the Mildmay Memorial Handicap Chase on him one year at Sandown, 'That was his type of race.' In 1965, however, the pair fell in a running of the race won by Freddie, his old Bogside rival; in 1967, the two-day meeting incorporating the Mildmay, in early January, was frosted off. Robinson was to have reason to wish that the next fixture at the Esher course on 10 and 11

February had been abandoned too. In a hurdle race, his mount Kirrie-muir crashed through the wing of the final flight, leaving the jockey with a broken leg. This left Robinson unavailable for Popham Down's ill-fated second attempt on the Grand National – and while Johnny Haine, his Scottish Grand National partner, rode him, again at Sandown, ten days before the Big Race, by this time Jeff King had also been injured, meaning Haine's services would be required to ride the strong-pulling Rondetto, King's regular mount, at Aintree.

It was as a result of this painful and all too typical game of musical saddles that Macer Gifford ended up sitting, however briefly, on Popham Down's back at Liverpool. Josh's younger brother, Macer, was at that time enjoying a run of success with a steeplechaser called Larbawn, owned and trained in Warwickshire by Michael Marsh, another of Mrs Turriff's many acquaintances. 'Macer suited certain horses,' Josh told me. 'They used to run for him.'

A popular figure, the younger Gifford brother was looking set to become a farmer, until 'out of the blue' he told Josh he had been offered a ride in a so-called members' race at Water Newton. 'I said, "Go on then – grab it!"' Gifford said, recalling how he put some breeches and boots in the post for him and then thought, 'Christ! Have I done the right thing?' He need not have worried. When they spoke that evening, it turned out Macer had finished third and last in the members' race, but picked up two 'spare' rides and won on both. 'That was it,' Gifford said. 'He was bitten.'

Though he was subsequently champion amateur jockey, Macer never attained the stature of his brother as a professional – few did. He died well before his time from motor-neurone disease.

Through her binoculars, Mrs Turriff – attired for the day in a specially made pink suit that matched her racing colours – watched anxiously as the now riderless Popham Down continued gamely on his way. By the time he was back in his stable lad's grasp, she would have bitten out all of the fingers of her gloves.

Chapter 18

A BLANKING
OF THE MIND

The spectacle of 40 or more mounted thoroughbreds streaming over a steeplechase fence is as thrilling as anything in sport. Yet racing exacts a heavy toll on its participants, human and equine. All first-fence casualties at Aintree that day got up unscathed. Back at the winner's enclosure, however, spectators would soon have cause to reflect on the risk jockeys run every time they swing themselves up into the saddle.

The blue Grand National ribbon was to be hung around the winner's neck by an impeccably groomed man in a sheepskin jacket who walked with a cane in each hand. Tim Brookshaw was a former jockey who had finished second in the 1959 Grand National, in a celebrated ride that saw him negotiate the last eight fences without the benefit of stirrups. This was after his right iron had broken on landing over Becher's Brook. Liverpool was also where Brookshaw had suffered a life-changing injury, breaking his back in a hurdle race in December 1963. Terry Biddlecombe, who won the race, saw Brookshaw fall 'straight onto his chest' after his mount had crashed through a wing of the fifth flight,

Foinavon as a yearling, Pallasgreen, County Limerick. The horse's breeder, Timothy H. Ryan, stands in the background.

Foinavon at four in Tom Dreaper's yard near Dublin with Peter McLoughlin who rode the horse to his second victory at Punchestown in 1964.

Side by side in the Scottish Highlands,
as their equine namesakes once were in
Tom Dreaper's yard (*from left to right*),
Foinaven, Arkle and Ben Stack.

Cyril and Iris Watkins. Cyril
acquired joint-ownership of
Foinavon with his partner
Mac Bennellick for 2,000
guineas in October 1965.

Mac Bennellick (*right*) talks to journalist Michael Litchfield at the time of the 'Great Pools Swindle'.

Mirabel Topham surveys her Aintree domain. Nothing on the racecourse was done at this time without her approval.

Wooden model from October 1965 of the 'Aintree Paddocks' housing development that might have been built at the racecourse. 'Somewhere near the location of fence number 12 is a cog-shaped school.'

The Queen Mother (*centre*) and Princess Margaret (*right*) in mohair tweed coat, in Liverpool for the 1965 Grand National. It was feared at the time that this might be the last National at Aintree.

The BBC's Ray Lakeland (*left*) with the 'Roving-Eye' – a camera mounted on a station wagon, used to bring viewers spectacular coverage of the race. The tool's value was enhanced by the skills of Don 'Mac' Mackay, its regular operator.

Many jockeys face a constant battle to ensure they can ride at the weights prescribed for their mounts. Here, Terry Biddlecombe, who won the 1967 Cheltenham Gold Cup on Woodland Venture, sits in his personal sweatbox, heated by 150-watt bulbs.

This scene at the Chair, the Grand National's biggest fence, captures the brooding atmosphere that hung over Aintree in 1966. Jockey Paddy Cowley sprawls in the foreground having been jettisoned from his mount; Jeremy Speid-Soote (*standing, centre*) struggles to keep hold of his 100/1 outsider Black Spot.

Jockeys Pat McCarron (*left*, Freddie), Nobby Howard (*centre*, Scottish Final) and Jack Cook (*right*, Ross Sea) queue to weigh out for the 1967 Grand National.

First fence drama: in the foreground jockey David Nicholson tumbles from the well-backed Bassnet. Though no one realised at the time, a more significant casualty was the 66/1 shot Popham Down. His rider Macer Gifford can be glimpsed in the act of falling on the extreme left of this photograph.

David Nicholson and Bassnet collect their thoughts after an early exit.

Disaster strikes at the 23rd as Rutherfords (*foreground*, sheepskin noseband) slams on the brakes, catapulting jockey John Leech from the saddle. Also in shot (*left to right*) are the riderless April Rose, Stan Hayhurst on Castle Falls (number 17), Johnny Haine on Rondetto (number 3) and Roy Edwards on Princeful (number 32).

John Buckingham and Foinavon approach the Canal Turn, the 24th, in glorious isolation but for three loose horses – Princeful (*left*), Rondetto (*centre*) and April Rose (*right*).

Jockeys John Lawrence (white and red colours) and Stan Mellor (blue and yellow) are sent flying at the 23rd fence as the race is stopped in its tracks. By the time John Buckingham and Foinavon thread their way through the melee ten seconds later, both riders have dashed to the relative safety of the outside rail.

A worried Pat Buckley (*left*) stands over his floored mount, Limeking, one of the victims of the pile-up at the 23rd fence. Remarkably, the huge horse was unhurt and able to walk back to the stables. 'I had a look around his legs,' the jockey recalled. 'No cuts, nothing.'

Moment of victory: on passing the winning-post it looked like all remaining strength drained instantly from jockey John Buckingham's body

The BBC's David Coleman (*left*) interviews John Buckingham (*centre*) and Honey End's jockey Josh Gifford (*right*) after the race.

Buckingham and Foinavon return in triumph to the winner's enclosure, led by stable lad Clifford Booth.

Just over an hour earlier at Worcester a similar scene had ensued, with the victorious Three Dons, ridden by Foinavon's trainer John Kempton, led in by head lad Colin Hemsley.

Guests of honour at a royal palace: holding up traffic on The Mall in central London are (*left to right*) Hemsley, Buckingham and Foinavon, Kempton, Susie the goat and Booth.

Children in Compton, the Berkshire village where Foinavon's stable was located, prepare to cheer the Grand National winner on his return home.

whereupon his legs 'jackknifed upwards towards his head,' bending his torso in a way it was never meant to be bent.

In a sport of hard men, Brookshaw was admired universally for his uncompromising riding style which was married to an amiable disposition. Arkle's jockey Pat Taaffe 'never met a man more nonchalant or casual over the high fences'. Brookshaw, the Irishman said, had 'only one method of going into a fence, kick, kick, kick and keep on kicking'. John Buckingham remembers him as 'absolutely fearless'. Going into the last obstacle in a race, he would give his mount 'one smack to take off, one in mid-air and one when he landed'. But Brookshaw was also the jockey who took the trouble to sit down and reassure Foinavon's future partner before his first-ever ride, at Wolverhampton – no doubt with his trademark greeting, 'How now, brown cow?'

Though you had to be unlucky to suffer an injury as debilitating as Brookshaw's, every rider thundering over Aintree's sodden turf that day knew that his next fracture was probably just around the corner. Here is an inventory of the career injury-records of some of the top jockeys of that time:

David Mould – broken collarbone (twelve times), leg fracture (four times), broken ribs, a punctured lung, damaged vertebrae. 'I was long and skinny,' he told me, 'I broke.'

Biddlecombe – 'I broke 47 bones and lost a kidney.'

Taaffe – fractured skull, fractured thigh, dislocated shoulder, broken collarbone (three times), broken leg, broken arm, broken ribs, broken wrist.

Barry Brogan – broken jawbones (both sides), broken cheekbones (both), broken nose, broken foot, broken thumbs (both), broken wrist, collarbone, shoulder and ribs (every one on his left-hand side).

Buckingham's tally, accumulated over 1,300-odd rides – he broke a collarbone, shoulder, arm, ribs, thumb, knee and ankle, and damaged his kidneys – almost makes it look like he got off lightly. Yet even he had to endure a nightmarishly comical drive after the final ride of his career in May 1971, when he fell off a horse called The Leaf at Wetherby, injuring his right knee. Another jockey, who Buckingham was driving home, had a broken left leg. They headed back south with Buckingham's left foot operating accelerator and brake, while the other jockey, from the passenger-seat, worked the clutch with his good right leg.

The sheer size of fences and field made the National a high-risk race for jockeys. It was only three years since Paddy Farrell had fractured his spine at The Chair in a fall that left his mount, Border Flight, suspended on his back on the fence above the spot where his stricken jockey was lying. Thankfully, quick-thinking spectators managed to pull Farrell clear before the half-tonne horse slid thrashing to the ground.

Ron Atkins remembers the scene among the jockeys after his first National ride, when he finished 13th. 'It was like the Battle of the Somme,' he says. 'That was the first thing that hit me after we'd finished: everybody was still slapping each other on the back, but it dawned on me – there were quite a lot of guys got hurt here.' After the 1965 race, Brough Scott, who sustained a suspected fractured clavicle, found himself in an ambulance being transferred to Walton Hospital with 'various people who were worse off than me'. These included Johnny Lehane, who was 'really quite badly hurt', and the Duke of Albuquerque, the persevering Spanish amateur rider, who was whisked off behind the hospital-curtains groaning about his knee. Entries for that year in the Aintree jockeys' book, which lists all injuries, show that no fewer than 11 of the 47 jockeys received treatment after the race, with Lehane given '¼ morphine'. After suffering another heavy fall in his seventh and final National ride in 1976, aged 57, the grand old Spanish duke reckoned he had sustained over a hundred fractures at Aintree alone.

Only one jockey – James Wynne in 1862 – has actually been killed in the Grand National and rider fatalities in jumps racing in general in the post-war era have been infrequent, though not unknown. Doug Barrott's death in May 1973 after a fall at Newcastle in a very prominent race, the Whitbread Gold Cup, is still perhaps the most widely remembered example. Fatalities in the sport did, however, happen often enough in the 1950s and 1960s for jockeys to be mindful of the risks they were running. Six decades on, Michael Scudamore still remembers how 'a boy called Ivor Beckinsale' was riding in front of him in a race at Wolverhampton when he hit a concrete upright. 'I didn't know until next morning it killed him.' Scudamore says that after this, 'we asked for and got' a falling-area to the inside of the course, allowing horses and jockeys to roll out of harm's way unobstructed. Nonetheless, it does make you wonder why, by 1967, safety wasn't taken a little more seriously.

Attitudes were different then. The sport was populated by military men who had known the reality of war and to whom, in comparison, the occasional broken bone suffered by those paid to do a much-coveted job must have seemed a trifling matter. Other sports were more dangerous too. Motor racing's attrition-rate at the time was, in retrospect, appalling: within a month of the 1967 Grand National, Lorenzo Bandini, the talented Italian driver, had sustained fatal injuries in a fiery accident at the Monaco Grand Prix.

The shared perils did engender a special kinship between jump-jockeys, even the bitterest rivals. Riders were often first to visit their fallen colleagues in hospital – sometimes for the eminently practical purpose of reuniting them with clothes and personal effects left hanging on their weighing-room peg. After Stan Mellor's mount trod on him in the course of another Liverpool fall, Biddlecombe and Bobby Beasley walked through the hospital ward where he had been taken, but failed at first to recognise their injured colleague whose head was 'swollen like a football'. Jockeys were also a superstitious bunch, in stubborn defiance of a large body of evidence suggesting that their quirks and rituals made not the slightest difference to the horrors that befell them. According to Pat Buckley, 'We would never put on a new set of colours without throwing them on the floor and having the jockeys step on them.' The 1972 Grand National winner, Graham Thorner, famously wore the underpants he had on that day in all his races for years to come.

In spite of the physical dangers they face, jump-jockeys tend to play down the suggestion that they must be imbued with raw courage in industrial quantities. I don't think this is false modesty. Rather, it is an acknowledgement of the drug-like hold that the desire to race-ride exerts on them, at least before the often harsh reality is drummed home. 'Being a jockey is something that you want to do desperately,' a reflective Jeremy Speid-Soote told me. 'It would almost be something that you need to do.' By this token, race-riding, much like writing, is a calling, not merely a profession. And since they are compelled to race, and therefore to fall, jump-jockeys are obliged simply to accept injury as an inevitability (what the French call *une fatalité*). They have no choice in the matter, so courage doesn't enter into it. As Pat Taaffe put it, writing in 1972, 'We will fall on an average once in every 15 rides and most of these falls will be painless. It's just the odd one where you get hurt ... You don't need a great deal of courage to ride under these conditions. It's more a blanking of the mind.'

This stoical attitude, combined with the precarious financial circumstances of all but a fortunate few, meant that professional jockeys reacted in an unusual way when they did get hurt. 'You don't lie on the other side of a fence thinking, "Ooh! I broke my leg. Oh deary me",' as Mellor, the first man to ride more than 1,000 winners over jumps, told me. 'You're thinking, "Damn it! I'll miss that bloody ride on Friday now. And I won't be able to go to such-and-such a course on Saturday. And that bugger will get in on that horse."' The way he puts it, a fractured limb for a jockey is a bit like a cancelled train for a commuter.

It was in the mid-to-late 1960s that thinking on safety did finally start to advance, under the influence of riders like Atkins and John

Lawrence. It was in the aftermath of Brookshaw's and Farrell's accidents indeed, that Lawrence came up with the idea that has become the Injured Jockeys' Fund. Not that every innovation made such a lot of difference. Buckley remembers riding while wearing 'a piece of polystyrene' on his back, 'fastened with a Velcro strap around the waist'. This, he said, was 'almost useless'. At least jockeys in the 1967 Grand National were equipped with proper hard helmets secured with chinstraps, as opposed to the cork 'skid-lids' that were standard headgear until only a few years before. Both Buckley and Buckingham can recall requiring head-stitches in wounds sustained while wearing the old-style caps. Says Buckingham, 'They never even numbed it.'

The bones of horses can also break when subjected to the rigours of Aintree. And since thoroughbreds cannot be immobilised like a human patient, injuries that are no more than a painful inconvenience for jockeys – a broken leg, say, or a broken shoulder – can often amount to a death-sentence for their mounts. A list of equine fatalities attributable to the Grand National, compiled by Mick Mutlow, a specialist on the race, runs to more than 100 names, starting with Dictator in 1839. One of these deaths occurred in 1967 at the third fence, the big open-ditch.

As the 41 survivors galloped towards the six-foot-wide ditch guarding this fence, Princeful, Castle Falls and Penvulgo were leading the way. Foinavon was no longer prominent. 'I took a pull after the first fence,' Buckingham recalls, 'and they were gone like bats out of hell.'

In around eighth or tenth place going over the obstacle was a horse called April Rose ridden by Major Piers Bengough, an Eton-educated cavalry officer who would go on to serve as the Queen's representative at Ascot racecourse. The pairing had finished 11th in 1965. Indeed, April Rose had jumped more than 200 Aintree fences over the years without once falling. According to Bengough, the horse had 'the most economical action jumping a fence. He would hardly pick his legs up, yet somehow the Liverpool fences suited him.' The 12-year-old gelding, who was trained by Bassnet's trainer Alec Kilpatrick, looked to have negotiated yet another Aintree barrier. A stride or two past the fence, however, the tall black-and-silver-clad figure of Bengough toppled over the horse's right shoulder, leaving his sure-footed mount to carry on without him.

With a fence so formidable, you can encounter big trouble if your horse doesn't take off from the correct distance away from the ditch, as two more jockeys discovered to their cost. John Edwards, another amateur rider, says that his mount, Dun Widdy, took off a stride too soon, yanking the reins out of his hands and sending them flying over the horse's head. He took a further stride on landing and trod on one rein, detaching it from the bit. 'I only had one rein and no steering,' Edwards recalls. 'I was a total passenger. All I could do was go with the others.' Edwards managed somehow to stay in the saddle for one full circuit and to pull the horse up after the water-jump. The story has a silver lining: having run only half a National, Dun Widdy was fresh enough to win a race at Cheltenham on Edwards's 21st birthday five days later.

Richard Pitman's mount Dorimont would normally have been partnered by owner Bill Shand Kydd, a keen horseman and powerboat-racer who was related, via their respective marriages, to Lord Lucan. But Shand Kydd – who had loaned Pitman a white Rolls-Royce to transport his bride Jenny to church on their wedding-day – had recently broken a collarbone twice in the space of a fortnight and was out of action.

In a symptom of his inexperience and, no doubt, excitement, Grand National debutant Pitman had forgotten that the fence he was approaching at speed was an open ditch. He remembered 'too late'. Dorimont stood off a stride, launched himself and 'to my horror started his descent before the fence had been reached. The noise was deafening as we crashed to the ground.' Afterwards, Pitman remembers wishing, like a cricketer bowled out for a duck, that time could be wound back, 'just so that I could have a second chance to prove myself.'

Pitman would get his second chance – and complete the course – 12 months later. But for a horse called Vulcano, this latest crack at the National – his third – would be his last.

Two years earlier, Vulcano had won the race at Baldoyle in which Foinavon had blotted his copybook so badly. He was then sold to Enid Chanelle who had built a successful retail business specialising in stylish but affordable women's fashion. A noted beauty, who was painted in oils by Sir William Russell Flint, Miss Chanelle was also a well-known public figure in her own right. She compèred the first fashion show at the Royal Albert Hall and hosted a television programme called *Dream Girls*. Vulcano was moved across the Irish Sea and installed in Captain Ryan Price's yard in Sussex. In the 1965 Grand National, he was pulled up a few fences from home; the following year, he showed decent stamina in the soft going and finished ninth. For the 1967 race, however, the yard's main focus was on Honey End. Vulcano was a largely ignored 40/1 chance, although he was tipped to win on the day of the race by the sports editor of the *Irish Independent*.

What happened to him that grey afternoon is a textbook illustration of how calamity can strike at any time in the National, and with almost no warning. All had seemed to be going smoothly, with Speid-Soote, his jockey, choosing a line near the inner and the horse jumping proficiently. Then Dorimont came crashing down. According to Speid-Soote, 'my little man had nowhere to go, but he jumped it well'. On landing perilously close to the fallen horse's flailing hooves, however, Vulcano was kicked on the stifle, a bone at the front of the hind leg. Says Speid-Soote, 'It was very clear something bad was wrong, so I pulled him up and jumped off.'

The horse's adrenalin was pumping and, with the rest of the field receding into the distance, it was hard to make him stand still. Nonetheless, the gloomy prognosis was swiftly delivered and, once his saddle had been removed, Vulcano was put down there and then beside the great spruce fence. Speid-Soote, feeling 'very sick', was met by the side of the course by Price, who would later have to break the bad news to Miss Chanelle. 'It's not a nice job and the vets hate doing it,' Speid-Soote reflects. 'The only thing I do think and hope is that for a few minutes the adrenalin is really, really rushing and possibly they don't get the pain that they would get after ten minutes. The one you must feel sorriest for is the girl or lad who looks after the horse and has an empty stable the next morning.' The episode appears to have earned Tophams a reprimand from the RSPCA. Minutes of the company's October 1967 board meeting allude to the travelling inspectors report 'sent to us by the HQ'. It was generally agreed, the minutes note, that the racecourse vet would have to be consulted over 'Vulcano's shooting without the use of approved screens'.

Dorimont himself was killed at Doncaster within a year, in a fall that Shand Kydd, who was riding him in a hunters' chase, remembers knocked him unconscious. He was 'a lovely old thing', he says.

Chapter 19

A SMALL BLUE-AND-WHITE DRINKING MUG

Leading the way over Becher's Brook was Penvulgo, another of Vulgan's progeny, ridden by the extrovert Cork-born jockey, Johnny Lehane, popularly known as 'Tumper'.

Less than two-and-a-half years later, in the stillness of early morning, at the obscure Devon yard where he had recently found work, Lehane appears to have drunk a musty-smelling liquid from what the police called a 'small blue-and-white drinking mug'. The liquid was Gramox-one W – paraquat. Having urged his employer's wife to get help, a vomiting Lehane, going downhill fast, was later rushed to hospital in Exeter, but found to be dead on arrival. He was 35.

What would drive a man who, much of the time, was, as his friend Terry Biddlecombe said, 'the happiest little jockey you could wish to meet' to condemn himself in this way to a painful and pitifully premature death? It is hard to be sure: not even the coroner, who recorded an open verdict, was altogether satisfied that Lehane meant to kill himself. 'My reason for saying this,' he explained, 'is that, apparently, having drunk this stuff, he set off and started enlisting help as if either he was going to be sorry for what he had done or, alternatively, because this was a way of drawing attention to himself because his hopes perhaps had gone astray.' Lehane's employer told the inquest that the ex-jockey said he had been drinking that night. And an engagement to a Honiton woman was in the process of being broken off. A lethal dose of paraquat can be very small. It is possible that this was more a misguided, drunken impulse than an act of despair.

The greatest day of Lehane's career had come three days before his 24th birthday, on 7 April 1958, when he rode a horse called Gold Legend to victory in the Irish Grand National. Soon afterwards, he followed the example of many of his compatriots, whether jockeys or not, by crossing the Irish Sea to try his luck in England. At first, things went well: Lehane finished fourth in the jockeys' championship two years running, with contemporaries remembering him as an outstanding natural horseman. But after steering Aintree specialist Mr What home third, in wet and wintry conditions, in the 1962 Grand National, his fortunes changed. It started to become clear that his most successful days were behind him.

In a sport full of strong characters, Lehane appeared to be one of the strongest. He had a flair for nicknames (although the origins of his own were unclear) and, like many other leading jockeys of the day, partied at least as hard as he rode. Biddlecombe remembers him crawling around the floor looking for his false teeth at his 21st birthday party. The Irishman was also on hand for a holiday in Majorca during which Biddlecombe and Josh Gifford went water-skiing in the sea on wooden lavatory seats.

Lehane was known too for his exceptional generosity. According to Richard Pitman, 'He delighted in buying drinks for everybody in the local whether he knew them or not. He would give toys to children in the street and presents to older people.' Tim Norman, for one, has reason to be thankful that this characteristic could also stretch to passing on spare rides to rival jockeys. 'If it wasn't for Johnny Lehane, I wouldn't have ridden Anglo,' the 1966 Grand National-winner told me, explaining how the Irishman walked into the weighing-room at Cheltenham in the week before Christmas 1965 and offered him a ride he could not take advantage of the following day on one of Fred Winter's horses at Windsor. That was Anglo – and Norman duly rode him to victory both on the banks of the Thames and, more importantly, at Aintree three months later. Anglo was not the only Grand National-winner Lehane rode. But though he was sometimes in the right place when it came to Liverpool horses, he never managed to be so at the right time.

The other side of the coin, insofar as his generosity was concerned, is that when he did have cash, it burned a hole in his pocket. 'When he had money, he couldn't keep it, he used to squander it,' Biddlecombe told me. And his lifestyle seems to have been peripatetic even by the standard of jockeys who thought little of driving 50–70,000 miles a season. According to Pitman: 'He had friends in every part of the country and would stay a short while with each, leaving behind him enough clothes to kit three men.' Another jockey told me that the boot of Lehane's car was 'just a mass of dirty clothes'.

There was also a darker, thin-skinned side to Lehane's personality. Bobby Beasley, another Irish jockey, whose taste for booze drove him to alcoholism, recalled a curious incident when he found Lehane 'giving his horse a fair old hiding' down at the start of a novice chase – a category of race viewed with apprehension by riders due to the inexperience of their mounts. When Beasley asked his rival what he thought he was doing, Lehane grinned and said he would 'rather frighten them before they frighten me.' According to Biddlecombe, though he was a sincere friend, Lehane 'took life seriously from time to time' and was 'sensitive to a degree', becoming 'really depressed' if he had a run of losing rides. 'I sometimes took him by the shoulders to shake him out of it.'

This more fragile side of Lehane's nature must have made it difficult to cope with the implacable highs and lows that are a jump-jockey's lot. But, when his career ended and he could no longer sweep away the darkness by doing anything as clear-cut as notching a winner, well, perhaps it just hung over him. Perhaps in those grim moments as he drank weedkiller from the small blue and white drinking mug, life had taken on the appearance of an unbreakable run of losing rides.

Lehane died on 6 September 1969. On 8 April 1967, however, the flame of ambition still burned as he led the field over the most famous fence in steeplechasing while nurturing hopes of steering home the first Grand National winner to be trained within 50 miles of Liverpool for 18 years.

With an unbroken view of the fence, Lehane and Penvulgo met Becher's perfectly, the Irishman knowing better than to be tempted by the treacherous inside line. Spared the severest drop and with his jockey thrusting his weight backwards to help him, Penvulgo scrambled for just a step or two on landing before getting back into his stride. In second place, Roy Edwards and Princeful took the obstacle just to the leader's inside. And on they went, thrilled and relieved to have Aintree's signature fence behind them, Lehane's white cap and gloves standing out in the afternoon gloom.

Trained in Cheshire by Dick Francis's elder brother Doug, Penvulgo was to race over Becher's once more, in March 1968. This time the encounter had a sombre outcome. When well in contention in the Topham Trophy, ridden on this occasion by a jockey called Jimmy Morrissey, the horse got Becher's wrong and shattered the bones behind both knees. This meant, in the words of *Sporting Life*, that 'to all intents and purposes only his hind legs were operational'. And yet Penvulgo cleared eight more Aintree fences and laboured home fourth of 16. Not surprisingly, on dismounting, his jockey said the horse seemed terribly groggy. X-rays then revealed the injuries. A decision was taken to put him down.

Of the 38 runners who made it to Becher's in the 1967 Grand National, all bar one negotiated it successfully, even John Edwards with his single rein. There were one or two close calls. 'I nearly fell,' Scottish Final's jockey Nobby Howard told me. 'He stood off too far, but he found a leg.' In the end, though, the sole victim was a horse named Border Fury ridden by another amateur jockey, David Crossley Cooke.

Lying in about 30th place and on the wide outside, Border Fury started to tack noticeably to the inner in the last few strides before the fence. He cleared it comfortably enough, but at an angle, making the landing particularly hard to judge. He duly crumpled and rolled ineluctably over onto his right flank, impeding Limeking and forcing John Cook's mount Ross Sea to execute a neat sidestep. If there was a consolation for Crossley Cooke – who eventually remounted and watched the rest of the race on horseback on the inside of the course – it was that there can rarely have been a more gentle fall at Becher's.

Clearing the fence just ahead of Crossley Cooke as gravity took over, the riderless and blinkered Popham Down was starting to make progress up through the field. Slap bang in the middle of the course and the middle of the pack was Foinavon, jumping solidly. Another jockey had told John Buckingham that he wouldn't recognise the fence as Becher's as he was galloping into it. It was good advice. 'When you get halfway over it – agh. That's Becher's,' Buckingham recalled. 'I mean the drop on the other side. You have to sit right back, like going over a mountain. One thing about Liverpool – the fences are so much bigger there. And you can feel the horses really going back and heaving over. You can feel the extra effort.'

Next up, though, was a fence widely regarded as the closest thing Aintree had to a soft touch. It was the fence where Michael Daley and his mates were standing, a fence so little regarded that its only name was a reference-point to its daunting neighbour. Next up was the 'one after Becher's'.

Chapter 20

AN UNDERSTANDABLE SLAYER

It is often said that the 'one after Becher's' is the smallest fence on the Grand National course. This needs qualifying slightly: both the first and last fences were – at 4ft 6in in 1967 – exactly the same height; the water-jump is technically the lowest fence of all, at just 2ft 6in, but this is, in effect, a long-jump for horses, with a 15-foot spring required to touch down on dry land.

What it is probably true to say is that, at 3.27pm or so on that dreary afternoon, as the 37 remaining runners thundered towards it, the gorse-dressed seventh fence was the most disdained obstacle on the Grand National course. This was attributable chiefly to its location, in the midst of Aintree's most daunting hazards, directly after Becher's and before the Canal Turn and Valentine's Brook. For Dick Francis, the former jockey turned journalist and racing-thriller writer, it was 'innocuous and simple: just a fence between Becher's and Canal Turn. No more.' In the previous year's race, it had caught out only Flamecap, a long-odds outsider; in 1965, only a horse called Leslie. Foinavon's trainer John Kempton's race had actually ended there in one of the two

Nationals he had contested as a jockey on Seas End, in 1962. But that was because he had opted to pull his tired mount up there; it was not the result of the fence bamboozling them.

However, as Francis also knew all too well, this had not always been the way things were at Liverpool. There had been a time, a decade or more earlier, when the Grand National's seventh fence warranted the very greatest respect. During this period, he wrote, it was 'an understandable slayer. I fell there twice myself … It used to lie in a slight dip and it trapped a horse or two on every circuit.'

Earlier still, in 1938, the fence would have prevented the making of Grand National history were it not for a chivalrous gesture by Fred Rimell, a jockey riding a horse called Provocative. A length ahead of Rimell going over the obstacle was Bruce Hobbs, aged 17 years and three months, aboard Battleship, an unusually small chestnut stallion. When Battleship pitched on landing, his young rider shot over his shoulder and would have hit the turf but for the intervention of Rimell, who grabbed him by the seat of his pants and hauled him back into the saddle with the immortal words, 'Where do you think you're going, mate?' As luck would have it, Provocative then fell at the Canal Turn, the very next fence, while Hobbs drove Battleship on to the narrowest of victories. In doing so, he became the youngest jockey to win a National, while his bloody-nosed mount became the first National-winning horse to be both American-owned and -bred.

In the four Nationals between 1949 and 1952, the 'one after Becher's' ended the chances of no fewer than 22 runners – the sort of toll you would expect of Becher's itself. At this time, however, not only did the fence lie in a dip, it was almost five feet high.

It was the grim Grand National of 1954 that led to the fence's apparent emasculation. No fewer than four of the 29 runners died. Afterwards, the furore – anticipating more recent controversies about the race's toughness or, as some would have it, cruelty – was such that questions were asked in the House of Commons and the home secretary invited members of the National Hunt Committee to meet him. The RSPCA also made proposals. Around six weeks before the 1955 National, Mrs Topham announced steps to ease the hazards on the course, focusing on fences six (Becher's) and seven. At Becher's, the ditch was simply made more shallow, in an attempt to reduce the likelihood of injury to horses which fell back into it. Alterations to the 'one after Becher's' were more substantial. As *The Times* reported, 'At number seven fence ... the height has been lowered by six inches to bring it to 4ft 6in, the minimum allowed by rule number 44 of the National Hunt Rules. This is a plain thorn fence which the runners meet just after turning left-handed, and facing towards the canal. The reduction will give some relief just after the runners have negotiated Becher's.'

A Mr A.W. Moss, chief secretary of the RSPCA, welcomed the changes, while observing that 'only by the test of this year's race will one be able to judge whether these modifications have the desired effect.' The League Against Cruel Sport did not feel satisfied that enough had yet been done to prevent 'the distressing casualties among competing horses which have so shocked the British public in recent years.' The jockeys who rode the first two home in the 1954 race begged to differ. 'I did not think it was necessary to alter any of the jumps at Aintree,' said Bryan Marshall. 'There is nothing wrong with the course; they should have left it alone,' said George Slack.

Even at the minimum height, the seventh fence ended the hopes of a further three runners – 10 per cent of the field – in the 1955 National, which was run in conditions so wet that the water-jump was omitted.

Ahead of the 1957 race, the RSPCA actually recommended that the seventh fence be removed altogether. This was to make room for the re-siting of the following fence, the Canal Turn, famous for the sharp, 90-degree change in direction runners are required to effect, either while clearing the obstacle or immediately thereafter. Eight days before Grand National day Mrs Topham announced the rejection of the RSPCA's latest recommendations. The National Hunt stewards, she said, had gone carefully into the question and, apart from a comment that the seventh fence should be lifted from a hollow, had nothing further to add. Were the Canal Turn fence indeed to be moved back, she added with trademark pugnacity, it might well prove more dangerous.

It was the removal of this 'slight dip' alluded to by Dick Francis that appeared to make the difference. In the intervening decade, casualties at the fence had been few and far between.

There was at least one man in the 1967 Grand National field who retained a healthy respect for the 'one after Becher's', however. For Terry Biddlecombe, it was 'a trick fence' that looked like 'a baby hurdle'. This meant it was not respected by the horses who, he said, 'flatten out over it'. When Norther, the horse running beside him at Aintree that day made a small mistake there on the first circuit, Biddlecombe shouted sympathetically across to his jockey, John Lawrence, in his West Country burr, 'That's a bastard, isn't it?' At the time, the close proximity of the Canal Turn would have rendered a longer discussion hazardous. But as the patrician Lawrence was to observe pithily in *Horse and Hound* the following week, 'Just how big a bastard neither he nor I could know!'

Diagram of Race Position at Second Becher's

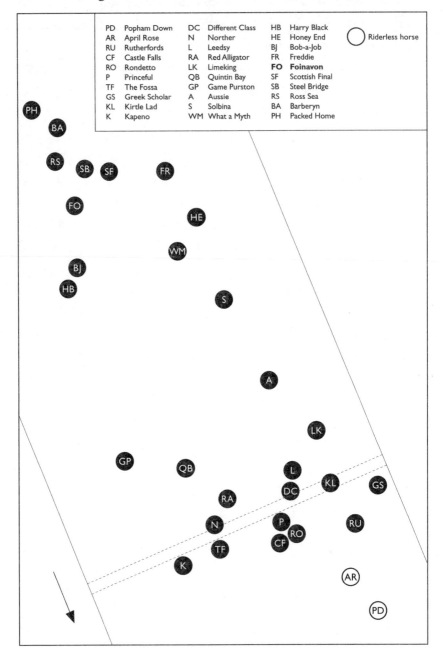

PD	Popham Down	DC	Different Class	HB	Harry Black
AR	April Rose	N	Norther	HE	Honey End
RU	Rutherfords	L	Leedsy	BJ	Bob-a-Job
CF	Castle Falls	RA	Red Alligator	FR	Freddie
RO	Rondetto	LK	Limeking	**FO**	**Foinavon**
P	Princeful	QB	Quintin Bay	SF	Scottish Final
TF	The Fossa	GP	Game Purston	SB	Steel Bridge
GS	Greek Scholar	A	Aussie	RS	Ross Sea
KL	Kirtle Lad	S	Solbina	BA	Barberyn
K	Kapeno	WM	What a Myth	PH	Packed Home

Riderless horse

Chapter 21

A CHAIN REACTION
OF RUIN

The record for the most finishers of a Grand National at this time was 22 runners, set in 1963, not long after the shape of the plain fences at Aintree had been altered. As the leaders in the 1967 race approached Becher's for the second time, this record looked in danger of being broken.

Steeling themselves again for the fence's disconcerting drop, 28 of the 44 starters were still in the race. No more than half a dozen of these seemed definitively out of contention. For John Lawrence, none the worse for that first-circuit mistake and lying handily in about tenth spot on Norther, the ingredients were in place for 'one of the finest, most spectacular contests in the National's history'. Had he been asked at that moment to name the winner, Lawrence subsequently wrote, 'My answer would have been Different Class.' Squinting into the Merseyside murk from the stands nearly a mile away, Gregory Peck must have felt like he had been nominated for another Oscar.

Besides first-fence casualty Bassnet, a further two of the more fancied runners had failed to make it this far. The 1966 winner Anglo, never prominent, had slammed into another horse at the fearsome

Chair fence at the other end of the course and been pulled up. Madame Borel de Bitche's Kilburn – the Welsh Grand National winner who had once refused to jump tiny *cavaletti* – had, meanwhile, simply failed to take off at the big open ditch that served as the 19th fence on the second circuit. 'He had a habit of not doing anything every now and then,' recalled jockey Tim Norman. 'He buried his head in it. I went over. When I got back, he was back-legs out of the fence, front-legs in. I trotted him back.' A further unwelcome surprise awaited Madame Borel de Bitche on her return to her hotel suite. Thieves had forced the door and stolen jewellery worth more than £4,000 from the drawer of a dressing table. Missing items included a square blue diamond solitaire ring, a pearl necklace and a bee-shaped brooch.

This was also the fence that ended the Galloping Grandad's race, saving Ladbrokes £900 plus that case of champagne in the process. The fading Penvulgo was out of the reckoning too, though Johnny Lehane reported that the horse had given him a 'super ride' until the 20th fence when he 'jumped right onto another one'.

Paul Irby, riding Ronald's Boy, was another whose Grand National had come to a premature halt. 'The Canal Turn was quite a shock because I hadn't appreciated quite how sharp the turn was,' he told me. 'Anyhow, we wheeled around and went gaily along until we came to the 12th. Much to my dismay we failed to leave the ground, ploughed through the bottom of the fence and it was the one time when there was a bloody great ditch the other side, so there was no coming back from that. I was really rather upset because I was beginning to enjoy myself. After that it was a bit of an anti-climax. I was sitting on the horse in the ditch … I hacked back down the five-furlong course at which point I was greeted by a couple of mounted policemen who said, "Excuse me, sir, but do you realise you've got most of that fence on your horse's tail?"'

Four horses – Princeful, Rutherfords, Castle Falls and Kirtle Lad – had joined Penvulgo in dictating a fast pace for most of the first circuit.

As they neared the stands, though, two new faces started to move up menacingly among the leaders. What is more, they were carrying substantially less weight than the pace-setting quartet. This is because they were running without the encumbrance of jockeys.

Early fallers they may have been, but Popham Down and April Rose had not, like Bassnet and Border Fury, been recaptured by their grounded riders. When left to their own devices racehorses will tend to try and follow the herd and, in those days, at Aintree there were very few places where loose animals could exit the course, even if they wanted to. So they kept on running, reins flapping. This was an extra problem for the jockeys still in the race, since an unpiloted racehorse can do wholly unpredictable things. 'A loose horse in front is a terrible thing to have,' according to Paddy Broderick, Kirtle Lad's jockey.

One possible exit-point comes as the field starts the second circuit, to the inside of the course, down towards the starting-area. Accordingly, as the blinkered Popham Down cruised up on Kirtle Lad's inside as he led the way back out towards the Melling Road, Broderick made strenuous efforts to shoo him away from the racecourse. Popham Down would not be told. He hit the front and led impressively over the 17th fence that had precipitated his downfall first time around. April Rose, for whom the Aintree fences held few terrors and no secrets, followed in his wake some lengths behind as John Leech (Rutherfords) and Stan Hayhurst (Castle Falls) tried to keep their distance.

As Popham Down and April Rose were moving up in the field, Foinavon had been dropping back, going through halfway in 31st or 32nd position. He was in good company though. According to John Buckingham, 'Up towards Becher's second time, Josh Gifford was only just in front of me on Honey End. That gave me a bit of confidence. Josh was probably one of the best judges of pace and I thought if Josh is there then I'm not in a bad position. When we jumped Becher's second time, he was only three lengths in front of me.' Two other good horses, What a Myth and Freddie, were in the same vicinity.

With the loose horses over and clear ahead of the field, two of the leaders breathed a particularly big sigh of relief on touching down safely at Becher's. One was Leech on board Rutherfords, who had taken a narrow lead. 'Paddy [Broderick] and I were talking around the course; we were talking about the loose horses,' he said. 'I remember going to Becher's and thinking, "God I hope those things don't stop here or we'll all get killed." They jumped Becher's and I said to myself, "Oh, we'll be all right now."' The other was Nick Gaselee riding a horse called Kapeno, who had fallen at Becher's in both previous Grand National attempts. 'I had gone to the middle of the fence,' Gaselee told me. 'He jumped it beautifully. I thought, "Here we go". His bogey had been laid to rest. I thought, "This could be it" – along with a lot of other people.' On Gaselee's inside, Stan Mellor, the former champion, was enjoying a model ride on The Fossa, appreciating his partner's jumping action. 'He used to get well out over his fences and well out the other side, which is nice at Aintree,' Mellor said. 'On landing, he was better than most because he would stretch out. He would land like on a cushion.'

Mellor could have made good use of a cushion a few moments later. Disaster for most of the field was now just seconds away.

It was a battlefield. It was a defeated cavalry charge. It was reminiscent of those blood-curdling 19th-century sporting prints. It was like cars in a multiple motorway concertina in fog. From a mile away, it was as though a film had broken down with a temporary cessation of all movement. It was a cauldron of furious activity. It was a chain reaction of ruin.

In the days that followed, all these metaphors – and more – were deployed by writers striving to convey the trauma of seeing one of the world's great sporting spectacles disintegrate into chaos in the blink of an eye. The tangled limbs, human and equine, the frenzy of confusion, with horses suddenly facing in all directions, the spraying clods and foliage – all of this was transmitted instantly to a goggle-eyed television audience. Some elements of the nightmarish tableau, though, could only be appreciated by eye-witnesses at this far end of the course, as well as the 28 men sucked into the maelstrom. There was the steam, a big cloud of which soon spanned the width of the course over the hot, thrashing bodies. There was the noise, both the disbelieving hubbub of the tightly packed crowd and the desperate, frustrated cries of riders and their mounts. And there was the sheer, forlorn helplessness. 'Everybody was just panic-stricken,' according to Freddie's jockey Pat McCarron. 'It wasn't the danger. It was just you were losing a grip on the race. The whole thing was falling apart and you couldn't do anything about it.'

So what happened? In a sentence, Popham Down, the loose horse who led the field along the line of wide fences all the way to Becher's, appears to have decided he had had enough. Approaching the one after Becher's with April Rose and the rest of them on his tail, he headed for the left-hand corner of the fence close to the inside rail. He may have been trying to run out, and there was a small gap in the rail just before the obstacle. Instead, at the last moment, he veered to his right across the face of the fence, causing April Rose to check, and triggering mayhem among his still-mounted pursuers. Since he was wearing blinkers, it is worth pointing out that Popham Down's view of what was behind him would have been restricted.

Mellor is not alone in surmising that though the pile-up did not take place at Becher's, the unexpectedly big drop there may have unsettled the loose horses. 'They were on the inside, the deepest part,' he told me. 'And I think what went through their mind was, "the floor wasn't there". Like when you step off the pavement and suddenly, bang, you get this jar because you didn't know the kerb was there. Next fence I think they thought, "Oh, not again!" and tried to run out.'

For a split-second, as he approached the 23rd, Mellor thought that the danger was past. 'I thought they could get out,' he said. 'They disappeared. I sat down and rode in. The next thing: they came out, one, two, just following each other at a half-trot. Donkey, donkey, donkey.'

The Fossa turned right. Mellor carried straight on – and landed on top of the gorse-dressed thorn fence. Realising the peril of his position, he quickly rolled off to the landing side and joined the ejected John Lawrence in sprinting to the safety of the outside rail. Still that wasn't the end of it. Mellor thought he saw a horse go by wearing his blue denim saddle-pad. So he gave chase. 'I legged it down to the Canal Turn. Nearly.' Too late he realised that it wasn't The Fossa. 'So I was out with the washing.' This didn't stop him ending the afternoon by winning the last race on the card, a Flat race featuring the likes of Paul Cook and Willie Carson. There can be no better illustration of this tough competitor's insatiable appetite for winners.

Mellor's was merely the most eventful of a score of hard-luck stories unfolding simultaneously before the incredulous eyes of passengers on the 'officers' special' and Michael Daley and his mates in their dark-blue 'mod macs'. 'We could not believe it as all the horses were falling on top of one another,' Daley remembered.

Of the quartet who had made most of the running, Broderick was probably the most unfortunate. Tucked in behind the others at the moment of disaster, he managed to stay in the saddle. Kirtle Lad, though, was stuck on top of the wrecked fence. Thinking fast, Broderick rolled off, just ahead of Mellor, onto the landing side and eventually extricated his mount. He shouted to an ambulance-man standing by the fence, 'Give us a leg-up, give us a leg-up. But he just stood there looking at me, dumbfounded.' Conspicuous in yellow silks and black cap, he did remount quickly enough to keep his hopes alive. But Kirtle Lad refused at the Canal Turn, the next fence. He had pulled a muscle in his hindquarters. Broderick was left to 'lead him back along the track'.

Princeful's jockey Roy Edwards and Stan Hayhurst also found themselves on the landing side. Edwards made a vain attempt to catch his dark-brown mount as he kicked himself clear and lolloped down to the Canal Turn. Castle Falls had bellied onto the fence, but been shoved unceremoniously over by the heaving pile-up of horses behind him towards the inner. Hayhurst 'landed sprinting on my knees and dashed to the inside thinking, "Oh God, there are 40 horses here". My fellow was on his back under the fence. Another horse had his front legs almost on Castle Falls's tummy.' The noise was deafening and from the take-off side of the fence equine heads were waving around, in the inimitable Lawrence's phrase, like 'demented serpents'. Nonetheless Hayhurst ran back in, grabbed the reins as the horse righted himself, but found they had got stuck under his breastgirth. By the time he was ready to ride on, he was far behind.

Leech, on Rutherfords, was closest to April Rose and had no chance when his horse slammed on the brakes. He was first to hit the deck and 'thought I was going to get kicked to death'. Luckily, he came to rest under the fence's wing. The riderless April Rose was such a consummate Aintree jumper that he actually managed to fiddle his way over the obstacle with chaos breaking out around him. This may have cost Johnny Haine, aboard the hard-pulling Rondetto, the race. The pair had been showing ever more prominently and were up into third alongside Princeful as the devastation started. Whether by luck or sheer brute strength, they cleared the obstacle – one of only three runners to do so at the first time of asking – and Haine immediately fell off. It is hard to be sure, but April Rose may well have played a part in his demise as the two horses jumped the fence together. Like Princeful, they then jogged off riderless to the Canal Turn. It was the stylish Haine who had ridden Popham Down to his Scottish Grand National victory. Perhaps he would have got the ride at Aintree if Rondetto's regular jockey Jeff King had not had to sit out the 1967 National with a fractured skull, and perhaps the course of Grand National history might have been changed.

A few strides further back in the field, Gaselee's satisfaction at surviving Becher's had been made instantly irrelevant. Kapeno hit the backside of another horse and came to a halt, still standing, but with his front feet in the fence. Gaselee 'went right up the horse's neck, but didn't come off. Two things struck me straight away, "Oh God, what a way to end"; but also, "Hey no one has got over it". You heard this extraordinary noise from the Canal Turn. I suppose it was people ooh-ing and ah-ing. I thought, "If I'm quick I can still do it". I pulled him back about five yards from the fence. The horse refused. For my second attempt we went back much further.'

Cruising one moment, David Mould and Different Class were at the eye of the storm the next. 'My brain was telling me it was going to happen,' he told me. 'But I couldn't do anything about it.' Different Class was knocked to the ground and Mould cannoned into the fence. 'We ended up being wrapped around bloody great spikes and everything … My horse was smashed into the floor. I couldn't find him. At the time I thought my horse had been killed … I think we all walked back. People were just walking about dazed really. I thought someone had to be killed. Guaranteed. It was just mayhem. By the time I got back, the winner was gone from the winner's circle. I hadn't a clue who had won.'

Though Mould could have been forgiven for thinking, like plenty of others, that the pile-up cost him the National, the outcome of the following year's race, when Different Class finished third, suggests he didn't quite have the staying power.

In the Sunday papers, some of the most dramatic pictures featured the massive bulk of Limeking, the biggest horse Pat Buckley ever rode, lying flat on his back under the fence, his concerned jockey standing beside him. 'I was exactly where I wanted to be,' Buckley, who was 13th going over Becher's, recalled. 'I got bumped in mid-stride. I was hoping my nag would go forward because then we would have got over.' Instead, the jockey was deposited on top of the fence. When he found Limeking stuck on his back on the take-off side, 'the Red Cross people were giving me advice. When the mayhem was finished, I gave him a smack around the arse. He got up and shook himself. I had a look around his legs. No cuts, nothing.' They walked back 'totally disappointed about the result'.

If the leaders had little control over their fate, those further back in the field at least had a sporting chance of picking a path through the pandemonium. Eddie Harty, aboard the speedy Solbina, was one of these. 'It all happened in front of me,' he recalled. 'It was a concertina effect. They just folded up.' Solbina did indeed get through to the fence, but his take-off stride coincided with a gust of noise from the crowd. He refused and threw the pale blue-jacketed Harty off. It was here that the jockey's injuries from earlier in the meeting came back to haunt him. 'I couldn't get back up,' he told me. Valuable seconds were lost before he was able to remount and address the fence again.

The mêlée also ended any lingering fancy that Freddie might finally win a National. He fought his way through at the third attempt, but by then was so far behind that, in McCarron's words, 'I was in the next parish'. It is possible Freddie – though 'a hell of a great animal to ride' – was a spent force even before the Aintree fates intervened. It felt to his jockey 'as if it was a bit lacklustre. As if he had done it all before and knew it. It's a hell of a thing to take on – four-and-a-half miles with a big weight on your back. It definitely leaves its mark. I came to the conclusion he had had enough.'

That said, Freddie jumped Becher's only marginally ahead of a horse whose name makes you realise that, had the cards fallen differently when the leaders started sandwiching into each other, the Scottish challenger might yet have pulled off what would have been an intensely popular victory. That horse was Foinavon.

Chapter 22

ONLY ONE GONE ON

It was just starting to appear that the baby hurdle would defeat all-comers, when a dark form skirted its way around the edge of the war-zone, approached the fence with short, chopping strides and clambered over, before continuing, almost apologetically, on its way. In the Canal Turn stand, John Pinfold remembers a rustling of paper as spectators tried to identify the escapee. Television viewers encountered no such problem. 'And now, with all this mayhem, Foinavon has gone off on his own,' Michael O'Hehir rattled out unerringly, no doubt thanking his lucky stars that he had approached John Buckingham during his vigil beside the red Avery Toledo scales in the weighing-room before the race.

'I just galloped into them,' Buckingham told me. At that stage, he still had one clear blue eye fastened firmly on the chocolate-and-white hooped cap of Josh Gifford, a few lengths ahead. 'Josh went into it and refused. I swung across and missed Josh's quarters. There was a small gap in the fence that was unaffected by the pile-up and we approached it at a 45-degree angle. Foinavon had reduced to a canter and jumped it off his hocks like a showjumper. I kicked on away from the fence.' The new leaders passed under the noses of Stan Mellor and John Lawrence standing at the outside rail. 'Stan Mellor was saying, "Go on Buck!

162

You'll win."' Even so, the penny didn't drop that he was in front until he had jumped the next fence, the Canal Turn, negotiated the right-angled corner and surveyed the approach to Valentine's. 'There was nothing there. I couldn't believe it.'

On one level, this feat of navigation was the product of outrageous good fortune: had Buckingham and Foinavon chosen any other route, or run the first three-quarters of the race any faster, their path would almost certainly have been blocked. Yet this was a pairing that bracketed a sensible, clear-thinking horseman with an unusually placid thoroughbred. Both deserve some credit. Buckingham, though hardly at the top of his sport, was an experienced jockey in the middle of his 805th ride. He had shown evidence of his coolness and independent-mindedness before, once winning a ten-horse race at Market Rasen after all his rivals had gone the wrong way and been disqualified. As for Foinavon, Pat Taaffe, twice a Grand National-winner and the jockey who had ridden him in most of his early jumps-races, subsequently had this to say, 'I think if you'd asked me to pick a horse in that race to find a way through I would have chosen Foinavon. The others might panic, but not this one.'

Among the jockeys who noticed Foinavon thread his way through were Gifford and Brian Fletcher. According to Gifford, Honey End, the favourite, was 'jumping like a buck', but 'absolutely froze' when he saw the 'tragedy' – note the choice of word. Gifford went on: 'I turned around three or four times. I thought, "Don't panic, don't panic" … I was turning around to wait to do something sensible and Johnny came by me. If I had waited another split-second, I'm not saying [Honey End] would have jumped it, but I'd have had a lead.' Fletcher, the teenager from the north-east riding his first Grand National on Red Alligator, was just behind the leaders as the pile-up happened and had no time to avoid being sucked in. 'I was thrown off the horse, but I kept hold of him and at the third attempt I was able to jump back on – he was a tall, rangy horse, so it wasn't easy,' Fletcher said. 'I saw John jumping the fence because, as I was scrambling to get back on my horse, I saw this thing come from nowhere. I was trying to get a clear piece of space to jump back up.' Fletcher finally got over the wrecked obstacle at the third attempt. Though Red Alligator was full of running, once Fletcher had got his bearings he realised he was a long way behind.

There was one other runner who managed to clear the 23rd fence at the first time of asking that afternoon. Tellingly, he had been even further back in the field than Foinavon. In fact, Packed Home, the US Ambassador to Ireland's horse, had been dead last at Becher's, the previous fence. Jockey Tommy Carberry, moreover, had been thinking about pulling up when he saw 'this carry-on in front of me' with 'more coming back towards me than going away from me'. He went straight up to the fence, jumped and duly landed on the other side. 'I was more surprised than the horse,' Carberry said. 'It was like the waters of the Red Sea parting.'

Carberry was one of a trio of Irish jockeys who, discounting the incapacitated Kirtle Lad, were first over in pursuit of the already distant Foinavon. The other two were Francis Shortt on a horse called Aussie and Jackie Cullen riding Quintin Bay, the old rival Foinavon had edged out to win the Foxrock Cup at Leopardstown two years before, in the race that qualified him to run in a Grand National.

Five years earlier, Shortt had been responsible for the best performance Pat Taaffe ever saw from a jockey at Liverpool, bringing Fredith's Son home in fifth place in the 1962 National. Taaffe wrote, 'This was the sort of ride you wouldn't have wished on your worst enemy. Fredith's Son didn't jump a single fence correctly. He jumped them crookedly, landed parallel to the fence, twisted and did just about everything but fall ... I don't believe there was any other jockey in the world who could have completed the course with him.'

In 1967, Shortt acknowledges that he 'wasn't going all that sweetly' when lying 16th at Becher's, some way behind the leaders. 'My goose was nearly cooked,' he says. And yet, once the pile-up developed, he came within an ace of stealing Buckingham's thunder, nearly squeezing through on the inside when Foinavon was still, if not a speck on the horizon, then a good few strides away. As the *Irish Field* reported, Shortt 'had time to pick his passage through to a gap in the fence. He was about to shoot through the gap when a loose horse, running down the fence, crashed into him. A split-second earlier, he would have been through and away.' As it was, he got over at the third attempt, with a leg full of thorns and Cullen just in front of him.

Hard on the heels of this Irish trio was Terry Biddlecombe on Greek Scholar, the handsome chestnut with the distinctive white diamond on his forehead, who, the jockey says, 'always wanted to please'. Just behind the leaders on the inside, Greek Scholar landed on top of the fence giving Biddlecombe grounds to hope they would be 'knocked over' to the other side by the horses behind them. As it was, the jockey had to turn around, back off and execute a small circle. Castle Falls' rider Stan Hayhurst then remembers the pair walking through what was left of the fence, with the effervescent Biddlecombe shouting, 'Come on lads! There's only one gone on.'

Looking on from the stand, the teenage Pinfold had a camera with him. Like other spectators, however, he was so transfixed by what he was witnessing that he didn't think to take a snap of Foinavon jumping the Canal Turn, surrounded by three loose horses, even though the runaway leader passed just feet in front of him. 'I did take one of the next couple,' he says.

The men in the jockeys' room at Worcester racecourse were similarly spellbound as O'Hehir distilled the drama into vivid commentary. 'He's about 50, 100 yards in front of everything else. They're all pulling up ...' Beside himself with excitement, John Kempton leapt up onto a table to get a better view. In his office in Rainham, a flabbergasted Mac Bennellick, Foinavon's former co-owner, could hardly believe his eyes – or that he hadn't staked a penny on the horse. In Buckingham's home village of Chipping Warden, the football match being played by the village team was abruptly halted so players could see if the local man held on to his lead. At home in Finchampstead, Cyril Watkins, perhaps rueing his decision not to try to get to Aintree, could not bear to watch. He retreated to the garden with Shoes and Socks, his Airedale terriers.

In Wealdstone, north-west London, 17-year-old Dennis Lewell was thrilled to bits. A few hours previously he had entrusted his friend Alan Sweeney with half-a-crown to place on Foinavon. Sweeney looked old enough to do business in the local bookie with no questions asked. Strangely, the wider Foinavon's lead stretched, and the more excited Lewell got, the more uncharacteristically quiet Sweeney became.

In the TV room on the Orion oil rig, two of Eric Brown's colleagues – the important one and the roustabout who had purchased the real Foinavon ticket in his sweepstake – were now roaring the horse home. Brown was desperately hoping one of the chasing pack would catch up while pondering how he was going to cope with being the equivalent of almost two weeks' wages out of pocket.

The issue now for Buckingham was keeping the horse going and on his feet over six tough fences in his unwonted state of glorious isolation. He talked to his mount. He pushed and kicked. He urged him on once or twice when he tried to duck out. He sweated pints, in spite of the foul day. He never stopped working. And all the time, underpinning the beat of his racing heart, he heard the drumming of Foinavon's hooves and felt the rhythmic motion of his flanks underneath him.

The last mile of the race resembled the plot of a spaghetti western, with Buckingham the bandit escaping with the loot, as author Vian Smith first observed, and the rest of the field the chasing posse. Biddlecombe went for broke on Greek Scholar, the first fancied horse to set off in pursuit, and caught up with the Irish contingent as they all converged on an inviting hole in the 28th fence, the third from home. Honey End was also eating up the ground near the inside rail, though Gifford narrowly avoided a very nasty moment when Popham Down crashed back onto the racecourse a few yards behind him, splintering the rail on impact. The loose horse had sneaked through the narrow gap before the 23rd that he had perhaps had his eye on all along while chaos was raging.

Going over Anchor Bridge and crossing the Melling Road for the fourth and final time, Greek Scholar moved into second, but Foinavon still had a healthy lead. It was on the long run to the second-last, with Honey End charging ahead like a six-furlong sprinter under Gifford's desperate urging, that you began to think they might just catch him – to the joyous relief of an army of punters. Buckingham jumped the last, sensibly enough, with particular deliberation, and the gap had been whittled down so much by this point that commentator Peter O'Sullevan declared, 'It may still be a race.' It was at about this time though, listening on the car radio at that Edinburgh point-to-point, that George Pottinger's frustration at not following his 750/1 hunch got the better of him. He hit the dashboard with his fist.

Pottinger's instincts turned out to be well-founded. Having reached the Elbow and regained the rail, Foinavon gathered himself and started pulling away for the first time since the chasing pack had finally conquered the 'one after Becher's'. Honey End had shot his bolt and it was Red Alligator, having surged through from towards the back of the field, who was finishing fastest of all up Aintree's famously strength-sapping run-in. After a final glance back, Buckingham reached the winning-post, whereupon it looked like all remaining strength drained instantly from his body. He had 15 lengths in hand. A deeply disappointed Gifford held on to second on Honey End from the fast-finishing Red Alligator with Greek Scholar a tired fourth. The US Ambassador to Ireland's horse Packed Home, the only other finisher to clear the 23rd first time, clung on dourly to fifth, in spite of a broken pedal bone. Popham Down crossed the line along with another loose horse in around eighth place, just in front of the gallant Nobby Howard, in his *National Velvet* colours, on Scottish Final.

Chapter 23

'THEY MIGHT CALL THIS THE FOINAVON FENCE'

For many followers of the race, Foinavon's shock victory triggered reactions ranging from astonishment to despair. Unlike the FA Cup where feats of giant-killing are widely celebrated, upsets on this scale in racing tend not to be much appreciated. They leave too many out of pocket. The spectrum of emotions felt by those actually connected to the horse was, of course, very different.

On the turf in front of Aintree's stands, an exultant Clifford Booth hurled the sheets he had been carrying into the air and set off to catch Foinavon and lead him in. With the less than pristine clarity of the Aintree sound-system at that time, it was only when he caught sight of his horse passing the Elbow that he had realised he was in the lead. A couple of minutes later, as he clutched the left-hand rein by the gelding's hot muzzle, Booth heard an unfamiliar voice, 'Here you are, son. You lost these.' The voice belonged to a policeman. The jettisoned quarter-sheets had landed on his head and dislodged his helmet.

In the jockeys' room at Worcester racecourse, John Kempton jumped into the air with what one witness remembers as an 'extraordinary screech'. The table on which he was standing creaked and groaned and, Kempton thinks, 'broke a bit'. He dashed out of the room in a state of high excitement. Driver Tony Hutt realised instantly that Foinavon's shock victory meant he would have to go and bring him back from Liverpool after all. He braced himself for another long journey through the night. In the event, head lad Colin Hemsley drove the horsebox carrying Three Dons back from Worcester to Compton, enabling Hutt to have a nap in the vehicle before unloading Foinavon's stable companion and heading north.

On venturing back in from his garden in Berkshire, Cyril Watkins found his wife Iris in tears. She had sat through the tense closing stages as the horse agonisingly picked his way one by one over the last six fences, although she did have to 'hide my face in my jumper once or twice', as one might during the scariest bits of a horror film. She later chided her husband affectionately as 'a big coward'. The telephone started to ring. And ring. One of these calls was from the flabbergasted Mac Bennellick. The message was effectively, 'Thank God you had the guts to go through with it.' Flush with the success of his bets, as well as the victory itself, Watkins told his erstwhile partner there and then that he would give him half the first-place prize money of £15,879 and 10 shillings. This was even though Bennellick had surrendered his half-share in the horse. 'I think it's the decent thing to do,' Watkins said. 'We have been good friends for years.' Arrangements were swiftly made for a celebratory dinner with family and locally based friends that evening at The George, a silver-service hotel in nearby Reading. This would be the first of a number of events hosted by the gratified owner to mark Foinavon's victory.

In Leamington Spa with her grandparents, Ann Buckingham could not stop shouting, 'He's won! He's won!' 'I must have said it 50 times,' she later recalled. Her grandparents, like Iris Watkins, were overcome with emotion. At another address on the same street, Ann's sister, like Cyril, couldn't bear to watch and had gone up to the bedroom while the race was on. 'She didn't watch at all. She just couldn't stand it.' As befits a moment of high drama in a family house in the heart of England, almost the first intelligible sentence uttered was, 'Let's have a cup of tea.' Soon the telegrams started to arrive. And the visitors.

Back in Liverpool, the Adelphi Hotel's Sidney Spofforth and Peter Laiolo, his fellow chef, were already hard at work on the chocolate horses for that night's banquet, oblivious to the narrow escape they had just had. Were it not for Foinavon's last-gasp change of colours, as spotted by Michael O'Hehir, Spofforth would have been left to reflect that his prayer for a winner devoid of tartan had gone unanswered. As it was, not only were John Buckingham's silks well within their creative compass, but the colours of the second man home, Josh Gifford, were easy-peasy – chocolate and white. Even so, they had no time to lose, with diners unlikely to linger long at Aintree on such an inclement afternoon.

Gifford was one of a number of jockeys who were convinced, understandably, that they would have won had it not been for the pile-up. 'I thought I'd catch him until I got to the Melling Road,' he said, 'and then I ran out of steam.' Another of these was Red Alligator's teenage rider Brian Fletcher, who went on to become one of the great Grand National horsemen, with a record of three wins, one second and two thirds from nine starts. 'I am adamant to this day that I would have won in 1967 if I had got a clear run around,' he told me. 'Another couple of furlongs and I'm sure I would have caught him.'

Seeing how much ground Red Alligator lost at the 23rd fence and how much he subsequently made back up, it is hard to disagree with Fletcher's assessment.

John Buckingham, drained but elated, was escorted in towards the winner's enclosure by two police officers, cloaked as well as mounted. While many were still cursing their luck, or trying to ascertain just what had happened at the far end of the course, first-fence faller David Nicholson at once congratulated Buckingham for a 'tremendously determined feat of horsemanship'. Peter O'Sullevan, the BBC's lead commentator and, then as now, a voice of unimpeachable authority on racing, also proffered credit where credit was plainly due. 'Here's the one that got away, that streaked away,' he told viewers. 'A really enterprising piece of jockeyship by young John Buckingham.' Not that he was under any illusion that Foinavon had undergone a sudden transformation into Champion the Wonder Horse. 'It really looked a waste of time for this one to be in the field,' he continued. 'Totally outclassed in the Cheltenham Gold Cup in which he just led the field on sufferance until the business started.'

With his girths undone and saddle removed, the extent of the gelding's exertions became clear as he panted hard and steamed like a New York subway grate. He made life a little bit hard for the sheepskin-jacketed Tim Brookshaw, nodding his head vigorously when the time came to don the blue ribbon in what was an oddly undecorous ceremony. This ended with the former jockey, who had intimated that he would be having 'a few bob' on Honey End, losing his balance and taking a tumble. As Booth circled with the horse, David Coleman, the regular presenter of *Grandstand*, the BBC's flagship Saturday afternoon sports programme, entered the enclosure for a sequence of live interviews. The first was with a wide-eyed Buckingham, who had already donned his jacket and trilby for the occasion. 'Everything seemed to stop in front of me,' he said, an edge of incredulity in his voice, like a man who fears he might wake up at any moment. 'I managed to pull onto the outside. I nearly got stopped by two loose horses ... After he jumped it, we were just out on our own. I couldn't believe it. It was wonderful.' They were joined by a stoical but 'terribly disappointed' Gifford, still in his jockey's colours, a curl of blue cigarette smoke pluming from one hand. 'When I got to Canal Turn, loose horses were three-deep and some coming back at me,' he said, in a first indication that, in his shock, he had misidentified the culpable fence. He later lost a small bet on the long journey home. 'Well, you couldn't dream it was going to be that fence, could you? I mean it's so small after jumping Becher's.' It was, of course, a further cruel irony that it should be his brother Macer's horse that caused the pile-up.

The absence of the winning owner on Grand National day was not unprecedented: neither Kilmore's owners in 1962 nor Ayala's the following year made it to Aintree. But for the trainer to be absent as well was highly unusual. Happily, Jack Kempton, John's father, was at the racecourse and ready to step into the breach, plummy vowels much in evidence, field-glasses around his neck. 'We have never had a long enough trip for him,' he told Coleman and his international audience, exuding bonhomie. 'We always thought he would stay for ever, but he hadn't got a colossal amount of foot.' Popham Down's owner, of course, was at Liverpool and, after the race, approached Kempton suggesting light-heartedly that she was owed half the prize-money in view of her horse's role in what had happened. Foinavon's former owner, Anne, the Duchess of Westminster, was also there and, according to John Lawrence – who must presumably have been rushing from weighing-room to press-room or telephone at the time – 'greeted those who sympathised with the words, "If he was still mine, he probably would have been running the Mullingar."'

Before coverage of the National was brought to a close – and Everton fans informed that their team was 1–0 up at half-time in the FA Cup tie in Nottingham – there was time for a short piece to camera by the stocky figure of O'Hehir standing beside the wreckage of the 23rd fence. As souvenir-hunters prepared to move in and collect pieces of gorse to act as keepsakes of a momentous day, the commentator, who had already covered himself in glory amid the chaos of the race, pulled out another prediction that has turned out to be bang on the money. 'They might call this the Foinavon fence,' he mused.

By this time it was becoming clear that all 28 men and 30 half-tonne quadrupeds who careered into the pile-up had somehow survived their ordeal more or less unscathed. The only name in the jockeys' book that was there to list all injuries was that of Stan Mellor, hurled onto the fence as the mêlée began. And he was well enough to win that last Flat race of the afternoon. Nobby Howard's horse Scottish Final had picked up a nick on one leg and the jockey was on his way out of the weighing-room to tend to him when the clerk of the scales asked him to escort a man to the stables. It was Gregory Peck. 'He was saying, "Did you see my horse? Was it going well at the time?"' Howard remembers. He duly located Different Class for the Hollywood star and left to tend to his own horse.

Back in the weighing-room, Buckingham had ordered champagne for the jockeys. Swallowing his disappointment, Gifford – who had earlier admitted to Coleman with commendable candour that he had been hoping Buckingham would fall in the race's closing stages – opened the first bottle, stuck half-a-crown in the cork and handed it to the winner, saying simply, 'Well done, John'. An envelope in the rack, addressed to The Winner, The Grand National was also drawn to Buckingham's attention. Inside was an invitation to appear on Sunday evening on *The London Palladium Show*, a variety show broadcast by ATV and compèred that night by Bob Monkhouse. This was the first sign that with victory had come, for a limited time, a new status: minor celebrity. As soon became clear, this was to apply to Foinavon as much as the man who steered him through the most spectacular pile-up in Aintree's history.

By this time, the course was emptying fast. John Pinfold, hooked for life as a result of what he had witnessed, was on his way back to Woolton, a sprig of gorse from the 23rd fence safely in his possession. Michael Daley and his mod mac-wearing friends were facing a dressing-down from their mums and dads. This was on account of whitewash from the railings at the top end of the course – the part vandalised over Easter – which had somehow found its way onto their clothes. *Sun* columnist Clement Freud, who had backed The Fossa ante-post at a tempting 200/1, was soon to discover that his house had been burgled.

Clifford Booth, facing another night on-site before Hutt arrived with the horsebox to pick him up, had been handed three pounds to tide him over by Jack Kempton. 'He said, "That will get you home," Booth recalled. 'And he said, "I'm not giving you any more because you'll only go spending it getting drunk or something." In spite of his landlady's suggestion of a night out in Liverpool, Buckingham and his brother were soon heading home to Northamptonshire, having phoned ahead to say they were on their way. On arriving they found that the neighbours had been busy, stringing up flags and renaming the house 'Buckingham Palace' with freshly daubed paint. They spent the rest of the night partying in the Rose and Crown, Buckingham's local pub. It was probably just as well that the victorious jockey and his brother returned from Aintree when they did. A newly minted celeb he might be, but he was still expected at work on the Courage estate on Sunday morning.

The absence of any of the winner's chief connections meant that the Adelphi Hotel's traditional Grand National gala dinner lacked much of its usual sparkle, for all of Spofforth and Laiolo's efforts. 'There were none of the usual riotous scenes,' wrote a '*Daily Post* Woman Reporter' with perhaps a tinge of disappointment discernible in her prose. 'As compared with former years, the atmosphere was almost subdued,' the journalist continued, going on to describe how the black, red and yellow ribbons on the traditional owner's top table were removed and replaced with more subtle red and yellow floral decorations in black bowls. The 350–400 guests were treated to a menu that included *huitres natures, chauchat suprême de volaille beau rivage* and *tartelette aux fraises Becher's Brook*, with the strawberries flown in from California. The 'tall, tousle-haired' trainer Toby Balding was there with the injured Highland Wedding's Canadian owner Charles Burns and was commended for his 'enthusiastic' dancing. But while Balding's pleasure in the occasion was shared by other members of the racing fraternity, 'one missed the energetic performances by the diminutive jockeys of the Twist which had been a feature in former years of this celebration.'

Beyond the Adelphi and the Rose and Crown, much of the country had switched focus to a younger and very different cultural institution, the *Eurovision Song Contest*, being broadcast that night from Vienna's Hofburg Palace with commentary by one Rolf Harris. In a win every bit as clear-cut as Foinavon's, Sandie Shaw, the bare-footed pop star from Dagenham, trounced the opposition with the unashamedly cheesy 'Puppet on a String'. Sean Dunphy, a Baldoyle-based Irishman, came second and Vicky Leandros, singing the enchanting 'L'Amour est Bleu' for Luxembourg, only fourth. It was the United Kingdom's first win in the contest's 12th year. Buckingham and Foinavon faced competition as the day's biggest newsmakers.

Chapter 24

FOINAVON AND THE WOMEN

During the 2010 football World Cup, Paul the Octopus became the most famous cephalopod in recorded history by predicting the outcome of matches. Well, the 1967 Grand National had its own Paul the Octopus. Her name was Peggy and she was a black half-breed Labrador from Thames Ditton.

On the day of the race, Peggy's owner Josephine Morris followed her usual practice by cutting out the names of the 44 runners and scattering them on the kitchen floor. Peggy was then admitted and asked to make her selection. Foinavon was the name on the first piece of paper she touched. At this point, Mrs Morris's son Christopher, a student accountant, read out the highly unflattering assessment of the horse's chances published in their morning paper. Mrs Morris, however, would not be deterred. She insisted that her son pop down to her local bookmaker to place her usual bet of £10 each-way on Peggy's selection. The tip seemed so fanciful that the idea of simply pocketing the stake did flash across Morris's mind. Fortunately he resisted the impulse: the gift his mother handed him from her winnings was the equivalent of nearly a year's wages for him at the time.

Several million people bet on the National that year. Yet only a tiny fraction emulated Peggy in singling out the winner.

The fourth floor of the Tote's New Bridge Street headquarters in London was where bets placed on any given race – from all over the country apart from the racecourse itself – were totted up and payouts calculated. Staff there were bracing themselves for the annual deluge of post-Grand National work when the pile-up occurred and Foinavon broke clear. One bet settler, Peter Chapman – one of the few staff members who neither smoked nor worked night-shifts as a telephone-exchange operator – remembers the reaction of his boss, Tony Barker, an East Ender with a centre-parting and a good war record that he never talked about, when Foinavon crossed the line. 'Tony came running back from the TV screen shouting, "Look at this!"' Chapman, who had never seen him so animated, recalled, 'He held up the slips for bets that had come in nationwide on Foinavon. I'd guess there were somewhere between 10 and 20. Then another shout, 'We've got nothing to do!"'

In contrast to bookmakers, who seek to attract punters' money by setting odds for each runner before a race, Tote payouts are calculated once the market is closed. They reflect the total staked on the winner as a proportion of the overall sum bet on the race. The smaller the amount gambled nationwide on the victor, the bigger the payout to each winning punter. So little had been bet that day via the Tote on Foinavon that the organisation paid a remarkable £445 for every pound staked on the horse to win.

Not everyone with money riding on Foinavon used the Tote. Many racegoers took advantage of the on-course bookies whose umbrellas stood out along the rails among the Aintree crowds. Others, no doubt far outnumbering the punters who placed specific wagers on the horse, drew the 'Foinavon' ticket in workplace sweepstakes, such as the one that left Eric Brown out of pocket on the Orion oil rig. And many, like Christopher Morris, visited a licensed betting-shop.

These high-street bookmakers, though they had taken the country by storm, were a recent innovation. The first had opened less than six years previously, on May Day 1961, with the entry into force of the new Betting and Gaming Act. This finally legalised off-course cash betting. Prior to that, betting was supposedly regulated by the Street Betting Act of 1906, whose intention was, as far as possible, to localise the activity on racecourses. It became an offence, therefore, to loiter in public places for the purpose of bookmaking or making and settling bets. Cue the arrival of a public telephone service and an example – by no means the first, or last – of a new technology making an ass of the law. The telephone made it possible, for the relatively well-off at least, to get around the restriction on off-course betting quite lawfully by setting up a credit account with a bookmaker and phoning bets in. Millions of working-class gamblers and the bookmakers who served them got around the law in a different way: by ignoring it. But in doing so, they ran the risk of prosecution. The result, as acknowledged by Home Secretary Rab Butler, when the new bill was debated by the House of Commons in November 1959, was 'differential treatment for different social classes of the community'. Butler cited a Royal Commission estimating that about half a million people bet off-course by telephone on credit with an average weekly stake of between £2 10 shillings (£2.50) and £3 10 shillings (£3.50). This compared with no fewer than 3.5 million who, in effect, flouted the law by betting in cash, with their average weekly stake a mere eight shillings (40p). The law, Butler admitted, had been brought 'into contempt'. Little wonder that Labour MP George Thomson described the situation before the reform as 'almost a classic example of one law for the rich and one for the poor.'

Betting shops, by spreading like wildfire – 7,000 opened in May 1961 alone – had changed all that by 1967. But a whiff of disrepute still lingered from the days when cash bets were routinely transacted on the sly in darkened doorways in the poorer parts of town. Nor were the new outlets, with their chalkboards and tense, smoke-filled interiors, exactly inviting. Not for nothing did Manchester MP Eric Johnson observe, 'the Bill seems to say that we are to make betting in a betting-office legal, provided that we make that office as uncomfortable as possible'. Derby day and Grand National day were still probably the only two occasions in the year when members of the English middle-classes could be seen in a betting-shop without some risk of disapproval from their peers. And while plenty of women bet on the 1967 Grand National, the usual practice, as with the Morrises, seems to have been for the bets actually to be placed by men. This was in spite of a reservation expressed by Lord Silkin during passage of the bill that, 'we are going to introduce wives to the mysteries of betting'.

One of the betting-slips in Tony Barker's hand would have related to Cyril Watkins's last-minute Tote wager. Taking into account the two ante-post bets – totalling £16 each-way – that he placed with book-makers, I very much doubt that anyone won more on Foinavon that day than his owner. By my estimate, his winnings must have been comfortably over £10,000, a very substantial sum in 1967 – and he told one journalist that Iris, his wife, had won £1,250 into the bargain.

It was, of course, a magnificent result for the bookies. According to William Hill, 'We could not have picked a better winner.' A Glasgow bookmaker called John Banks was reported to have made £25,000 on the race. Even so, a sprinkling of lucky, or supremely insightful, individuals around the country did manage to back Foinavon. And a strikingly high proportion of those were women.

In Liverpool, Lucy Geddes managed to win twice over on the horse, even though she was not a lover of the Grand National. First off, one of her daughters came home from work on the eve of the race with two tickets for a sweepstake at Ayrton Saunders, a pharmaceutical wholesaler. One ticket, for one of the favourites, her daughter kept; the other, for Foinavon, she presented to her mum. Mrs Geddes then had to endure an evening of light-hearted ribbing from the men of the house about what a hopeless case she had been given. She said nothing at the time, but on the morning of the race when her husband asked which horse she wanted him to back for her, she replied, 'Foinavon'. That evening, she was able to repay the previous day's mickey taking with interest.

Helen Dillon, a regular London-based punter with interests in five-card stud and 18th-century English porcelain, spent Grand National day with friends at their oast-house in East Hoathly, a village in Sussex. She noticed that an elderly local woman called Lily, who helped in the house, was pacing around and muttering, 'Foinavon's going to win, Foinavon's going to win.' Dillon rang the Tote and put on a four shillings (20p) each-way bet. After being paid her winnings, she was at a cocktail party in Flood Street when she met a woman with a stall at Chelsea Antiques Market. She asked her if she would like to share the stall. Within a week, she had taken up residence, together with her modest porcelain collection.

A Liverpool supermarket worker called Vivian Humphries and four friends had the bright idea of using a Ouija board to find the winner the week before the race. Gathered among the cereal boxes in the shop's storeroom, the glass they were using duly spelled out the first letters of 'Foinavon'. Four of them, three of whom were women, staked five shillings (25p) each-way, while the fifth attendee wagered double that. He won enough for a tape-recorder, while Humphries herself bought a leather coat with her winnings. They were too scared to try it again the following year.

Other women who gambled successfully on the horse included Nan Toone, a £9-a-week shoe-machinist and mother of three from Leicestershire, who staked four shillings on a racing pools coupon with the first three finishers in the right order. Then there was Martyne Millington, also from Leicestershire, who won a VIP day at Aintree in a *Daily Mirror* competition and followed that up by earning £52 from Foinavon's victory. A nurse at the Royal Berkshire Hospital where Cyril Watkins had been admitted also risked a few shillings on her patient's horse and treated colleagues to cream cakes for tea when the bet paid off.

Another pocket of support for the rank outsider came from the network of Avon ladies who sold beauty products door-to-door, helped by one of the decade's most enduring catchphrases, 'Ding dong, Avon calling!' This was primarily because of the coincidence of the horse's name. It is not altogether surprising that Avon lady Alison Grant should have staked a shilling each-way on Foinavon: she is also John Buckingham's sister-in-law. But she told me that a Stratford-based manager of hers called Yvonne Jones had a much bigger bet. The horse was also said to have attracted wagers from staff at the company's operations in Corby. Back in Liverpool, Margaret Nolan had 'about 2/6d' (12½p) each-way on Foinavon, not because she was an Avon lady herself, but because a colleague at work in the Liver Building had recently become one. She spent the race at the swings in the local park with her nephews and didn't hear the result. When she got back, the men who had earlier been pulling her leg about her choice were stunned. She won about the equivalent of a week's wages. 'It was absolutely hilarious,' she says.

Foinavon's youngest backer may also have been a girl. According to a blog posted in 2010, in 1967 the then nine-year-old Patricia Rogers staked 'two bob' (10p) on the horse since she thought it had the nicest name. She also had to put up with plenty of teasing, but stuck to her guns – and won 'ten whole pounds'. As she wrote, 'Ten pounds was a lot of money to a nine-year-old girl in 1967, it meant a drawer full of chocolate and a whole new wardrobe for my Sindy doll'. Eleven-year-old John Warham also picked out the winner after Foinavon got a mention in a regional news programme he was watching. With his dad away at the football, his winning sixpence (2½p) each-way bet was laid by his grandmother. And 13-year-old milk-boy Nigel Everett had a shilling each-way too, after taking a break in a steamy-windowed Mitcham café and reading in a paper that Foinavon jumped 'like another Arkle', or words to that effect. Tom Sculley, the milkman Everett assisted on his round, had a rather larger bet.

I have been told about three houses in England and Wales called Foinavon: one in Compton, one on a cliff overlooking the sea in Criccieth and one in South Yorkshire. The last of these was built by Sam and Joyce Sowerby who ran a poultry and egg business on Doncaster Corn Exchange market. Sam was also a course bookmaker, and in the bookmakers' draw for the 1967 Grand National he drew Foinavon. The Sowerbys were, I am told, so disappointed with their horse that they informed any customers who enquired that they had got Honey End, the favourite. This draw must have been valuable because they used the winnings to build a house, Foinavon, on a smallholding they owned near Doncaster. Sowerby would rescue ponies and donkeys and keep them at the site while they awaited permanent homes.

Much the best-known backer of the winner was another man with a house called Foinaven (though in his case named after the Scottish mountain), Chay Blyth. The future round-the-world yachtsman 'just had to have a bit on'. Birmingham-based David Radford, like the Sowerbys, drew Foinavon in a sweepstake. He tried to sell the ticket to colleagues who had been unable to participate and actually bet on Honey End. Luckily for him, no one would accept his offer. The *Sunday Times* said a 'Sussex man' had picked the first three horses in the correct order and collected £1,125 for a one-shilling (5p) stake. The *Sunday Post* declared Jack Haggerty, a Glasgow barman, the 'luckiest punter of the day' for scooping £625 with a £2 bet. Wiltshire farmer Ernest Sharps got less favourable odds, but must have matched those winnings with his £5 each-way bet. The wager was inspired by a dual coincidence: the farm straddled the river Avon and its 100-acre size matched Foinavon's starting-price. Sharps used his windfall to acquire more acres and hence, presumably would have had to scour the racecards of future Nationals for outsiders with even bigger prices.

Alan Whitehead, a *Daily Mirror* reader and engineering apprentice at Metal Box, about ten minutes' walk from the racecourse, had come across the interview with John Kempton published in Ron Wills's column. It was his custom to read the paper while having lunch at his bench next to a short cut to the staff canteen. With the National just 24 hours away, it was the main topic of conversation and he kept being asked for tips by those walking past. At first, he had answered Bassnet, but by the time he had digested the interview, he was getting 'a bit fed-up' with repeatedly being asked the same question. So he started saying that, according to what he had just read, Foinavon was going to win. Whitehead had planned to go to the race with a friend, but they were put off by the weather. Instead, he went to the local bookie where he bet £2 to win on Bassnet – and sixpence (2½p) each-way on Foinavon. He collected just over £3.

Bob Knight, a painter and decorator from Romford, was perhaps the one man in the country who placed a bet on Foinavon yet ended up feeling as if he had missed out. In the weeks running up to the race, Knight had a recurring dream of Foinavon winning the National. He felt someone was telling him to back it and kept pointing out to his family that the odds were 500/1 ante-post. The household was not well-off and Knight's wife would not normally have supported such an out-and-out punt. Yet so insistent was the dream that she encouraged her husband to have a really sizeable wager. In the event, he could not bring himself to take such a risk with the family finances and made do with an affordable bet of a shilling or two each-way. One of Knight's sons had gone to Margate to watch a football match and was unaware that he had scaled down his bet. When he heard what was happening at Aintree on the radio, 'I was jumping up and down and telling everyone my dad had won a fortune.' He found a phone-box and called home as soon as the race was over, only to be told the disappointing news. Not surprisingly, the first time this son went to Aintree, he was more interested in seeing the 23rd fence than Becher's Brook or The Chair.

There were other hard-luck stories. A bookie in the Banbury area agreed to let a customer place a bet even though the race had started. It was a hefty each-way wager on Foinavon. In Wealdstone, the reason for Alan Sweeney's reticence became clear soon after Dennis Lewell had finished calculating his winnings as Foinavon passed the winning-post. Sweeney had been so convinced that Lewell's selection stood no chance that he had kept his half-a-crown (12½p), stood the bet himself and now couldn't afford to pay up. As their friend Graham Sharpe, also present, recalled, there was a stunned silence before Lewell, who at least got his money back, went through the motions of being annoyed. His heart wasn't really in it, however, and the three teenagers trooped off to play football.

In the FA Cup quarter-final at Nottingham, Everton had failed to hang on to their half-time lead, going down 3–2 to Forest in a thriller in front of a full house of 47,500, with a young forward called Ian Storey-Moore scoring a hat-trick. It had made ultimately frustrating watching for Michael Walters and his fellow Everton fans. Then again, Walters had the considerable consolation of having won the National sweepstake conducted on the coach on the way to the game. After a while, though, when the stranger who supervised the sweepstake had still not reappeared at the coach, which was waiting to take them back home, it started to dawn on Walters that he would have to face up to another piece of bad news: the sweepstake man had absconded.

Chapter 25

WELL DONE, FOINAVON

As a weary Tony Hutt, Woodbine on his lip, turned at last into the lane that led down to Chatham Stables and the Ridgeway beyond, scores of village children gave a high-pitched cheer and started waving their Union Jacks. It was Sunday lunchtime, nearly 24 hours after Foinavon's scarcely believable victory, and the unlikely hero was making his triumphant return.

In an early sign that winning the world's most famous steeplechase was not going to sweep away all life's problems, however, the morning after the Kemptons' day of days had been surprisingly fraught. There were two issues. The first was the condition of the horse. In Liverpool first thing, on going to load him into the horsebox that Hutt had driven through the night to pick them up, stable lad Clifford Booth had found the gelding 'lame as anything'. This meant there was no question of parading him through part of the village of Compton, as originally intended. Instead, people would have to come to the yard. The second issue was the time of Foinavon's arrival. The post-race visit to the Grand National winner's stable was a tradition for the press, anxious for a fresh angle for their Monday morning stories, as much as local well-wishers. And with a victor as surprising as this, a big turnout was guaranteed. It would not do to keep the men from the *Telegraph* and the *Mail* waiting for hours on end in the middle of nowhere in the now dry but still far from spring-like weather conditions. As a result Hutt and Booth had to stop and phone in progress reports from red telephone boxes along the way at regular intervals, stuffing shillings and silver sixpences into the slot.

In the end, the hassle was worth it. The villagers, including a group of 11 children crammed on top of a Land Rover with its spare tyre on the bonnet and a sign reading 'WELL DONE FOINAVON' across the front, had a memorable afternoon and the Kemptons got a salvo of the sort of publicity you just cannot buy. Foinavon's lameness – caused by a strained suspensory ligament in a foreleg no doubt as a result of the exertions of the race – had eased during the long journey, enabling him to be walked off the horsebox without undue fuss. An evocative photograph of the scene graced the front page of *The Times* the following morning. Flanked by excited locals, the horse, displaying the blue Grand National ribbon bestowed on him by Tim Brookshaw, is being led carefully up the driveway into the yard by Booth, sporting flat cap and tie. Beside them, John Kempton, in a distinctive and rather dashing check jacket, is keeping a firm grasp on Susie the white goat. 'The one-speed winner of the Grand National was too stiff to parade through his flag-bedecked village,' James Lewthwaite of the *Mail* informed his readers. 'So the villagers came to see him.' The *Telegraph* sagely advised that each week the horse consumed 'a dozen packets of Polos'. Kempton, for his part, confided that, while he might be one-paced, Foinavon jumped 'like a cat' and was 'tremendously intelligent'. Once settled into his 30mph gallop, he added, 'nothing can change it. If somebody tries to speed him up, he goes all over the place.'

Behind-the-scenes, the yard's other equine residents were getting agitated at the unaccustomed intrusion. Head lad Colin Hemsley spent most of the afternoon making sure that the visitors kept their distance, in particular from Three Dons, the prized but excitable colt who was recuperating from his successful efforts at Worcester. By about 3.30pm, their curiosity sated, the villagers had drifted away and Hemsley and Booth started to settle the horses down for the night. At the same time, wage-packets for by far the most successful week the yard would ever know were distributed. As Booth picked up his envelope, Jack Kempton took it and extracted the £3 he had given him to tide him over in Liverpool. 'I was on £5 for the week – and £2 10s (£2.50)of that was the digs money I gave my mum,' Booth recalls. It was another small indication that not as much was going to change at Chatham Stables as you might think.

Newspaper opinion on the race was remarkably polarised. *The Times* racing correspondent Michael Phillips declared it 'a sad chapter in the history of National Hunt racing'. His downbeat assessment was widely shared. The *Daily Mirror*'s Peter Wilson observed tartly that he had 'rarely seen a less satisfactory Grand National – and I have seen about 25.' Hotspur in the *Daily Telegraph*, meanwhile, struck a more pragmatic tone, emphasising that 'most visitors left Aintree insufficiently informed, besides being wet and out of pocket.' Yet the *News of the World* had proclaimed the pile-up 'the most fantastic moment in the most fantastic horse race ever run', publishing a large front-page photograph, snapped by '*News of the World* reader John Williams of Southport', of 'that second of sensation which brought millions of you out of your TV chairs'. And Don Cox writing in the *Sun*, 'the independent newspaper' as it styled itself then, argued forcefully against changing the rules to try to prevent such accidents happening. 'We must accept the Grand National for what it is … or let it die!' Cox wrote. 'The National is there, we must accept what happened on Saturday as part of the risks that jockeys take and we as punters share.'

Ron Wills's Spotlight column, which had run that short interview with John Kempton on the eve of the race, now seemed almost bashful about what it could have portrayed as a major coup. True, the phrase 'The column that gave you Foinavon' had been added, but in surprisingly small type. The accompanying text showed similar restraint, describing Kempton's Aintree hero with scrupulous accuracy as 'the horse Spotlight DIDN'T write off as a no-hoper'. At Mullingar, the small Irish racecourse-town, a resident recalls that a moral dimension had been introduced into the story via a newspaper headline along the lines of 'Lazy Horse Wins Grand National'. 'Well, there's hope for some of you then', one of the sisters at a local convent school was heard to remark to her class when the topic was broached the following week.

For a really considered assessment of the 1967 Grand National and its legacy, the racing public had to wait a few days longer for the appearance of the first issue of *Horse and Hound* to post-date the race on 15 April. The article contributed by John Lawrence to the magazine that day was witty, erudite, original, authoritative, all of the above. It would have constituted sports journalism at its best even without the ingredient that gave its writer an unfair edge over other contemporary chroniclers of the great pile-up: as Norther's jockey, he was slap bang in the thick of it.

It is worth dwelling on some of the points raised in Lawrence's tour de force. First, he had recalled a precedent in the shape of the 1928 Grand National won by another long-odds plodder, Tipperary Tim. On that occasion, the Canal Turn alone, then an open-ditch, accounted for more than half of the 42-strong field. Only one other horse finished – and it had to be remounted to do so. Given that a further 17 runners ultimately trailed Foinavon home in 1967, the earlier race undoubtedly had a greater attrition rate. Newsreel footage suggests, however, that the 1928 pile-up was not as spectacular.

Lawrence gave short shrift to calls for a tightening up of qualification standards for the National, arguing that loose horses were the issue and 'loose good horses are just as dangerous as loose bad ones'. He went on, 'The answer surely is to get the loose horses out of the way as quickly as possible – and that means doing away with (or leaving wide gaps in) the inside rail.' He was not the first one to argue this case. In the wake of the 1928 incident, *The Times*, no less, suggested extending and enlarging exits from the course, 'so as to reduce the number of riderless horses remaining in the race for lack of an obvious way of escape.'

The journalist-jockey also underlined how 'heartily thankful' all involved should be that the 1967 pile-up happened where it did and not a fence earlier, at Becher's Brook. 'Popham Down could just as easily have chosen Becher's,' he wrote, 'and had he done so, the probable results do not really bear thinking about.' Nonetheless, there was 'absolutely nothing wrong with the race … The occasional total turn-up, however painful at the time, is perhaps a salutary reminder that this is still the National – a contest in which literally anything can happen.' This was, he added, 'the best Grand National field for years and would have produced a magnificent race. Fate decreed differently – but there will be other days.'

Finally, like commentator Peter O'Sullevan, Lawrence had seen enough steeplechasing to know how much credit the winning horse and jockey deserved for sidestepping the chaos and making it to the winning-post intact, even if their victory was widely seen as a fluke. 'It is true,' he wrote, 'in a way, that Foinavon won the National because he was too slow … But that does not detract either from John Buckingham's cool horsemanship or from Foinavon's courage.' In a couple of years' time, he went on, in common with other jockeys, 'I expect I shall feel pretty certain that Norther "should" have won – but the name in the record books will still be Foinavon and that, really, is that.'

As his mount was making his way gingerly back to his stable in Berkshire, the cool horseman in question was heading for London for his brush with show business – and feeling anything but cool at the prospect.

For all his new status as a Grand National winner, Buckingham's Sunday morning had indeed started with a shift at the stables on the Courage estate. Unlike any previous shift, however, this one culminated, fittingly enough, with a champagne celebration. Later, when he arrived at the Palladium, Bob Monkhouse, the show's compère, took him into his dressing-room and showed him a big board detailing their planned routine. The smooth-as-silk comedian explained that he, Monkhouse, would go on stage sporting top hat and binoculars, talk about having been up to the Grand National and say that Foinavon had won. He would then call Buckingham out onto the stage.

You might have thought that a man capable of navigating a stubborn half-tonne animal over 30 fearsome obstacles with bedlam a possible consequence of the slightest mishap would take a little scripted banter in his stride. Not so. 'I was more nervous than I had been at any other time of my life, and they virtually had to push me on to the stage!' he later recalled. 'Thank God you can't see anything because of the lights.' Nervous or not, he steeled himself and did his duty, even delivering a punchline that, while not worthy of Morecambe and Wise, did the job by providing a cheesy link to the next act on. 'How did Freddie jump?' Monkhouse inquired with mock seriousness. 'He didn't jump very well today,' the novice stand-up replied, 'but he will be jumping well tonight.' Another question from Monkhouse, 'Are you talking about Freddie the horse?' 'No, Freddie and the Dreamers!' Cue the arrival onstage of the well-known pop group fronted by the bouncy, bespectacled – and jockey-sized – Freddie Garrity.

Less than 24 hours after that, Buckingham was back on the tread-mill, going all the way to Wye for ride number 806 – a horse called Easter Speaker in the Dover Handicap Chase over two miles, value £340. They came in seventh and last. Next day, it was the train to Plumpton, the tight Sussex course next to the railway station, where he had a second and two thirds – and Ron Atkins and Bruce Gregory, two of the jockeys who had ridden Foinavon and might have had the ride at Aintree had things panned out differently, caught up with and congratulated him. It was on the way to Plumpton that Buckingham got another taste of the consequences of his new-found celebrity. First, the mother of an importuning small boy asked him for his autograph on the Underground. Then, at Victoria Station, the barber where he dropped in for a haircut and shave declined payment, saying, 'That's all right, Mr Buckingham, there'll be no charge.' There were undoubtedly many more autographs to sign between then and 27 May, when he partnered Jolly Signal in an obscure hurdle race at Towcester. But that was his next winner, seven weeks to the day after his greatest triumph. For Buckingham, like the staff at Chatham Stables, the rhythm of life after Aintree would carry on much as before.

After the frenzy of post-race interviews, during which they pledged to keep Foinavon 'for ever', the Watkinses set about celebrating their good fortune – with gusto. A few days after their dinner at the George, their local silver-service hotel, Cyril hosted a black-tie party at the Savoy with oysters on the menu and dancing. Some time after that, there was another glitzy London celebration, this time at the Talk of the Town, the well-known cabaret-restaurant on Charing Cross Road.

For Cyril's erstwhile partner, Mac Bennellick, there was the very considerable consolation of half the prize money, along with the satisfaction of being designated one of three 'Faces in the News This Week' by the *Havering Recorder*. (The other two were Patricia Lefevre, Romford's new carnival queen, and Dennis Simmons, who lost both legs in a road accident but still marked his 45th birthday by swimming two lengths of the Harold Hill Pool.) 'Mr Watkins and I have always had a complete understanding on the question of prize money won by any of our horses,' Bennellick told the *Recorder*'s reporter, adding, 'I would rather have won the National than the Derby.'

The second Sunday after the race, Bennellick and Watkins visited Compton together to see their now famous horse. 'We were there for about an hour and a half or two hours,' Booth remembers. 'They gave me £2.'

Chapter 26

THE WORLD OF WILLIAM HICKEY

It is one of those photographs that demands a second look. Yes, that really is Buckingham Palace in the background, which means that the three pedestrians holding up the 1960s traffic are at the top of The Mall. But why are they accompanied by a horse and a nanny goat in a jacket? The animals add a comic touch to what might otherwise be a faintly menacing scene. These are not military men, but they must surely have a certain standing for a mounted policeman to be stopping traffic for them in this precise location. And then there are those uniform, dark *Reservoir Dogs*-style ties.

The giveaway is the horse's rider. He is dressed in the same distinctive jockey's silks he was wearing when he burst out of obscurity at Aintree 17 days before. Now John Buckingham, along with Foinavon, his owner and his main handlers from Compton, are on their way to meet a member of the royal family.

It is an eye-catching and unorthodox way of arriving for a St James's Palace reception in the presence of Her Royal Highness the Duchess of Kent. So it should perhaps come as no surprise that the Grand

National-winning team had been roped into a publicity stunt. The reception marked the launch of National Cancer Day Ascot, a charity race meeting due to take place at the end of September. About 300 guests had been invited in total, including a good sprinkling of dukes, ladies, earls and other establishment figures.

The newspapers lapped it up, with the *Mail* describing Foinavon as 'the first horse to be guest of honour at a royal palace'. The duchess, evidently a good sport, went outside to greet the unlikely Liverpool hero, and feed him some carrots. Susie the nanny goat, unusually, spurned the offer of real food, but took a fancy to a piece of plastic grass that had been laid out with the aim of beautifying the occasion. Not everyone in Foinavon's retinue made it into the reception. One who did was the Rolls-Royce-driving scrap-metal dealer and long-time supporter of the yard, Gordon Passey. Some time later, Foinavon's horsebox-drivers, who had been waiting outside, saw Passey coming back towards them carrying something in his hands. 'This was the best I could do for you,' he said, holding them out so they could see what he had. They were full of peeled prawns. 'I've just gone off fish,' murmured one of the drivers. Nonetheless, it was a considerate gesture.

That this was the grandest occasion graced by Foinavon's presence, there can be no doubt. But the newly minted equine celebrity was to do an awful lot of this sort of thing in the months following his shock National victory. Already he had been paraded around the Reading Football Club stadium at Elm Park, proving as unperturbed by the noise of the crowd, there to watch the home team take on Workington in the old third division, as by the chaos he had encountered at Aintree at the 23rd fence. Soon there would be visits to Wasps rugby ground at Sunbury-on-Thames, to Stratford-upon-Avon, where he started a donkey derby at the racecourse involving jockeys and Coventry City footballers, and to Malvern, where he was scheduled to open the Pony of the Year Show. Other engagements were slated to include a show at Shaftesbury in Dorset, the Royal Duchy of Cornwall Show and the Wokingham Carnival. There was also a photo-shoot in Compton for the 1968 Schweppes racing calendar in which Foinavon would be Mr April. Burnished like a mahogany sideboard, the horse posed, ears pricked, with Buckingham on his back again in full Grand National garb. Susie had left her mark here too, flattening a small bush that acted as the yard's centrepiece. 'We had it all held up with string,' stable lad Clifford Booth remembered. 'If you look very closely, you can see the string that was holding it all together.'

'Since Foinavon surprised everybody, including himself, by avoiding all the setbacks of the Aintree track, he has become more socially accept-able than even his old stablemate Arkle,' commented the *Daily Express*. This article was headlined, 'Foinavon moves into the World of William Hickey', traditional nom de plume of the newspaper's gossip columnist.

This was just fine with Cyril Watkins, who appeared to relish his new status as Grand National-winning owner. 'He is the most popular horse in the country at the moment,' Watkins proudly told one reporter. 'He's booked up for charity appearances every Saturday until the end of September. He won't be racing again this year.'

However, the effect of Foinavon's crowded social calendar back at Chatham Stables as the weather improved and the days lengthened was altogether less benign.

To put it bluntly, the frequent jaunts to one event or another in England's leafier shires became a distraction the small yard with its still meagre resources could ill afford. The extra work – and extensive travel-ling – were not appreciated by staff, whose hours were already long and anti-social. And because the functions were, for the most part, charita-ble, it was usually difficult for the Kemptons to recoup their expenses, let alone charge any sort of appearance fee. Of course, they recognised that the causes they were helping were good and were happy to do their bit, acknowledging that fortune had smiled on them at Liverpool. But, at the same time, they felt hemmed in, unable to say 'No' for fear of appearing uncaring or making Watkins look bad, while all too aware that these extra-curricular commitments were a source of friction in the yard and risked undermining any chance they had of building on the victory to improve their racing operation.

In truth, there were other tensions too. On 21 January, John Kempton had married Patricia Minter at St Mary's Church in the nearby village of Shaw-cum-Donnington. The couple rented a small house a few miles away from Chatham Stables, so John was no longer quite so close to the horses. The intention was that this arrangement would be temporary, with John and Trish eventually taking over the bungalow across from the yard while John's parents went to live at the small house. But this never actually happened. 'It was always going to be "This year, this week, next week",' John Kempton recalls. Over time, the failure of the move to take place imposed increasing strain on relations between John and his father.

Engines rather than horses had always been the two men's shared passion. They would often be seen working on some car together, occasionally a classic, their tools laid out neatly like surgical instruments. Now, there was no longer time for such pleasurable pursuits.

It was at about this time that Clifford Booth left, going to work for Fred Winter in one of the elite National Hunt yards of the era. Adding to the pressure, the Kemptons had had another small stable-block installed, anticipating inquiries from new owners attracted by all the post-Grand National publicity. These vacancies now needed filling. On 17 August, the *Evening News & Star* reported that Kempton was advertising for more horses to train. 'But unlike most trainers, he wants bad ones – jumpers who can't jump properly or horses who are difficult to manage. He thinks there are more Foinavons about … and would like the chance to prove it.' It was an original pitch, seeking to highlight his and Colin Hemsley's knack for equine psychoanalysis, and some occupants did eventually move into the new block. But the glory day at Aintree never did yield much of a dividend in terms of new business. The nature of Foinavon's victory was, it seems, just too outlandish for outside owners to conclude that the skills of the horse's training team had much to do with it.

By the end of the summer, Foinavon fever had cooled sufficiently for the horse to leave the world of William Hickey and go back into training. The yard had had a couple of winners by then, which was two more than they had mustered by a similar stage of the previous season. No sooner had the equine celebrity made his belated seasonal debut on 1 November at his local course at Newbury, however – a solid but pedestrian fourth place in a three-mile chase won by Bassnet – than a new problem arose. And this time its impact was industry-wide.

It was actually a few days before that race, on 25 October, that the first case of foot-and-mouth disease was diagnosed in Shropshire. This was not particularly unusual at the time. Yet five weeks later, on 28 November 1967, with the worst such epizootic of the century now raging, all horse racing in Britain was cancelled until further notice. It did not resume until 5 January.

Chapter 27

10 MILLION TO ONE

More than 60 race-meetings in Britain and Ireland were lost before something approaching normality was restored. More to the point, well over 400,000 farm animals were destroyed, with the prime dairy country of Cheshire losing nearly a third of its cattle. The geographic spread of the devastation was smaller than in 2001, the next occasion on which the UK endured a serious foot-and-mouth outbreak. But in afflicted areas, the deadening effect on day-to-day life was all too similar.

Over the five weeks when there was no racing at all, bookmaker William Hill said it stood to drop £1 million a week in turnover. At Aintree, the chief concern was over whether the field for the 1968 Grand National would be unacceptably weakened by the absence of horses deprived of the chance to qualify for the race. Mrs Topham and her colleagues actually asked the National Hunt stewards if they would agree to a fortnight's extension of the usual early January cut-off point. In the event though this idea was discarded, there being only two extra qualifying races in the proposed lengthened period. When the handicap was published on 25 January, there was a more than adequate list of 102 entries. On it were 27 of the 1967 field, including the first three home: Foinavon, Honey End and Red Alligator.

This was the start of tougher times all round for Britain, with the long post-war boom petering out. Ten days before horse racing was halted, on 18 November, came the shock of devaluation. This was the occasion of Harold Wilson's famous 'pound in your pocket' broadcast. The prime minister told a shaken nation that the cut, from \$2.80 to \$2.40 in the value of the pound, 'does not mean that the pound here in Britain, in your pocket or purse or in your bank, has been devalued.' Among the things it did mean was that imported goods would cost more – as Mrs Topham was soon to discover to her cost. A discussion with a Colonel Livingstone Learmouth about catering arrangements for the 1968 spring meeting yielded the doubtless unwelcome news that Letheby & Christopher would have to raise prices, 'since devaluation had automatically increased prices of champagne' and other imports. The cost of the Grand National trophy would be higher than in 1967 too.

It was fully three months on from his first outing of the season in early November before Foinavon again found himself travelling to a racecourse. It was a marathon journey, all the way to Newcastle for the Eider Chase, one of very few races in the calendar apart from the National that was over four miles long. Highland Wedding, a leading fancy for the 1967 National prior to his injury, had won the last two runnings. He had not come to attempt a hat-trick. Instead, Foinavon would be up against Red Alligator, the local Bishop Auckland-based horse which jockey Brian Fletcher was convinced would have won the 1967 Grand National had the pile-up not intervened, and Master of Art, another leading National prospect trained in Sussex by Captain Ryan Price. Johnny Lehane had been booked to ride Cyril Watkins and Mac Bennellick's gelding, who would be carrying just 9st 7lb.

If the threat from foot-and-mouth disease was subsiding, however, racing still had to contend with Britain's capricious climate. On wakening on Saturday morning, head lad Colin Hemsley was dismayed to find that the landscape had turned white. The snow and frost meant that not only had they undertaken a 500-mile round-trip for nothing, but that he would probably have to repay some of the four days' worth of expenses he had brought with him from Berkshire. Since he had already spent the bulk of the money on a mini shopping-spree for his wife at C&A, this came as an unwelcome realisation.

It took Foinavon's training team almost a further three weeks to finally get another race into his legs. On another bitterly cold day at Ascot, he trailed in last of six having gone to post as top weight. Few would even have noticed, sports fans' attention being fixed at the time on the accident that had befallen Middlesex cricketer Fred Titmus in the Caribbean. The mishap cost the off-spinner four toes.

The Grand National was now just five weeks away and Foinavon had managed only two outings since his victory in the previous year's race, finishing last and last. He squeezed in two more runs before his return to Aintree, but showed nothing to suggest there was the slightest prospect of his emulating Reynoldstown, the last horse to win two consecutive Nationals, in 1935 and 1936.

After another long trip to West Yorkshire, he was again last of four finishers in a three-and-a-half-mile chase at Wetherby. But the race did offer grounds for hoping he was running into better form, as he came in a semi-respectable 16 lengths behind the winner, Rutherfords – a horse with sound National credentials, as he had demonstrated, for 22 fences, 11 months earlier. These hopes were largely extinguished the following week at Sandown. Having jumped off in front, Foinavon was soon overhauled and eventually pulled up by Lehane. The race was won by Different Class, another of his past – and future – Aintree rivals.

Three days later, as the Cheltenham festival got under way in blustery but clear conditions, the world of politics once again imposed itself on racing. The first Budget by Roy Jenkins, the new Chancellor of the Exchequer, who had replaced Jim Callaghan soon after the pound was devalued, was an absolute stinker. And among a series of tax hikes that *The Times* judged 'nasty but necessary' was a doubling to 5 per cent of the betting duty levied on stake money. Jenkins described this as 'the maximum' he was advised the tax could bear at that moment.

As in 1967, the identity of Foinavon's Liverpool jockey was not settled until a few days before the race. His winning partner, John Buckingham, was not expected to be available this time around, since his employer, Edward Courage, would be running a horse called San Angelo at Aintree and would want the jockey to ride him. In fact, Buckingham broke an arm falling from a John Kempton-trained horse called Churby at Worcester on 12 March. Sidelined as a result, he ended up watching the National from a vantage-point beside The Chair.

Lehane appeared to be next in line, having ridden Foinavon, albeit without success, in two of his races in the run-up to Liverpool. He had been expected to partner him at Wetherby as well. However, he had suffered a fall in the first race of the day and did not ride again that afternoon. A Midlands-based jockey called Phil Harvey had stepped into the breach and piloted him to his most impressive – or least unimpressive – run of the season. Whether dissatisfaction with Lehane's subsequent performance at Sandown was a factor, or if there was haggling over the jockey's fee as in 1967, one cannot be sure. But over the last week before the National, it became clear that Harvey, not Lehane, was going to get the Aintree ride.

As the sport's leading lights converged once again on Merseyside, the future of the racecourse was still technically open to question. There was a sense, though, that while it remained unknown who the new long-term owners would actually be, the threat that Becher's Brook might be paved over and the Grand National forced to move or die had been averted. As the three-day meeting was in progress, a story broke that Liverpool Corporation was to pay £1.5 million to take over the racecourse. The story was denied, although Sports Minister Denis Howell acknowledged that discussions were 'moving along'. Michael Phillips, *The Times* racing correspondent, reported that the National took place in a 'much better atmosphere' than for several years. 'There was a feeling that, in spite of all the denials, the future of the great race and its birthplace was safe,' he wrote.

After the prolonged cold snap, the weather was as spectacular as it had been atrocious the previous year. 'Summer in spring continued yesterday,' read a front-page picture caption in *The Times* on Grand National morning. A temperature of 76.3°F was recorded in Suffolk. If there was a reminder of the mounting industrial and economic problems confronting the country, it was a Liverpool bus strike that was in its third week as the meeting got under way. The strike was said to explain why Liverpool Football Club had not sold out their allocation of tickets for the impending away game at Manchester United, their bitter rivals. It also cast doubt on the wisdom of the decision by Mrs Topham and her colleagues to advertise the National meeting on 5 million bus tickets.

One man especially glad of the fine weather was Colin Hemsley, assigned to look after Foinavon this year. He arrived in Liverpool only to find that no one had booked him a bed for the night. So he slept in the horsebox, prior to getting up at dawn and exercising the horse over Aintree's vast open spaces. Having had to miss his great moment the previous year, John Kempton reached the racecourse good and early this time around. It was a special day for the young trainer whose horse had defied the odds last time, even though he was under no illusion about the likelihood of lightning striking twice. 'I know it's about 10 million to one against it happening again,' he had told one journalist. 'But that doesn't matter. There is a special privilege in even entering a horse for this unique race and I shall be delighted if Foinavon finishes in the first ten – if only to silence the knockers.'

One memorable new product of the times had discounted the gelding's chances of achieving even a top-ten placing. The dawning realisation that the future prosperity of industrialised societies such as Britain would depend on harnessing new technology was stimulating interest in computers. Not the sleek, ultra-light laptops of today, but vast whirring, beeping machines fresh from the realm of science fiction. This growing fascination, plus the hiatus in the jumps-racing season forced by the foot-and-mouth epizootic, had created a propitious environment in which to try sömething new: computerised horse races. The voice of racing, Peter O'Sullevan, had been deployed to commentate on a computer version of the Massey Ferguson Gold Cup, usually run at Cheltenham in December, when no racing was taking place. This was a pleasing enough bit of fun, with an Atlas Computer capable of 500,000 calculations a second producing a wholly plausible result.

But, of course, it is one thing to simulate a race that has been cancelled, quite another to broadcast a computer version of a Grand National that is soon to be run, large as life. Like it or not, the ability of the great machine to see into the future, with slick-looking paper printouts and spools of magnetic tape taking the place of a crystal ball, was on the line. And, while O'Sullevan vested the occasion with his usual effortless charm, concluding it was the first time that 'the horses have ever finished a lot fresher than the commentator', the computer flunked the test. Gregory Peck would have liked the result, which had Different Class winning from Rutherfords, Master of Art and Bassnet. But the real-life winner, like Foinavon, failed to feature in the first ten past the computer's virtual winning-post. It is tempting to imagine the bookies sharing a knowing chuckle over this cutting-edge confirmation of real life's fathomless complexity.

Another way in which modernity was entering people's homes was through the medium of colour television. The BBC had effected the first official colour broadcast in Britain from Wimbledon the previous July. TV critic and Conservative politician Julian Critchley remarked that the eye was 'caught by incidentals such as a bright green towel or a bottle of orange squash'. BBC2 Controller David Attenborough said everything was perfect, 'the weather, the transmission and the prospects'. The American company RCA was reported to be poised to begin production of colour television tubes at its new £1 million factory in

Skelmersdale New Town, not a million miles from Aintree. This technical and cultural revolution still lay in the future as far as the Grand National was concerned, however. Red Alligator's dominant 1968 victory would be the last to be broadcast on television solely in black and white.

You would not have given much for jockey Brian Fletcher's chances of riding the Grand National winner if you had seen him 24 hours earlier. He took a crashing fall from a horse called JFK at the first fence of the Mildmay Chase. 'He didn't know whether it was Christmas or Easter,' recalls Stan Mellor, who was down to ride French Kilt, one of the favourites, in the big race. Fletcher, though, was one tough customer, even by the singularly elevated standards of 1960s jump-jockeys. 'In today's world, I would never have been allowed to ride in the Grand National,' he admitted to me. As it was though, he went to Southport, to the 'sauna baths', to 'get myself cleaned out. I was fresh as a pin, but still had a thumping great headache ... I remember passing the [winning] post and saying, "Well, Brian, you have done it." I was on the crest of a wave.'

The result – and the 20-length winning margin, even wider than Foinavon's the previous year – clearly hardened Fletcher's conviction that he and Red Alligator would have won in 1967 as well if it weren't for the pile-up. The third-placed jockey, David Mould, by contrast, concluded from his 1968 experience that Different Class would not have won 12 months earlier even if he had not been capsized by the chaos at the 23rd fence. 'He didn't get the trip,' he told me. 'He jumped the last three fences on sheer guts. He was absolutely gone.'

As for Foinavon, well, the 1968 National made plain that he had exhausted his fund of Aintree luck. Kitted out with the same highly distinctive blinkers, but with Harvey sporting new orange and blue silks, the shock 1967 winner was far from disgraced, however.

'He was a hard old ride,' the jockey recalls. 'Going down the first straight, he would have pulled up if he could.' Nearing halfway, though, he had picked up momentum. Then, as they streaked past the stands, misfortune struck. 'He flew The Chair,' Harvey continues. 'I was tracking Bassnet, one of the favourites. Going to the water, I was right up Bassnet's backside. I thought I should give myself some room, so I gave him a length. Bassnet tripped over the water. His neck came out to the side and tripped Foinavon up. If I had stayed right behind him, I would have got through.'

Harvey permanently damaged his left shoulder in the fall, but Foinavon was right as rain. He might, indeed, have been inclined to follow the other runners out for the second circuit were it not for Hemsley, who had seen what had happened on a television screen near the entrance to the racecourse and come hurrying out shouting Foinavon's name. He thinks it was the yellow plastic bucket he was carrying that did the trick. This was the receptacle from which the horse often slurped his eagerly awaited ration of goat's milk. He may therefore have associated it with a treat. Whether for this, or some other impenetrable, horsey reason, he cantered straight over, more like an obedient gun-dog than a flighty thoroughbred, senses scrambled by the adrenalin-rush of race-day. 'Cor, you've got him well trained!' said the relative of Harvey's with whom Hemsley had been standing. Pat Taaffe might have recognised it as the same reflex that had caused him to crop grass at Baldoyle.

Two other horses – Ronald's Boy and Champion Prince – were brought down in the same incident. One of them, Champion Prince, had exhausted his Aintree luck too. His jockey, Andrew Wates, had just pulled over towards the inside rail and jumped the fence when his horse's legs were taken away from under him by one of the other victims. 'It was like being catapulted into the air,' Wates recalled. He escaped unhurt; Champion Prince sustained a broken neck.

Chapter 28

LAST HURRAH

It was just another ordinary late spring day behind the sturdy black steel gates of Blackrath farm. Stud groom Dermot Whelan was in the back field exercising the establishment's most precious asset on the end of a lunge-line as he had done hundreds of times before. Vulgan, though now 25, was inflamed with the impulses of the season, charging and bucking around like a two-year-old, as he nearly always did.

It was May 1968, Paris was simmering and Frank Latham's little Kildare stud was at the peak of its fame, with Vulgan entrenched as the leading sire of jumpers in Great Britain and Ireland. Though he was now firmly in the veteran category, the most productive brood-mares were still being driven up the white-walled driveway as regularly as ever for their assignations with the pocket-sized stallion. And his strike-rate remained outstanding: four mares in every five who visited him in 1966 were successfully impregnated. Most important of all, his offspring went on and on winning: in the four seasons to 1966/67, his stock won over 160 races. Foinavon's quota was just four.

Then in the blink of an eye it was over. An over-exuberant kick, a shriek of surprise and anguish and rage and one of those awesomely powerful hind legs had buckled irreparably, its hock shattered. The vet was summoned, but a horseman of Whelan's experience knew all too well the inescapable verdict. 'His hock was shaking like a child's rattling-box it was in that many bits,' he told me, the moment still etched on his mind across four decades. 'When a stallion gets to that age, the hock gets very thin from getting up on the mares. It's very easy to break a hock. He was still strong as an ox.' When he was injected, although the drugs knocked him out straight away, it took a quarter of an hour for the great stallion's heart to stop.

Back in England, Foinavon was preparing for his last race of the season, a three-mile chase of little consequence at the stiff but scenic Northamptonshire course of Towcester. He was pulled up in a race he had finished third in two years before. This meant that in 1967/68 he had run seven races altogether, been pulled up twice, been brought down or fallen twice and finished last three times.

It could have been the end of the road. And yet after his summer break, this time blissfully free of county show-opening duties, and reunited with John Buckingham, the patient, clear-headed rider who had partnered him to Grand National glory, the ten-year-old bounced back to such effect that he pieced together his most consistent run of results for four years. It was to be his last hurrah.

His season opened, just as it had two years earlier, in the West Country. In the space of four weeks, Foinavon and Buckingham contested three races at the Devon & Exeter course on the Haldon Hills. They performed better each time, coming fourth of seven in the horse's seasonal debut, then third, overhauling one rival on the line. Unlike some of the other jockeys who rode him, Buckingham seemed content to bide his time, confident that his old partner's stamina would carry him through the field in the race's latter stages as others tired. This approach was seen to good advantage in the John Lumley Handicap Chase on 18 September. In a field of just four on a course they now knew intimately, Foinavon and Buckingham hit the front at the second-last fence and stayed on to win by a comfortable two-and-a-half lengths. 'Foinavon's first since Aintree,' said a headline on the front page of the next day's *Sporting Life*. 'Foinavon got into the winner's enclosure at Devon & Exeter yesterday for the first time since his 1967 Aintree triumph.'

Less than a week later, the pair were involved in one of those sporting match-ups that, while it was hardly Arkle versus Mill House or War Admiral versus Seabiscuit, tend to capture the imagination of the sporting public. 'It will probably be a long time,' wrote journalist Len Thomas with little fear of contradiction, 'before we again see a winner of the Grand National and the runner-up of the same year competing for a mere £580 in a three-mile chase on this course.'

A year and a half after the jockey's hopes were dashed at Aintree, Josh Gifford and Honey End were finally to have their chance to exact a measure of revenge. If the earlier clash had been in the spotlight of racing's Broadway, however, the re-match was in the provincial theatre of Plumpton in the Sussex countryside. And, figuratively as well as literally, autumn was setting in.

Foinavon's recent victory in Devon had actually left such an impression that *Sporting Life*'s Man on the Spot tipped him once again to get the better of his Ryan Price-trained rival. 'Foinavon had a poor season last season,' he wrote. 'But his form has perked up this season and he won in convincing style at Devon & Exeter recently.' Honey End had 'also had a poor season last year and I well remember him running very slovenly in this race last year'. (He finished third.)

On the spot he may have been, but in this case the *Sporting Life*'s 'Man' was also wide of the mark, as Honey End romped home by five lengths from Buckingham's mount. A mistake at the water was said to have taken 'much of the steam out of Foinavon'. Problems at water-jumps, indeed, were to be a recurring feature of the gelding's final races.

The outcome of this duel, however, was at once overshadowed by an incident in the next hurdle race. At the third-last flight, Gifford tumbled from his mount, Hot Ice, but his left foot got stuck in his stirrup, causing him to be dragged 'several yards' before he was able to free himself. Carried into the ambulance-room on a stretcher, he was soon smoking and 'smiling cheerfully'. But a broken ankle was diagnosed.

'Gifford may be out for a long time,' said the headline above Thomas's *Sporting Life* article.

Deciding when to stop is one of the hardest things for any public figure to get right. Money often has more of a say in the decision than it should. Sometimes it prompts stars to outstay their welcome, which may be why boxers and rockers rarely seem to bow out with grace; sometimes to depart too soon, as when top Flat racehorses are retired to stud well before the racing public is ready.

Owned by the widow of the richest man in England, there was never the slightest chance that money would be permitted to influence Arkle's retirement date. And when the announcement that lowered the curtain on steeplechasing's golden age finally came on 8 October, nearly two years after the horse's last race, it was greeted with relief as well as disappointment and sadness. Anne, Duchess of Westminster, had decided against a Christmas-tide comeback by her great chaser not, she said, because he was unsound but simply because of the passage of time. Just short of his 12th birthday, she had concluded, 'not even Arkle, with his immense courage, could be expected to reproduce his old brilliance'. When, next day, his great rival Mill House fell in an obscure four-horse race at Ludlow, it seemed to vindicate the decision.

Having finished in the first three in each of his last three starts, there must have seemed little reason why Foinavon should not soldier on. By now, though, he had run nearly twice as many races as Arkle and was only a year younger. When on 4 October he was found to be lame on his off foreleg on arrival at post for the start of a three-mile chase at Wincanton, it could be interpreted, with the benefit of hindsight, as a sign that the end was near for the 1967 Grand National winner too.

With two fences to jump in the Consolation Handicap Chase at the Staffordshire course of Uttoxeter eight days later, you would have said that evidence of decline was becoming more compelling. True, Foinavon was set once again to finish in the first three, but only because half the six-strong field had fallen. Having jumped poorly throughout, he was well adrift of the two leaders as they approached the penultimate obstacle, accompanied by a loose horse.

Admiral Pennant, who had come down at the seventh, had been declared to run in no fewer than three races that day. The riders of the two leaders were about to have reason to wish his trainer had chosen one of the others. According to *Sporting Life* reporter Doug Newton, Admiral Pennant, running loose, impeded his rivals as they approached the fence. 'Jenin, who had been three lengths clear, hit the fence and toppled over,' Newton reported. 'As Paddynoggin reached the obstacle, the loose horse ran across and carried him out.'

As at Aintree 18 months earlier, Buckingham and Foinavon suddenly found themselves with an unassailable lead in a race they had no right to win. And this time there were just two fences between them and the winning-post. Having navigated his way safely home over half a circuit at Liverpool, Buckingham was not about to slip up here. Spectators in Uttoxeter's new 1,800-capacity grandstand, opened only in May, raised the roof. 'The crowd were going mad,' Buckingham remembers. 'I never heard such applause.' Of course, with Foinavon sent off at 9/2 third-favourite, a lot more of those watching in Staffordshire that afternoon backed him than had at Aintree when his triumph produced a confetti of discarded betting slips.

With Apollo 7 in orbit and the opening ceremony for the 1968 Olympic Games in exotic Mexico City about to start, Foinavon's sixth and last victory was far from big news – even with its faint but unmistakable echo of his and Buckingham's great day at Liverpool. After 63 races and over 150 miles raced, mostly over steeplechase fences, that would have been the perfect moment to retire, following the last of his sporadic visits to the winner's enclosure, with the cheers of an enthusiastic Saturday afternoon racing crowd ringing in his ears. It would also have been too good to be true. And so, six weeks later, it was on to Warwick – and a race that had been won two years running earlier in the decade by a horse called Popham Down.

Chapter 29

A CERTAIN MILEAGE

It is a metaphor that the Kemptons, with their mechanical bent, would have appreciated. 'A horse,' said Vincent O'Brien, the great Irish trainer, 'is like a car: he has only got a certain mileage.' The particular horse that the master of Ballydoyle had in mind was Nijinsky, a sleek roadster, but the comparison held just as true for jalopies like Foinavon.

Rain-clouds hung low and menacing as the small field of six lined up for the Crudwell Cup, a race that Popham Down had once dominated. It was the second-most valuable contest of the day at Warwick and some useful chasers had been attracted, notably Domacorn, big, black, leggy and error-prone, and San Angelo, the Edward Courage horse who had finished 12th in the 1968 Grand National.

It was late November and Britain was bracing itself glumly for winter while moaning about Chancellor Roy Jenkins's latest bombshell. This took the form of a swathe of duty increases – petrol and cigarettes, whisky and beer, the usual suspects – announced the previous day. 'Putting up the price of Christmas,' said *The Times*, sounding a factual, but uncharacteristically populist note. 'Resign!' bellowed Conservative MPs on the opposition benches.

John Buckingham had extra cause to be despondent. A bright new prospect from the Courage stables was emerging called Spanish Steps.

Buckingham, who had schooled the horse, had triumphed on him the previous month on his first outing of the season, but had then been beaten into second place in a race he admits he should have won. Spanish Steps was running again that afternoon in the big race of the day at Ascot, the Black and White Gold Cup Chase. But this time Buckingham would not be riding: shortly after that defeat, another jockey, Jack Cook, was sitting next to Mrs Courage at a dinner, pitched for the ride and got it. This was part of the game – as Buckingham has acknowledged, any 'sensible' jockey would have taken the opportunity. Nonetheless, he says, 'it broke my heart'.

For the only time in the horse's last seven races, Buckingham was not riding Foinavon either. Richard Pitman, one of the third-fence fallers at Aintree in 1967, would be his 16th and final jockey. It was to be a breakthrough year for Pitman, but this was not one of the races that contributed to it. With two wins in his last five outings, the form-book must have looked promising to Foinavon's stand-in jockey. In reality, his mount had reached the end of his tether. After leading to the second fence, he soon fell behind in a race won by Domacorn with News View, yet another son of Vulgan, second. Pitman remembers an 'incredibly hard' ride. Another jockey, Tony 'Geordie' Mawson, aboard San Angelo, was taken by surprise when his rival nearly stopped in his tracks ahead of him. 'Foinavon tried to refuse at the water,' he says. 'I went into his back and knocked him over the jump. I didn't expect him to refuse.'

It was more than two months later, on 1 February 1969, that Foinavon, now 11, ran his final race. Like his former stable companion Arkle, this last run came at Kempton Park, a course where he had gone well in the past, in a race – the Royal Mail Handicap Chase – he had contested twice before.

The television cameras were at Kempton. The story of the day, though, was not the inexorable silting up of Foinavon's carburettors, but the return of Persian War after a hock injury. The hurdler was probably the closest thing jumps-racing had left to a horse with Arkle-like star quality.

Foinavon's race was soon run: a mistake at the third, in the rear of the sparse four-horse field by the fifth, down at the tenth – the problematical water-jump. Reunited one last time with the horse who had carried him to immortality, Buckingham could tell well before their fall that the spark had gone. 'He jumped the water, which was just past the stands, then did the splits,' he says. 'I felt the horse wasn't enjoying himself at all – it was obvious. I told them I didn't want to ride him any more. I think the horse had had enough.'

Chapter 30

GHOSTS AND THE GREAT POOLS SWINDLE

Two old steel wheels, lichen-stained and mounted on bricks, have been wired to the wooden fence that now separates the bungalow from the L-shaped stable-block. A metal chimney stack has started to corrode. Battleship-grey paint still coats the stable-doors. Rain pours down and the air is thick with ghosts.

It is 9 April 2012 – 45 years to the day since Foinavon returned from Liverpool as the most famous horse in England, posed for photographs and walked stiffly past the pressmen and locals to his stable on my left. You would never guess that this bedraggled yard, with a traffic cone and two green wheelbarrows on one side and a three-step mounting-block on the other, had once housed a Grand National winner. Nor that a patch of grass by the fence, where two seed-trays lie waterlogged, is his burial plot.

Foinavon was duly retired after that feeble last run at Kempton Park and lived on contentedly enough at Chatham Stables for a couple of summers. In April 1970, he was said to be spending 'grazing hours' with the Kemptons' other Grand National horse, Seas End, then 18 years old. A horse's digestive system is a surprisingly delicate part of its anatomy. When it stops racing, the transition from the energy intensive diet it has consumed for years to a regime appropriate to its new, more sedentary lifestyle must be carefully managed. In those days, this meant replacing the oats that the horse would have required when in work with the correct balance of bran, grass and other low energy foodstuffs. This would often have entailed a certain hard-heartedness: the retired chaser might crave its accustomed diet, particularly when, as in Foinavon's case, it still lived among active racehorses munching their way through pounds of oats every week. The consequences of indulging the animal, though, could be severe. 'If you give a racehorse that is not working oats, he becomes uncontrollable, or he gets colic,' Colin Hemsley, the former head lad at the stable, told me. Then as now, colic – severe abdominal pain – could be a death sentence for horses.

Unfortunately, while the yard enjoyed some success in the aftermath of Foinavon's retirement, the underlying tensions were proving more and more disruptive. A frustrated Hemsley, tired of Jack Kempton's condescending attitude and frequent attempts to intervene in racing matters he did not really comprehend, took the opportunity to leave in 1970, when offered a plum post with George Beeby, another local trainer. John Kempton eventually grew so fed up with waiting to move into the bungalow beside the yard with Trish, his wife, that he departed too, accepting a job as assistant to David Barons, an up-and-coming trainer based in South Devon. This left John's parents to keep Chatham Stables ticking over as best they could. At some point, as they were struggling to cope, it seems that Foinavon's retirement diet went awry and the horse contracted colic with fatal consequences. Like Arkle, he was just 13. He was buried in the yard beneath the centrepiece that had been held up with string in 1967, when the cameraman taking shots of the burnished horse for the Schweppes racing calendar came to call.

John Kempton stayed with Barons's expanding operation for around five years. During the couple's third year in the West Country, a farmer-friend who had once been an amateur jockey, introduced them to scuba diving. From then on the sea began to exert its pull, as well as their desire to be their own bosses. 'We had the bright idea of buying a boat and taking diving parties out,' Kempton says. 'Even though the yard was quite successful, we had this hankering to work for ourselves. We had a house in Kingsbridge that came with the job, which meant we could take out a mortgage to buy a 42-foot boat. We launched off with that. The first year, we just did it in the summer, during jumps-racing's rest season. I taught myself navigation around the kitchen table.'

They attracted sufficient custom that first summer to take the plunge and turn their back on racing for good. The business proved viable enough to sustain them for 28 years, far longer than the time John Kempton had worked with horses. Throughout this period, they spent nearly the whole summer at sea, shuttling back and forth from the Channel Islands and Scilly Isles, returning to base each Friday night to re-stock and pick up new passengers. 'We went from the 42-footer to a 55- and then a 65-foot boat,' Kempton says. 'It was very hard work because we used to take 10 or 12 people at a time and cater for them three meals a day. Trish had the rough end of the stick because she would be cooking solidly all winter as well as working the boat. The business worked because she did it so well. People kept coming back year after year.'

Jack Kempton took out his own trainer's licence and managed one winner – a horse called Tandem at Towcester on 27 May 1972. Hemsley, who had reluctantly left Beeby's to work in a pressed steel factory by then, because he needed a job capable of supporting a mortgage, remembers answering a knock on his door one spring evening. To his surprise it was Jack Kempton who asked him sheepishly if he would school the horse, a difficult character that Hemsley knew from his time at the yard, before the race. This he agreed to do.

In the minutes before the off, the horse gave jockey Tony 'Geordie' Mawson a taste of what to expect, dumping him on the lush Northamptonshire turf in front of the grandstand. 'He was the type of horse if you asked him to go left he wanted to go right,' Mawson recalls. 'He wouldn't parade properly, so I let him go down to the start and got fined £10 for my trouble.' Perhaps not surprisingly after these antics, Tandem went off a distant 33/1 outsider in a five-horse race.

'I got him out very quickly and led going to the first,' says Mawson, who retains a detailed recollection of the unexpected victory. 'I just sat on him and let him run. He slammed the brakes on before the first but jumped it. He did exactly the same before the second and third. I realised then I was as safe as houses because he was really looking after himself. The fourth was the ditch. I let him slam the brakes on then belted him one. He took off so fast I nearly fell off backwards.'

The pair were still clear tackling the demanding climb before the finish, but Stan Mellor, riding one of the favourites, Main Hill, was gaining ground. Mawson describes how he manoeuvred his mount to block the former champion's attempts to pass on both the inside and the outer. 'Then I took off and won by miles.'

That was as good as it got for Jack Kempton as a racehorse trainer. Two days later, Tandem ran again and trailed in fifth. After they had finished, one of the other jockeys asked Tandem's rider how he had managed to win a race on the horse. 'I always believed every horse had a key,' Mawson says. 'it was just a question of finding it.'

If any jockey could be said to have unlocked the secret of making Foinavon run well, it was of course John Buckingham, who managed three wins, a second, a third and a fourth in his eight rides on the horse with which his name will always be associated.

Buckingham rode in the Grand National on three more occasions, finishing every time, although he did suffer a particularly disappointing fall on his last appearance in 1971. Riding Limeburner in the race for the second time, he was in with a chance when coming down at the second from home. He remounted to finish 12th.

He remained a well-known figure in the weighing-room for many years after his painful last fall at Wetherby a month or so later, notching up three decades as a valet, working most of this time with his brother Tom. For all the more genteel associations of the word, this was as demanding a trade in its own way as being a jump-jockey. The risk of broken bones and extended hospital visits was no longer a preoccupation, but a jockeys' valet faced a similar grind of early mornings and countless miles on the clock. Plus now the good days meant not glory and a stupendously potent adrenalin rush, but a smaller-than-expected pile of boots to polish or mud-spattered breeches to wash. Buckingham continued to view his domain, nevertheless, as 'almost a sacred place ... the holy of holies ... the best place to be'. And, as a gregarious character as well as an ex-rider, he could relate to the maddeningly capricious ups and downs that his clients had to cope with like few others. This must have been a big advantage – and a great help to them. He still inhabits the house he was living in that cloudy morning not far off half a century ago when he took John Kempton's surprise phone call asking if he would ride Foinavon at Aintree. The Rose and Crown is still his local.

Two days before Buckingham's last Grand National, on 1 April 1971, Iris Watkins collapsed towards the end of a typically busy day engaged in chores around the property at Nine Mile Ride and died of a stroke. She was just 54. Cyril stayed on at the bungalow for some months after her death, but then moved with the brood-mares to a former pig farm in the New Forest. Coincidentally, the new house – Yew Tree Farm at Stoney Cross near Lyndhurst – was almost next door to a hotel called the Compton Arms. Events had evidently taken their toll. Tiggy Partridge, a local teenager who looked after the horses for him, describes him as 'quite a recluse. A very nice man, very quiet.'

On 24 October 1974 Partridge had tonsillitis and was too unwell to tend to the horses. Her indisposition coincided with the day when Cyril's diseased heart finally gave out on him. He was found on the property at the wheel of his car. He was a month short of his 66th birthday. Partridge (now Tiggy Aubin) recalls that the property, originally two separate farm workers' cottages, was subsequently auctioned in Lyndhurst for £25,000. It was bought by the director of a carpet company.

Of the people most closely associated with Foinavon, the only one who made news again in any significant way was, ironically, the co-owner who gave up his interest in the horse in the months before he hit the Aintree jackpot. Football pools concessionaire Mac Bennellick had made the front page of the *Havering Recorder* in the wake of that victory. Six years later – just a week before Red Rum's sensational first Grand National win – he found himself on the front page of the *News of the World*.

'The Great Pools Swindle' proclaimed the headline in capital letters more than an inch high. 'Four men and a woman have confessed to the *News of the World* that they have pulled off the gambling swindle of the century,' the story, by reporter Michael Litchfield, began. 'They filled in football pools coupons after learning match results from phone calls across the world and collected top dividends for weeks on end.'

McIntyre 'Benny' Bennellick was said to be 'Mr Big' of a syndicate whose alleged exploits provided an object lesson in how technology, in this case the international telephone network, was starting to shrink the world.

For some years, the football pools organisations in Britain had made use of the Australian football results to enable them to keep going in summer when the European leagues were not functioning. I still have hazy recollections of these scores being read out on the afternoon sports programmes, monotonous as the speaking clock, interminable as the shipping forecast. Under the scheme outlined by the newspaper, Bennellick and his associates had realised they could 'beat the clock' by exploiting the time difference between Australia and England to phone over the results and fill in and deliver a coupon before the pools companies' deadline for receiving weekly entries. The plan entailed heavy upfront cost: two members of the team were said to have been dispatched to Melbourne with £3,000 in their pocket. But the newspaper said their aim was to make 'at least £100,000 every season' from a system they regarded as 'a champagne pension for life'.

By today's standards, the infrastructure at their disposal seems impossibly primitive. A call from Bennellick to his Melbourne associates needed to be booked for 8.35am South Rainham time, 25 minutes before the deadline for coupons to be delivered to the pools company's offices. Two further members of the team, one an accredited pools agent, would then be waiting with a blank coupon for Bennellick to call them at 'a phone in a public kiosk outside Blackfriars station'. The newspaper helpfully included a small photograph of the London phone box in question. In a touch of cloak-and-dagger, the calls to Australia were said to deploy a special code. 'No team was ever mentioned.'

Almost four decades on, Litchfield remembered Bennellick as being 'quite shabbily dressed' with a fairly thin face and hair 'all over the place'. The extensive *News of the World* spread quoted a Mr Leslie Payne, managing director of Copes Pools, as saying, 'If it is at all possible, we shall certainly want to prosecute them all.' One can only presume that it was not possible. 'I expected there to be prosecutions, but it was never mentioned again,' Litchfield told me.

Quite how much Bennellick and his associates actually made from what the newspaper described as 'Britain's most audacious gambling coup' is unclear. But it was not enough to provide Foinavon's former owner with a pension for life, 'champagne' or any other variety. He and his wife Peggy moved to Ashford in Kent, where they bought a 60-acre farm in an auction. They built a four-bedroom house, kept chickens and sold their eggs. His son and daughter-in-law used to grade the eggs for him. By 1975, though, he and Peggy were divorced. Another relationship broke down when the woman moved to South Africa where her husband was working. He bought three greyhounds, which he raced at Romford. He used to place bets at £200 a time, but rarely if ever won. As he struggled to make ends meet, he sold the gold Grand National trophy Foinavon had won for just £200. In 1984, now renting an apartment in Gravesend, he fell ill with prostate cancer and was taken into hospital. While there on 29 May, as the miners' strike raged, he had a heart attack and died. He was 67 and had hit rock bottom financially. His son Colin survived him by only a year, dying in July 1985 at just 36 years of age.

Foinavon's miracle day at Liverpool didn't change the lives of those closest to him – except in the very short term; but it has touched those of plenty of strangers, myself included. From the very start, the Grand National has been a race of incredible stories – and stories such as Foinavon's and the pile-up he eluded helped stimulate the interest that kept the race alive when its future was under severe threat. Now the advance of technology that seems to have helped Mac Bennellick to place bets on the football pools while already knowing some of the results, has created conditions in which the value of broadcasting and sponsorship rights for world-renowned sports events like the National have been able to spiral.

As this book goes to press, it looks like the 2014 renewal may be the first Grand National worth £1 million in prize money. And if the race's future is still not entirely secure, it is because of the highly emotive issue of horse welfare, and not financial pressure. So much has been invested at Aintree that Mirabel Topham would scarcely recognise the place (and would no doubt be less than thrilled to find her old house turned into a restaurant). Time, in short, has moved on. There is now a limit on the size of the Grand National field and a chaser with Foinavon's record would have no chance of making the cut. Yet no one – and nothing – has benefited more from his one great exploit than the National itself and of course, the fence after Becher's now bears his name. I hope those now running Aintree can feel the presence of those ghosts.

Notes on the Text

8 April 1967 ...

4   Copious prize money – the total prize fund for the 2012 Grand National stood at £975,000, with £418,860 earmarked for the winning owner.

4   High-profile Flat race in the Middle East – the race was the Dubai Gold Cup and the horses were Fox Hunt, Bronze Cannon and Grand Vent. The race was restaged after being declared void when Fox Hunt sustained his fatal injury.

6   Freddie foaled in County Offaly – *A Horse Called Freddie*, Vian Smith, Stanley Paul, 1967, page 9.

6   One in six Britons watch the Grand National – BBC coverage of the 2012 race was watched by an audience that peaked at 10.89 million viewers.

6   Freddie's 'furious refusal to give in...' – *A Horse Called Freddie*, Vian Smith, Stanley Paul, 1967, page 56.

7   One racehorse that shared its name with an even more striking Scottish mountain was Ben Nevis, the 1980 Grand National winner.

Chapter 1

9   US troops at Aintree – *Gallant Sport – the Authentic History of Liverpool Races and the Grand National*, John Pinfold, Portway Press, 1999, pages 202–5.

9   Vulgate's journey – email correspondence with Guy Thibault, French bloodstock expert.

9   Failed mating – French Stud Book, volume 26.

10   Madame Lambert, death of Commander Lambert – *Auteuil, hier et aujourd'hui*, volume 2 (1916–2003), Guy Thibault, Editions du Castelet, 2003.

10   First race – ibid.

10   Group 4, Group 2 – the group system is a way of benchmarking the quality of the best races. The lower the group number, the better the race.

10 Wartime racing – the only English Flat-racing Classic to be missed was the 1939 St Leger, although the two Epsom Classic races moved to Newmarket. In 1942, King George VI remarkably won four of the five Classics, with only the Derby eluding him. Jumps-racing was harder hit: there was no Cheltenham Gold Cup in 1943 and 1944; no Grand National from 1941–45; and Kempton Park was closed for racing.

10 Mr H. Coriat/Gloucestershire Hurdle – *Sporting Life*, 3 March 1948.

10 John de Moraville's war record – war diaries of 4th (Queen's Own) Hussars; telephone interview with his son, also John.

11 De Moraville's thumb – face-to-face interview with Sir Peter O'Sullevan, former racing commentator; telephone interview with his son.

11 Newmarket sale – *Ruff's Guide to the Turf*, 1951 edition, page 807.

11 Dermot Whelan – telephone and face-to-face interviews.

11 Frank Latham's early plans for Blackrath – *Whelan and The Griese Valley & Beyond*, Barbara Sheridan (ed.), Millbrook Press, 2003, page 111.

12 Coping with Vulgan's temper – Whelan face-to-face interview.

12 Vulgan's initial and final fees – Whelan.

12 Fees in intervening years – *Register of Thoroughbred Stallions*.

12–13 Blackrath and leading National Hunt sires – *Statistical Abstract* and *The Statistical Record Annual*. The method of counting changed about halfway through Vulgan's career. So did the period covered, from the 12 months to 30 June to the calendar year.

Chapter 2

14 Coolmore stud – base of the great stallion Sadler's Wells, now deceased, and many others.

14 Timothy H. Ryan personal details – telephone and face-to-face interviews with his daughter, Jill McCormack.

15 The K Club – the Kildare Hotel Spa & Country Club, host of the 2006 Ryder Cup.

15 Ecilace breeding record – *Bloodstock Breeders' Review*, 1967, page 112.

16 Captain Charles Radclyffe's acquisition of Foinavon – telephone and face-to-face interviews with Capt. Radclyffe himself.

16 Details of regime at Lew – interviews with Capt. Radcliffe and Patrick Foley, household manager at Lew House farm.

16 Corbiere – winner of 1983 Grand National, third in 1984 and 1985; Zongalero – second in 1979 Grand National; State of Play – fourth in 2009 Grand National, third in 2010, fourth again in 2011.

16 May 1960 sale – Grosvenor Estate records.

17 The auction for Arkle – *Peter O'Sullevan's Horse Racing Heroes*, Sir Peter O'Sullevan, CBE, Highdown, 2004, page 8.

17 Arkle – winner of three Cheltenham Gold Cups between 1964 and 1966; the greatest steeplechaser in history.

17 Taken to Bryanstown – Grosvenor Estate records.

17 Sent to Greenogue – Grosvenor Estate records.

Chapter 3

18 The two most highly rated steeplechasers – Timeform puts Arkle's best rating at 212 and Flyingbolt's at 210. This compares with Mill House 191, Desert Orchid 187 and Best Mate 182. Each point's difference equates approximately to 1lb in weight.

18 Flyingbolt's brucellosis – *Go Down to the Beaten*, Chris Pitt, Racing Post Books, 2011, page 149.

19 Tom Dreaper's 1964 winnings – *Arkle – the Classic Story of a Champion*, Ivor Herbert, Aurum Press, 2003, page 131 (first published in 1966 by Pelham Books).

19 Queen Mother Champion Chase – originally the National Hunt Two-mile Champion Chase.

19 Dreaper's seven consecutive Irish Grand Nationals were with Olympia (1960), Fortria (1961), Kerforo (1962), Last Link (1963), Arkle (1964), Splash (1965) and Flyingbolt (1966).

19 Horses rarely long out of boxes – *Arkle – the Classic Story of a Champion*, Ivor Herbert, Aurum Press, 2003, page 97.

19 'We used to go out at nine … ' Peter McLoughlin – face-to-face interview.

19 Fairyhouse fences – a reference to the racecourse where the Irish Grand National is held.

19 Pat Taaffe on the 'baby' fences – *Arkle – the Classic Story of a Champion*, Ivor Herbert, Aurum Press, 2003, page 74.

20 'A car with four flat tyres' – face-to-face interview.

20 Taaffe, 'He moved so terribly … ' – *Arkle – the Classic Story of a Champion*, Ivor Herbert, Aurum Press, 2003, page 57.

20 Trace clip – a clip that leaves more of the horse's coat on than when in racing mode; suitable for light work.

20 Unnamed in 1962 Horses in Training – *Arkle – The Story of the World's Greatest Steeplechaser*, Sean Magee, Highdown, 2005 pages 27–8.

20 A Munro is a Scottish mountain over 3,000 feet; Foinaven's height is 2,989 feet.

20 Among the young Foinavon's stablemates at Greenogue in 1962 was Castle Falls, who was destined to be one of the 1967 Grand National's unlucky losers.

20 Irish bumper races in the 1960s – *Arkle – the Classic Story of a Champion*, Ivor Herbert, Aurum Press, 2003 pages 59–60.

21 Foinavon 'a bit one-paced' in first race – Tony Cameron telephone interview.

21 Tony Cameron's appearance in 1964 Olympics – *Go Down to the Beaten*, Chris Pitt, Racing Post Books, 2011, page 95.

21 'Little is known of Foinavon… ' – *The Times*, 16 Nov 1962.

22 'Arkle seemed almost embarrassed…' – *Peter O'Sullevan's Horse Racing Heroes*, Sir Peter O'Sullevan, CBE, Highdown, 2004, page 9.

22 Cheltenham ground as soft as dough – *Arkle – the Classic Story of a Champion*, Ivor Herbert, Aurum Press, 2003, page 89.

22 'I don't think I ever met a horse with less ambition' – *My Life and Arkle's*, Pat Taaffe, Stanley Paul, 1972, pages 69–70.

22 Vincent Slevin – telephone interview.

23 'Growing during the winter' – Grosvenor Estate records.

23 Official sixth birthday – for official purposes, all racehorses are considered to have been born on 1 January.

23 Baldoyle not a course for 'young, green' horses – *Arkle – the Classic Story of a Champion*, Ivor Herbert, Aurum Press, 2003, page 75.

24 Bobby Beasley – winner of the 1961 Grand National. Quotes on tough racing tactics taken from *Second Start*, Bobby Beasley, W.H. Allen, 1976.

24 First victory at Naas – Paddy Woods telephone interview.

25 Second win at Punchestown – Peter McLoughlin telephone interview.

25 'Looking awfully well' – Grosvenor Estate records.

25 Johnny Kelly – *Arkle – the Classic Story of a Champion*, Ivor Herbert, Aurum Press, 2003, page 178.

25 Baldoyle today – personal visit by author September 2011.

26 Fatal insurance notification – *Baldoyle – the Racecourse Village*, Michael J. Hurley, 2002, page 51.

26 Atmosphere at the course – ibid.

26 Michael O'Hehir – arguably the best-known voice in Ireland, he would famously encounter Foinavon again at Aintree two years later.

26 Delayed last race – The *Irish Field*, 9 Jan 1965.

26 The bald facts – the race was won by another son of Vulgan's called Vulcano. The two horses would meet again 27 months later at Aintree with a very different result.

26 A heavy fall – The *Irish Field* reports that Foinavon fell at the third fence. Course historian Michael Hurley says this was called Rooney's Hill, after a family who lived beside it. He describes it as 'the worst fence … as it was met on rising ground that then fell away again.' Taaffe had already suffered one fall that day, in the first race at the very first fence.

26 'On a day at Baldoyle … ' – *My Life and Arkle's*, Pat Taaffe, Stanley Paul, 1972, page 69.

27 Tony Cameron – telephone interview.

27 Peter McLoughlin – telephone and face-to-face interviews.

Chapter 4

28   Except where stated, the main sources for this chapter were face-to-face or telephone interviews with individuals present at the yard in the 1960s, including: John Kempton, trainer; Colin 'Jake' Hemsley, head lad; Joy Smith (née Douglas), stable girl; and Frank Whittle, jockey.

29   Kempton had learnt to shoe horses – the young trainer shod his own racehorses throughout his career. The racing plates worn by Foinavon in the 1967 Grand National were hand-made by him.

29   Captain Ryan Price – Champion National Hunt trainer five times between 1954 and 1967.

30   Lockinge – where Best Mate was based in his Cheltenham Gold Cup-winning years.

30   Peek Frean – known particularly for the Garibaldi biscuit.

30   Seas End's race record – 'With Nothing in his Mouth' by Lieut.-Colonel Tom Nickalls, *The Field*, 4 February 1965.

31   Paddy Prendergast – quoted in *Great Racehorse Trainers*, Tim Fitzgeorge-Parker, Pelham Books, 1975, page 128.

31   Gordon Passey – face-to-face interview with Edward Saunders, Passey's nephew, and other sources.

31–2   Horse slaughterer to Her Majesty – a publicity poster for the Oxford-based business proclaims, 'The utmost value given for live & dead horses, cows &c., and fetched away on the shortest notice.' It adds, 'Best harness oil & cart grease.' The poster incorporates a ditty, the first verse of which runs:
> *William Passey in his business is a man of great renown;*
> *He always gives best prices, both in country and in town;*
> *And if you want to try him, you may bear this in your mind,*
> *That for promptness or attention he's the best you'll ever find.*

32   Mick the Miller – twice winner of the English Greyhound Derby in 1929 and 1930.

32   Prendergast on betting – 'I had to bet to exist. I used to bet quite a lot, particularly long-price ante-post bets. But I'm in the happy position of not having to do so now [in 1966]. Obviously the majority of trainers have to bet to live.' Quoted in *Great Racehorse Trainers*, Tim Fitzgeorge-Parker, Pelham Books, 1975, page 128.

33   Seedier side of racing – *The Barry Brogan Story – In His Own Words*, Barry Brogan, Arthur Barker, 1981, pages 61–2.

33   As a 17-year-old in 1965, Brogan became the youngest trainer to saddle a horse in the Grand National; it refused at the 20th fence.

Chapter 5

35 'One chilly morning' – telephone interview with Colin Hemsley.

35 Cab proprietor's son – father's profession cited on Cyril and Iris's marriage certificate.

35–6 Sources for personal details on Cyril and Iris Watkins and Mac Bennellick include Lyn Shelton and Paul Nixon, Iris's niece and nephew, Chris Compton, Mac's daughter-in-law, Zelda Blackadder, family friend of the Watkins, and Tony Bennellick, Mac's nephew. Information gathered via email exchanges, as well as telephone and face-to-face interviews.

37 7¾ million football pools customers – Frederick Peart, MP for Workington, House of Commons debate on the Pool Betting Act, 29 January 1954.

37 Reginald Paget – House of Commons debate on replacement of the 1853 Betting Act, 5 May 1960.

37 Cheapest tax in the world – John Tilney, MP for Liverpool Wavertree, House of Commons debate on a National Lottery, 1 July 1968, 'Last year [the pools] produced £30 million revenue and next year it will be £40 million, at a cost of £2,500. Pools betting duty must be the cheapest tax in the world.'

37 Significant source of employment – figures stated by John Tilney, MP for Liverpool Wavertree, House of Commons debate on a National Lottery, 1 July 1968.

38 The young gelding had won a race for them – it was a good day for John Kempton, since he also won the previous race, riding Seas End. In a melancholy footnote, In Tune, a horse that used to be at the Kemptons' yard, pulled up with a broken fetlock in Seas End's race and had to be put down.

38 McCrimmon obliged to run in better races – novices' hurdles are for horses who have yet to win a race over obstacles. Once an animal has won such a race, he is clearly no longer eligible to enter them in future. However, in those days, National Hunt racing operated a six-week entry system. Victorious novices could still run in any races they had been entered in before their victory. McCrimmon's second win, at Folkestone, was also in a novices' hurdle.

38 Handicaps not wide enough – there were exceptions but, broadly speaking, in jumps racing horses carried at least ten stone in weight (deemed the minimum a jockey with saddle could be expected to ride at) and at most 12st 7lb (the most it could reasonably be expected to hump around in race conditions). If the relative merits of two horses in a race differed so much that this weight-range was insufficient to 'equalise' their chances of winning, the inferior horse would have to carry ten stone, even if its true weight should have been significantly less. One pound was deemed broadly to equal one length in handicappers' terms.

38 Watkins' and Bennellick's appetites whetted – another early acquisition was a horse called Saucerstown, which they renamed Ben Wat, hence turning it into the equine equivalent of a personalised number plate.

Chapter 6

39 No children of her own – she did, in effect, adopt the orphaned children of her husband Ronald's cousin, but, while James Bidwell-Topham was a Tophams director and, for a time, clerk of the course, neither he nor his sister Patricia possessed Mrs Topham's leadership qualities.

40 Mrs Topham performed wonders – *Gallant Sport – the Authentic History of Liverpool Races and the Grand National*, John Pinfold, Portway Press, 1999, pages 207–8. Pinfold writes, 'That the course was restored to a condition fit to be used in a mere six weeks was possibly Mrs Topham's finest achievement.'

40 New horse-racing course with easier fences – the Mildmay course, named after Lord Mildmay, a noted amateur jockey who drowned in 1950 and is credited with stimulating the Queen Mother's keen interest in jump racing.

40 Paddock Lodge – now converted into a restaurant.

40 Mrs Topham's bell-pull – face-to-face interview with Ray Lakeland, former BBC producer.

40 Ossie Dale – face-to-face interview.

40 Tight grasp on purse-strings – in November 1963, directors agreed to buy a replacement sewing machine 'as the present one was now dangerous owing to being so worn'. Minutes of Tophams Ltd board meetings, volume XII.

40 Steve Westhead – minutes of Tophams Ltd board meetings, volume XIII.

41 Topham Ltd financial information – gleaned from company report and accounts.

41 Devon Loch was ridden by Dick Francis, later a journalist and best-selling author.

41 Shareholder dividends – as at 1 January 1968, there were 1,125 shares in Topham Ltd, the family firm set up in 1899, in issue. Mrs Topham and James Bidwell-Topham owned 544 of these between them.

41 Mrs Topham's London house – *The Grand National, Anybody's Race*, Peter King, Quartet Books, 1983, page 93.

41 50 per cent salary rise – minutes of Tophams Ltd board meetings, volume XII. Mrs Topham's salary increase was from £500 to £750 per annum, with a yearly expense allowance of £300. Miss Bidwell-Topham's fee as 'wardrobe mistress' was increased by £100 to £250 per annum at the same time. 'Although Miss Bidwell-Topham functioned under this title, it was generally accepted that she dealt with 101 jobs for which she was absurdly paid,' the minutes note.

41 Buildings in poor repair – the minutes of a Tophams Ltd board meeting, 28 November 1964, allude to a crack in the rear wall of Tattersalls stand.

42 Sale of Grand National rights – minutes of Tophams Ltd. board meetings, volume XII.

42 Leslie Marler – information sources include interviews with his daughter, June Robinson, and cousin and former colleague at Capital and Counties, Dennis Marler.

43 Marler, 'Not a question of destroying the Grand National' – *Liverpool Daily Post*, 2 July 1964.

44 'The houses not the horses' – *Liverpool Echo*, 2 July 1964.

44 Birmingham racecourse closure – *A Long Time Gone*, Chris Pitt, Timeform, 2006.

44 Bogside allocated no more fixtures – Hansard, 9 July 1964, vol. 698, cc 610–2.

44 Capital and Counties share price – *Liverpool Echo*, 2 July 1964.

44 Mrs Topham's letters – minutes of Tophams Ltd board meetings, volume XIII.

44 Sefton family owned Aintree for 750 years – *Liverpool Daily Post*, 6 October 1964.

44 Lord Sefton hates prospect of no racing at Aintree – *Liverpool Echo*, 3 July 1964.

44 Lord Sefton's restraining order – *Liverpool Daily Post*, 4 July 1964.

45 Lord-in-Waiting to Edward VIII – *The Grand National, Anybody's Race*, Peter King, Quartet Books, 1983, page 85.

45 Levy Board capable of controlling the sport – *Rien Ne Va Plus*, Martin Crawshay, The Memoir Club, 2002, page 74.

45 'Grandees of the Jockey Club' – ibid., page 56.

45 Court reports – *Liverpool Echo*, 2–6 October 1964 and *Liverpool Daily Post*, 7 October 1964.

46 Mr Justice Stamp's ruling – *Liverpool Echo*, 30 October 1964.

46 Death of a staff member – minutes of Tophams Ltd board meetings, volume XIII.

46 No substitute Grand National – *Liverpool Echo*, 14 November 1964.

46 Decision to appeal judgement – minutes of Tophams Ltd board meetings, volume XIII.

47 112 entries – numbers inevitably come down to more manageable levels in the weeks leading up to race-day. In the event, there were 47 runners in the 1965 Grand National, a big field but not the biggest ever.

47 John Leech – telephone interview. Leech rode a horse called Coleen Star. They got as far as the 9th fence.

Chapter 7

48 'Tom Dreaper's Grand National hope' – *Irish Field*, 2 January 1965. Under the pen-name 'Formor', the newspaper's correspondent tipped Foinavon to win the race. 'While he has never quite lived up to the promise of his good looks, Foinavon is a fair type in this company and can score,' he wrote.

49 Tom Dreaper's illness – *Arkle – The Classic Story of a Champion*, Ivor Herbert, Aurum Press, 2003, page 125.

49 The Grand National always eluded Dreaper – his horses came second at Aintree in both 1970 and 1971, when his son Jim piloted Black Secret. Arkle never ran

in the race; the Duchess of Westminster would not risk him.

49 Foinavon falls at the last at Naas – *Irish Field*, 16 January 1965.

49 Peter McLoughlin – telephone interview with author.

49 Pat Taaffe's jockeys' title – *Arkle – The Classic Story of a Champion*, Ivor Herbert, Aurum Press, 2003, page 131.

49 Well beaten at Leopardstown – *Irish Field*, 23 January 1965.

49 Peter McLoughlin – telephone interview with author.

50 Barker yet to win a steeplechase – *Irish Field*, 13 February 1965.

50 Quintin Bay – would go on to run in four Grand Nationals, being pulled up in 1965 and finishing 6th, 11th and 17th in the three subsequent years.

50 Foinavon 'magnificently ridden' – *Irish Field*, 13 February 1965.

50 Vincent Slevin – telephone interview with author.

51 Princess Margaret's Aintree outfit and other race-day details – *Liverpool Echo*, 27 March 1965.

51 Freddie's nostrils inflamed like anemones – *A Horse Called Freddie*, Vian Smith, Stanley Paul, 1967, page 99.

51 Takings similar to 1958 – minutes of Tophams Ltd board meetings, volume XIII.

52 'Court proceedings inevitably take a long time' – *Illustrated London News*, 3 April 1965.

52 Sources for personal details about Jack White include Aline White, his widow, and Tim Hyde, a former friend now owner of Camas Park Stud in County Tipperary.

52 White pays £1,800 for Foinavon – Grosvenor Estate records.

52 Tony Cameron offers to buy Foinavon – telephone interview with author.

53 Decision to apply for 1965/66 fixtures – minutes of Tophams Ltd board meetings, volume XIII.

53 1966 Grand National is on – *Liverpool Daily Post*, 23 June 1965.

53 Taking the case to the House of Lords – minutes of Tophams Ltd. board meetings, volume XIII.

Chapter 8

54 Anne, Duchess of Westminster's sensitive handling – for example, she would not agree to allow Arkle, her most gifted horse, to be subjected to the rigours of the Grand National.

54 John Kempton, 'He was very clean on the legs' – face-to-face interview with author.

55 Anglo, winner of the 1966 Grand National, was sold for $42,000 in February 1967; Rutherfords was sold for around £15,000 in March 1968.

55 Expected to work a lot harder – details of the regime gathered from telephone

and face-to-face interviews with John Kempton, Colin Hemsley, head lad, and Joy Smith (née Douglas), stable girl.

56 Sandy Jane II – *Second Start*, Bobby Beasley, W.H. Allen, 1976, page 93.

56 The Fossa – The *Liverpool Daily Post* ran an article on The Fossa and Amelia just two days before the 1967 Grand National on 6 April. The horse had finished fourth in the 1966 race.

56 Clifford Booth – face-to-face interview with author.

57 Rondetto's best placing in the Grand National was third in 1969 as a veteran 13-year-old.

Chapter 9

59 Brough Scott – face-to-face and telephone interviews with author.

60 Josh Gifford – face-to-face interview with author.

60 Terry Biddlecombe, *This is Your Life!* – *Winner's Disclosure*, Terry Biddlecombe with Pat Lucas, Stanley Paul, 1982, pages 215–6.

60 Gloucester baths routine – ibid., pages 38–9.

61 Cheapest bed in London – Richard Pitman, face-to-face interview with author.

61 Pat Buckley – email exchange with author.

61 Buckley could hardly stand – *Kings for a Day*, Reg Green, Mainstream Sport, 2002, page 69.

61 Awful smell – *Winner's Disclosure*, Terry Biddlecombe with Pat Lucas, Stanley Paul, 1982, page 80.

61 Biddlecombe's personal sweatbox – ibid., pages 30–40.

62 Biddlecombe's 'usual' – ibid., page 38.

62 Barry Brogan in Edinburgh baths – *The Barry Brogan Story – In His Own Words*, Barry Brogan, Arthur Barker, 1981, page 33.

62 Brogan not eating a crumb – ibid., page 34.

62 Biddlecombe preferred the rigours of wasting – *Winner's Disclosure*, Terry Biddlecombe with Pat Lucas, Stanley Paul, 1982, page 38.

62 'I'd chew the steak and spit it out' – face-to-face interview with author.

62 Brogan 'gulping Lasix pills by the handful' – *The Barry Brogan Story – In His Own Words*, Barry Brogan, Arthur Barker, 1981, page 33.

63 Pitman seven stops in 60 miles – *Good Horses Make Good Jockeys*, Richard Pitman, Pelham Books, 1976, pages 96–7.

63 Laxatives 'unpleasant but effective' – ibid., page 95.

63 Brogan's 'favourite trick – *The Barry Brogan Story – In His Own Words*, Barry Brogan, Arthur Barker, 1981, page 64.

64 Biddlecombe's irrigation – face-to-face interview with author.

64 John Kempton taking tablets and running – face-to-face interview with author.

64 Henry Blythe – *Daily Mail*, 26 February 1966.

65   Tim Norman – telephone interview with author.

65   Guarding the Grand National trophy – *Liverpool Daily Post*, 23 March 1966.

Chapter 10

66   Jeremy Speid-Soote – face-to-face interview with author.

67   Ken White – telephone interview; *Go Down to the Beaten*, Chris Pitt, Racing Post Books, 2011 page 163.

67   Jeff King, 'He was left hanging there ...' – ibid., page 139.

67   'That of a spy story' – *Liverpool Daily Post*, 28 March 1966.

68   'Aintree Can Be Sold For Housing' – *Liverpool Echo*, 30 March 1966.

68   Denis Howell, 'The future of Aintree ...' – *The Times*, 31 March 1966.

68   Mrs Topham, 'a moral victory' – *Liverpool Echo*, 30 March 1966.

68   April Fools' day meeting of Tophams board – minutes of Tophams Ltd board meetings, volume XIII.

69   Leslie Marler letter – *The Times*, 20 April 1966.

69   Mrs Topham's disapproval & co. – minutes of Tophams Ltd board meetings, volume XIII.

69   Sales proposition sent to the council – minutes of Tophams Ltd board meetings, volume XIII.

69   Proposed American advert – minutes of Tophams Ltd board meetings, volume XIII.

69   1967 Grand National is on – *Liverpool Echo*, 2 August 1966.

70   1966 financial details – minutes of Tophams Ltd board meetings, volume XIII.

71   Watkins and Bennellick keen for Foinavon to run in big races – John Kempton, face-to-face interview with author.

71   Britain's worst spring blizzard for 16 years... – *The Times*, 15 April 1966.

71   John Buckingham – never sat on a horse until he was 15 – *Tales from the Weighing Room*, John Buckingham, Pelham Books, 1987, page 3.

71   The best-known Courage horses included the mares, Tiberetta and Tiberina, and the tough steeplechaser, Spanish Steps.

72   Bobby Beasley's 'angora finger' – *Second Start*, Bobby Beasley, W.H. Allen, 1976, page 163.

73   Commentating one-liner – Kenneth Wolstenholme's 'They think it's all over ... It is now.'

74   Mac Bennellick's attempt to sell his share in Foinavon – *Havering Recorder*, 14 April 1967.

74   The Aberfan disaster occurred when a slag heap collapsed on to a Welsh village, killing 144 people, mostly children.

74   Kempton Park's Pay TV experiment – *Arkle – the Classic Story of a Champion*, Ivor Herbert, Aurum Press, 2003, page 187.

74 Biddlecombe's frustration – *Winner's Disclosure*, Terry Biddlecombe with Pat Lucas, Stanley Paul, 1982, pages 120–1.

75 The articles say Pettitt had been doping his horses – the *Sun*, 17-21 November 1969. However, a law report in *The Times* nearly four months later says that the then manufacturers of Collovet 'accepted a statement and apology over publication in the Sun of articles by a horse trainer describing it as "dope" and an "illegal mixture"' – *The Times*, 12 March 1970. The report says: 'The defendants wished to make it clear that Collovet, when used as directed in accordance with the instructions always enclosed therewith by the manufacturers, was neither illegal nor harmful; nor was it in any sense "dope".' Pettitt had contravened Jockey Club rules. However, the defendants "had not intended to attack or belittle the product Collovet or Crookes, and they apologized for any such imputation".

75 Jeff King on Dormant – *Go Down to the Beaten*, Chris Pitt, Racing Post Books, 2011, page 140.

75 Clifford Booth's arrangement with Peter McLoughlin – face-to-face interview with author.

Chapter 11

77 Nobby Howard – telephone interviews with author; also interviewed by Clement Freud in the *Sun*, 8 April 1967.

79 Paul Irby – face-to-face interview with author.

80 John Kempton didn't make it to Aintree start-line in 1967 – nor, as it happened, did the Duke of Albuquerque, though he had pulled up only four fences from home the previous year on a horse called L'Empereur.

81 Ron Atkins father's shoe shop – *Go Down to the Beaten*, Chris Pitt, Racing Post Books, 2011, page 177.

81 Foinavon wearing blinkers – John Kempton face-to-face interview with author.

81 Foinavon 'ducking the issue a little bit' – Ron Atkins face-to-face interview with author.

82 Bobby Beasley's farm – *Second Start*, Bobby Beasley, W.H. Allen, 1976, page 144.

83 Atkins, 'What's the deal?' – face-to-face interview with author.

83 Bruce Gregory also rode Out and About to 14th place in the 1964 Grand National.

83 Bruce Gregory's car – Terry Biddlecombe face-to-face interview with author.

83 Bruce Gregory in France – Toby Balding, telephone interview with author.

84 'Nothing was going better' – *Sporting Life*, 23 February 1967.

84 Man looking for Foinavon's bit – Clifford Booth face-to-face interview with author.

84 'Cheltenham without Arkle …' – *The Times*, 15 March 1967.

84 Fort Leney – Dicky May was also running, meaning that all three horses looked

after by the Dreapers' stable lad Vincent Slevin in 1964/65 (Fort Leney, Dicky May and Foinavon) were in the eight-strong Gold Cup field.

85 Paul Kelleway grabbing Bobby Beasley – *Second Start*, Bobby Beasley, W.H. Allen, 1976, pages 18–9.

85 Terry Biddlecombe's difficult start to the Cheltenham festival – *Winner's Disclosure*, Terry Biddlecombe with Pat Lucas, Stanley Paul, 1982, pages 121–2.

85 Alberto Giacometti (1901–66) – Swiss sculptor, known for his attenuated figures.

86 'Oceanic' power of Mill House – *My Life and Arkle's*, Pat Taaffe, Stanley Paul, 1972, page 50.

86 At 100/8, Woodland Venture was the longest-priced Cheltenham Gold Cup winner since 1955.

86 Appearance of Terry Biddlecombe's doctor – *Winner's Disclosure*, Terry Biddlecombe with Pat Lucas, Stanley Paul, 1982, page 124.

86 Harry Collins's cow – ibid., page 124.

Chapter 12

87 Dave Patrick – telephone interview with author.

87 Clifford Booth – face-to-face interview with author.

88 Litany of items damaged by vandals – *Daily Mirror*, 29 March 1967.

88 Four figure bill – minutes of Tophams Ltd board meetings, volume XIII.

88 No arrests have been made – *The Times*, 1 April 1967.

89 Cyril Watkins being treated in hospital – email correspondence with Eileen Spragg, who worked at the Royal Berkshire Hospital in Reading in 1967.

89 Colin Hemsley – face-to-face interview with author.

89 Gregory 'must be congratulated on completing the course' – *Sporting Life*, 3 April 1967.

90 801st ride – John Buckingham's private riding log.

90 Buckingham picks up the phone … – *Tales from the Weighing Room*, John Buckingham, Pelham Books, 1987, pages 18–9.

90 Sailaway Sailor won next time out at Market Rasen on 15 April to give Kempton his fourth and final winner of the season. The horse's rider on that occasion was a certain Macer Gifford, enjoying a better day than he had the previous Saturday.

91 'Foinavon hasn't yet turned out as well as we thought he would …' – *Daily Mirror*, 7 April 1967.

91 Pat Taaffe on Foinavon – *My Life and Arkle's*, Pat Taaffe, Stanley Paul, 1972, pages 69–70.

91 Honey End's nickname – telephone interview with John 'Jinks' James, former apprentice with Capt. Ryan Price at Findon in Sussex.

Chapter 13

92 Tony Hutt and Geoff Stocker's coin toss – Geoff Stocker face-to-face interview with author.

93 Newbury Racehorse Transport was a sideline of Gordon Passey, the local scrap metal dealer who was one of the Kemptons' most loyal customers.

93 'You could hear it coming …' – Colin Hemsley face-to-face interview with author.

95 An excited John Buckingham – face-to-face interviews with author and *Tales from the Weighing Room*, John Buckingham, Pelham Books, 1987, page 19.

96 Maurice Kingsley – *A-Z of the Grand National*, John Cottrell and Marcus Armytage, Highdown, 2008, page 412.

96 Red Rum – the most famous Grand National horse of all. Won the 1973, 1974 and 1977 Nationals and was runner-up in the two races in between. 'Rummy', a local horse trained in nearby Southport, is now buried beside the Aintree winning-post. His trainer Donald 'Ginger' McCain died in 2011. It being a selling plate, Red Rum was bought in for 300 guineas following this Aintree debut on 7 April 1967. There was no bid for Curlicue.

96 Liverpool's manufacturing growth – *Liverpool 800*, John Belchem (ed.), Liverpool University Press, 2006, page 409.

96 Alan Ball and Alex Young at Aintree – *Liverpool Daily Post*, 7 April 1967.

96 'Thimbleful of spectators' – *The Times*, 7 April 1967.

97 Problems on Topham Trophy day – *The Times*, 7 April 1967.

97 Paint job problems – minutes of Topham Ltd board meetings, volume XIII.

97 Johnny Lehane's sore ribs – *Irish Independent*, 8 April 1967.

97 Eddie Harty's versatility – *Kings for a Day*, Reg Green, Mainstream, 2002, pages 105–6.

98 Spearhead's fall – *The Times*, 7 April 1967.

98 Harty's injuries – telephone interview with author.

98 Harty's 'heavily bandaged hand' – *Irish Independent*, 8 April 1967.

98 Ossie Dale sleeping in the loft – *Ossie Dale's Grand National Scrapbook*, Reg Green, Marlborough, 1992, page 13.

98 Escaped goat – telephone interview with Ossie Dale.

99 Foinavon's box – I am indebted to Aintree's current stable manager, Derek Thompson, who spared the time to show me around the yard on a very busy day.

99 Leedsy's rough flight – *Liverpool Daily Post*, 6 April 1967.

99 Reg Tweedie's blood-splashed breeches/Freddie staying at Haydock – *A Horse Called Freddie*, Vian Smith, Stanley Paul, 1967, pages 23 and 131.

99 Clifford Booth's night at the Sefton Arms – face-to-face interview with author.

99 John Buckingham's lodgings – *Tales from the Weighing Room*, John Buckingham, Pelham Books, 1987, page 20; also *Daily Express*, 30 March 1968.

99 Veronique Peck – telephone interview with author.

100 Gregory Peck 'a chance I have to take …' – *Liverpool Daily Post*, 8 April 1967.

100 Peck's bet with John Gaines – 'Disaster at a Thorny Barricade' by Whitney Tower, *Sports Illustrated*, 17 April 1967.

Chapter 14

101 Early 19th-century races for hunting horses – *Portrait of a Sport – The Story of Steeplechasing in Great Britain and the United States*, Elizabeth Eliot, Countryman Press, 1957, page 24.

102 'The first example …' – ibid., page 25.

102 'Up to this date …' – ibid., pages 35–6.

102 Aintree's first jumps races – *Gallant Sport – the Authentic History of Liverpool Races and the Grand National*, John Pinfold, Portway Press, 1999, page 72.

102 When his years of dominance in the saddle were over, Becher worked as a sack inspector for Great Northern Railway.

102 South-west Lancashire's reputation for hare-coursing – *Gallant Sport – the Authentic History of Liverpool Races and the Grand National*, John Pinfold, Portway Press, 1999, page 45.

103 Financial pressure on Lynn – ibid., page 76.

103 First use of the phrase 'Grand National' – ibid., page 105.

103 'The race was run …' – ibid., pages 76–7.

104 A galloping racehorse breathes up to 40 litres of air per second – *Inside Nature's Giants*, Channel 4.

104 'Internal blood doping' – 'Efficiency of Equine Express Postal Systems', Alberto Minetti, *Nature* vol. 426, 18–25 December 2003. Minetti, a physiology professor at the University of Milan, has also shed light on the limits of a racehorse's endurance when operating at high speed, identifying a decline in performance, when running on the flat, at distances greater than 10km (6 miles). He says this is normally due to glycogen depletion.

105 Becher and the filthy taste of water without brandy – *The Grand National – Anybody's Race*, Peter King, Quartet Books, 1983, page 32.

105 Dick Francis at Becher's – ibid., page 29.

106 The Chair 'impenetrable as a prison wall' – ibid., page 28.

106 Third fence like the 'Grand Canyon' – John Lawrence (Lord Oaksey) in the foreword to *Ossie Dale's Grand National Scrapbook*, Reg Green, Marlborough 1992. Lawrence came second in the 1963 Grand National riding Carrickbeg.

106 Falls at the first fence – *Nature*, vol. 428, 25 March 2004. (Data from the previous 15 Grand Nationals analysed by Christopher Proudman, Gina Pinchbeck, Peter Clegg and Nigel French.) The start for the 2013 Grand National is expected, at time of writing, to be moved closer to the first fence.

107 Grand National course alterations selected from timetable of significant changes compiled by Grand National specialist Mick Mutlow.

107 'In the past …' – *Second Start*, Bobby Beasley, W.H. Allen, 1976, page 133.

107 Reduced number of fallers – *The Times*, 1 April 1963.

107 Brough Scott – face-to-face interview with author.

107 'Like crossing the equator – *The Grand National – Anybody's Race*, Peter King, Quartet Books, 1983, pages 28–9.

108 Highland Wedding withdraws – *The Times*, 1 April 1967. Highland Wedding would go on to win the 1969 Grand National.

108 'The best Grand National field for years' – *Horse and Hound*, 15 April 1967.

109 Kilburn's switch from showjumping – telephone interview with Isabelle Jekey, Madame Borel de Bitche's daughter.

109 Glass in Rutherfords's foot – 'Disaster at a Thorny Barricade', Whitney Tower, *Sports Illustrated*, 17 April 1967.

Chapter 15

110 Pat Buckley, 'A typical day …' – telephone interview with author.

110 Peter O'Sullevan there at 7am – face-to-face interview with author.

111 Ray Lakeland, producer of the BBC's 1967 Grand National outside broadcast, says the broadcaster was quick to acquire a 12-inch Sony Trinitron for O'Sullevan once the product, acclaimed for the brightness of its images, became available. This would not have been until a year or two later, however.

111 Upon conclusion of the 1958 deal in October, Mrs Topham had proclaimed, 'In the dim and distant future, we may consider televising the National.'

111 Football League chairmen turn down live television proposal – *Liverpool Daily Post*, 4 April 1967.

111 Tophams 1960 profits £2,000 up – minutes of Tophams Ltd board meetings, volume XII.

111 Estimated 50 million television viewers etc. – *The Times*, 5 April 1967.

112 Ray Lakeland and the BBC's 'roving eye' camera – face-to-face interview with author.

112 The Lincolnshire Handicap was moved from Lincoln to Doncaster in 1965 when Lincoln racecourse was closed.

113 Nicolaus Silver's engine-oil – *Ossie Dale's Grand National Scrapbook*, Reg Green, Marlborough, 1992, page 34.

113 'Lord Derby in the middle …' – face-to-face interview with Ray Lakeland, former BBC outside broadcast producer.

114 'A seat of the pants guy' – ibid.

114 Sidney Spofforth – *Liverpool Daily Post*, 8 April 1967.

115 Cyril Watkins in his office – details sourced from his wife Iris's niece, Lyn Shelton, and nephew, Paul Nixon.

116 Three Dons's temper and good looks – face-to-face interview with Colin Hemsley, former head lad.

116 Frank Reynolds's personalised number-plate – *Coventry Evening Telegraph*, 5 September 1968.

116 Snow in the Cotswolds – face-to-face interview with Colin Hemsley, former head lad.

116 Southport Turkish baths – *Winner's Disclosure*, Terry Biddlecombe with Pat Lucas, Stanley Paul, 1982, pages 35–6.

117 John Buckingham's landlady – *Daily Express*, 30 March 1968.

117 The scene at the Adelphi – 'Disaster at a Thorny Barricade', Whitney Tower, *Sports Illustrated*, 17 April 1967.

117 Tim Durant's past and cancer operation – *A-Z of the Grand National*, John Cottrell and Marcus Armytage, Highdown, 2008, pages 145–6.

117 Ladbrokes telegram – *The Times*, 8 April 1967.

117 Charles Benson's Horse by Horse Guide – *Daily Express*, 8 April 1967.

Chapter 16

118 Information on train arrivals sourced from Phil Prosser and other railway enthusiasts.

118 Multicoloured trouser suits – *Liverpool Daily Post*, 10 April 1967.

118 John Buckingham, 'I never have lunch …' – *Daily Express*, 30 March 1968.

119 John Pinfold – face-to-face interview with author.

119 14 shillings – 70p.

119 Michael Daley – email correspondence with author.

120 'Officers' special' train – email correspondence with railway enthusiasts Stuart Daniels and Phil Prosser. The last 'officers' special' ran in 1976.

120 Graham Goode first live commentary – telephone interview with author.

120 Three Dons's unusual whip – face-to-face interview with Colin Hemsley, the Kemptons' head lad.

121 Three Dons takes lead approaching the last – *Worcester Evening News*, 8 April 1967.

121 Buckingham collecting autographs – *Daily Express*, 30 March 1968.

121 Richard Pitman, 'One buttock on the bench' – face-to-face interview with author. Pitman would twice finish as Grand National runner-up: in 1969 on Steel Bridge and in 1973 on Crisp.

121 Buckingham, 'All sitting down …' – *Daily Express*, 30 March 1968.

121 Pitman always went to church – face-to-face interview with author.

121 John Lawrence's glucose and orange quarters – *Good Horses Make Good Jockeys*, Richard Pitman, Pelham Books, 1976, page 126.

121 Biddlecombe, 'I have never seen so many …' – *Winner's Disclosure*, Terry Biddlecombe with Pat Lucas, Stanley Paul, 1982, page 36.

122 Time to weigh out: in any one of the previous 16 years, Michael Scudamore would have been in that line of jockeys. Instead, five months after a freak fall at Wolverhampton that left him with chest and facial injuries serious enough to end his career, he had been booked to do a radio commentary on the National for the BBC World Service and found himself 'in the tiniest room with the tiniest television.'

122 'Johnny, what's this you're riding?' – a recording of Michael O'Hehir's account of this incident can be listened to at: http://www.youtube.com/watch?v=5kA_FmPuXz4

122 Mullingar – Kieran O'Donnell, letter to author.

122 George Pottinger – he meant, of course, that he fished at the mountain in Sutherland after which the horse was named, though it is more normally written Foinaven nowadays. Details of the story came from a telephone interview with Piers Pottinger.

123 Michael Walters – telephone interview with author.

123 Eric Brown – telephone interview with author.

123 Cyril Watkins's bets – *Evening Post*, 8 April 1967 and *Sunday Express*, 9 April 1967.

123 Mac Bennellick watching in his office – *Havering Recorder*, 14 April 1967.

123 Scene in Cyril's Tilehurst pet-shop – email correspondence with Lyn Shelton, Iris Watkin's niece, and interview with Paul Nixon, Iris's nephew.

123 Bennellick's future daughter-in-law – email correspondence with Chris Compton, widow of Bennellick's son Colin.

124 The Flat race that preceded the National – the Hylton Handicap Stakes.

124 False start and 16-minute delay – *Evening News & Star*, 8 April 1967.

125 Raymond Guest – A better-known horse of Guest's, L'Escargot, would win the Grand National in 1975, beating Red Rum in the process.

126 Marie Christine Ridgway/Chay Blyth – telephone interview with Marie Christine Ridgway, also *Sporting Life*, 10 April 1967.

126 Chay Blyth in 1971 achieved even greater fame after sailing non-stop westwards around the world.

126 Clifford Booth's attempt to bet on Foinavon – face-to-face interview with author.

126 Ten bob – 50p

Chapter 17

127 Brough Scott – writer and former jockey; face-to-face interview with author.

128 David Nicholson, 'I have never had …' – *Liverpool Daily Post*, 8 April 1967.

128 John Buckingham, the preliminaries 'seemed to take ages …' – *Tales from the Weighing Room*, John Buckingham, Pelham Books, 1987, page 20.

129 Richard Pitman, 'So heavily showered with dust …' – *Good Horses Make Good Jockeys*, Richard Pitman, Pelham Books, 1976, page 43.

129 Bob-a-Job was ridden by Chris Young rather than the unfortunate Dave Patrick (see Chapter 12).

129 Paul Irby, 'I bloody nearly fell off.' – face-to-face interview with author.

130 Bassnet's fall – *The Bloodstock Breeders' Annual Review – National Hunt Season 1966/67*, page 111.

130 David Nicholson, who died in 2006, came third in the jockeys' championship in 1964/65 and was twice champion jump-racing trainer in the mid-1990s. The Grand National eluded him in both guises, however.

130 The embankment – this was built from rubble and debris left from Aintree's wartime occupation and first used in 1952. It allows a view of the first three Grand National fences.

130 Peter Jones – telephone interview with author. Jones, who rode Bassnet over the National fences in the 1966 Topham Trophy, finishing second, remembers that Becher's 'frightened the life out of' the horse. 'He hardly left the ground at the next,' he says.

130 Andy Turnell, 'I was fine …' – face-to-face interview with author. Turnell said he had taken a middle-to-outer line because his father, the trainer Bob Turnell, who also rode in several Nationals, "got cross with you if you went up the inner."

131 Mrs Charles Turriff – face-to-face interview with author. (The former Mrs Turriff now goes by the name of Georgina Galt.)

131 Taught to race-ride by Fred Winter – Winter's first Grand National winner as a jockey – Sundew (1957) – was trained on a farm at Henley-in-Arden owned by Mrs Turriff's mother.

132 1964 Scottish Grand National – *A Horse Called Freddie*, Vian Smith, Stanley Paul, 1967, page 51.

132 1964 was a banner year for Walwyn, who had already captured the Aintree Grand National with Team Spirit. *The Times* reported after the Scottish race that the Lambourn trainer's horses 'have now won £66,959 compared with the earlier record of £40,950 by H.R. Price.' Walwyn's haul was achieved in spite of Mill House's Cheltenham Gold Cup defeat by Arkle.

132 Armitage Shanks – the British bathroom fixtures company.

132 Popham Down foaled on the Marlborough Downs – Georgina Galt believes the foal was actually born on Popham Down. I have no reason to doubt this, but have been unable to trace anywhere with this name in the vicinity of these downs.

132 Willie Robinson, Mildmay was Popham Down's 'type of race' – telephone interview with author.

133 Kirriemuir – winner of the 1965 Champion Hurdle at Cheltenham.

133 Larbawn – twice winner of the Whitbread Gold Cup.

133 Josh Gifford, 'Macer suited certain horses …' – face-to-face interview with author.

133 Macer Gifford was champion amateur jockey in 1964/65.

Chapter 18

134 Tim Brookshaw's horrifying fall – *Winner's Disclosure*, Terry Biddlecombe with Pat Lucas, Stanley Paul, 1982, page 79.

135 Pat Taaffe on Brookshaw – *My Life and Arkle's*, Pat Taaffe, Stanley Paul, 1972, page 35.

135 John Buckingham, Brookshaw 'absolutely fearless' – face-to-face interview with author.

135 Brookshaw, 'How now brown cow?' – *Winner's Disclosure*, Terry Biddlecombe with Pat Lucas, Stanley Paul, 1982, page 84.

135 David Mould injury-record – face-to-face interview with author.

135 Terry Biddlecombe, 'I broke 47 bones …' – face-to-face interview with author.

135 Taaffe injury-record – *My Life and Arkle's*, Pat Taaffe, Stanley Paul, 1972, page 32.

135 Barry Brogan injury-record – *The Barry Brogan Story – In His Own Words*, Barry Brogan, Arthur Barker, 1981, page 125.

136 Buckingham's injury-record – included in an interview published in the Gus Dalrymple Column on 8 April 1972.

136 Buckingham's journey back from Wetherby – *Tales from the Weighing Room*, John Buckingham, Pelham Books, 1987, page 51.

136 Paddy Farrell's fall – *The Times*, 23 March 1964.

136 Ron Atkins, 'It was like the Battle of the Somme …' – face-to-face interview with author.

136 Brough Scott ambulance ride etc. – face-to-face interview with author.

136 Duke of Albuquerque's 107 Aintree fractures – *A-Z of the Grand National*, John Cottrell and Marcus Armytage, Highdown, 2008, page 18.

137 One Grand National fatality – ibid., page 163 and pages 551–2.

137 Michael Scudamore, 'A boy called Ivor Beckinsale …' etc. – telephone interview with author.

137 Stan Mellor's head 'swollen like a football' – *Winner's Disclosure*, Terry Biddlecombe with Pat Lucas, Stanley Paul, 1982, page 68.

138 Pat Buckley – email correspondence with author.

138 Jeremy Speid-Soote, 'Being a jockey …' – face-to-face interview with author.

138 Pat Taaffe, 'We will fall …' – *My Life and Arkle's*, Pat Taaffe, Stanley Paul, 1972, page 32.

138 Stan Mellor, 'You don't lie …' – face-to-face interview with author.

138 Atkins was made Safety Officer for the Jockeys' Association towards the end of the decade.

139 Buckingham, 'I took a pull …' – face-to-face interview with author.

139 Queen's representative at Ascot – this role included deciding ultimately who would be granted admittance to the Royal Enclosure (*Daily Telegraph*, 23 April 2005).

139 April Rose had jumped more than 200 Aintree fences without falling – *A Horse Called Freddie*, Vian Smith, Stanley Paul, 1967, page 129.

139 Piers Bengough, 'The most economical action …' – *Go Down to the Beaten*, Chris Pitt, Racing Post Books, 2011, page 70.

140 John Edwards – telephone interview with author.

140 Shand Kydd's loan of Rolls-Royce to Richard Pitman – *Good Horses Make Good Jockeys*, Richard Pitman, Pelham Books, 1976, page 32. Jenny Pitman would go on to become the first woman to train a Grand National winner – Corbiere in 1983.

140 Bill Shand Kydd's broken collarbone – telephone interview with author.

140 Richard Pitman, 'I remembered too late' – ibid., page 44.

141 Enid Chanelle – telephone interview with Kara McCulloch, Miss Chanelle's granddaughter. In later years, Miss Chanelle's attentions would switch to the performing arts. She became president of a company that acquired a string of theatres around southern England including the Theatre Royal Haymarket in London's West End. By a quirk of history, this was the very venue where, in the early 1920s, Mirabel Topham had made her last stage appearances.

141 Vulcano tipped to win – *Irish Independent*, 8 April 1967.

141 Vulcano at the third fence – face-to-face interview with his jockey, Jeremy Speid-Soote.

142 RSPCA report – minutes of Tophams Ltd board meetings, volume XIII.

142 Shand Kydd, Dorimont 'a lovely old thing'.

Chapter 19

143 Johnny Lehane's death – the *Western Times & Gazette*, 12 September 1969 and 14 November 1969.

143 Terry Biddlecombe, Lehane 'the happiest little jockey …' – face-to-face interview with author.

144 Coroner's remarks – the *Western Times & Gazette*, 14 November 1969.

144 1962 Grand National – Lehane's mount Mr What had won the race in 1958 and finished third in 1959. The first three home in 1962 were all aged 12, leading the race to be dubbed, 'the success of the veterans'.

144 False teeth/holiday in Majorca – *Winner's Disclosure*, Terry Biddlecombe with Pat Lucas, Stanley Paul, 1982, pages 57 and 76. Biddlecombe writes that he is 'not quite sure' how Lehane came by the name of 'Tumper', but thinks it was through his habit of 'addressing everyone and everything with the word "tumping"'.

144 Richard Pitman, '[Lehane] delighted in buying drinks …' – *Good Horses Make Good Jockeys*, Richard Pitman, Pelham Books, 1976, page 20.

145 Tim Norman, 'If it wasn't for Johnny Lehane …' – telephone interview with author.

145 Terry Biddlecombe, Lehane 'When he had money ...' – face-to-face interview with author.

145 Pitman, 'He had friends ...' – *Good Horses Make Good Jockeys*, Richard Pitman, Pelham Books, 1976, page 20.

145 Bobby Beasley sees Lehane giving novice chaser 'a fair old hiding' – *Second Start*, Bobby Beasley, W.H. Allen, 1976, page 161. Beasley reveals in the book that it was on the night of his mount Nicolaus Silver's 1961 Grand National victory that he 'got tight' for the first time in his life.

145 Biddlecombe, Lehane 'took life seriously ...' – *Winner's Disclosure*, Terry Biddlecombe with Pat Lucas, Stanley Paul, 1982, page 84.

146 The last relatively locally trained Grand National winner had been Cheshire-based Russian Hero in 1949. He never won another race.

146 Penvulgo's fatal injury – *Sporting Life*, 30 March 1968.

147 Nobby Howard, 'I nearly fell ...' – telephone interview with author.

147 John Cook later won the 1971 Grand National on Specify.

147 David Crossley Cooke watching the rest of the race on horseback – telephone interview with author.

147 John Buckingham, 'When you get halfway over ...' – *Daily Express*, 30 March 1968.

Chapter 20

148 Because the Grand National consists of nearly two full laps of a 16-fence course, the first fence is also the 17th, while the last is also the 14th. The water-jump is cleared once only, as the 16th fence. The 'one after Becher's' is the 7th fence on the first circuit and the 23rd on the second.

148 Dick Francis, 'Innocuous and simple ...' – *Sunday Express*, 9 April 1967.

149 Francis, 'An understandable slayer ...' – ibid.

149 Fred Rimell – later a very successful trainer who saddled four Grand National winners. His representatives in the 1967 race were The Fossa and Princeful.

149 Bruce Hobbs and Battleship – description of incident with Rimell draws on both *Second Start*, Bobby Beasley, W.H. Allen, 1976, page 45 and *A-Z of the Grand National*, John Cottrell and Marcus Armytage, Highdown, 2008.

149 Battleship was also one of the very rare blinkered Grand National winners.

149 22 casualties – figures supplied by Mick Mutlow, Grand National specialist.

150 'At number seven fence ...' – *The Times*, 15 February 1955.

150 The League Against Cruel Sport not satisfied – *The Times*, 16 February 1955.

150 Views of jockeys Bryan Marshall and George Slack – ibid.

150 RSPCA recommends removal of seventh fence ... – *The Times*, 22 March 1957.

151 In the 1970s, the 'one after Becher's' came close to claiming at least two high-

class victims. In 1971, Jim Dreaper was nearly knocked off Black Secret there in a collision with another horse (*Go Down to the Beaten*, Chris Pitt, Racing Post Books, 2011, page 151). Black Secret finished a narrowly beaten second. Four years later, Tommy Carberry found himself up around his mount L'Escargot's ears after the gelding surprisingly clouted the fence hard (*Kings for a Day*, Reg Green, Mainstream, 2002, page 121). The pair went on to win the race from the great Red Rum by 15 lengths.

151   Terry Biddlecombe, 'A trick fence ...' – face-to-face interview with author.

151   Biddlecombe, 'That's a bastard ...' – *Horse and Hound*, 15 April 1967.

Chapter 21

153   John Lawrence, 'One of the finest ...' – *Horse and Hound*, 15 April 1967.

153   Anglo slams into another horse – 'Disaster at a Thorny Barricade', Whitney Tower, *Sports Illustrated*, 17 April 1967.

154   Tim Norman – telephone interview with author.

154   Stolen jewellery – *The Times*, 10 April 1967.

154   Johnny Lehane's 'super ride' – *Sunday Express*, 9 April 1967.

154   Paul Irby, 'The Canal Turn ...' – face-to-face interview with author.

155   Paddy Broderick, 'A loose horse ...' – face-to-face interview with author.

155   John Buckingham, 'Going past the stands ...' – face-to-face interview with author, *Financial Times*, 5 April 2003.

156   John Leech, 'I remember ...' – *Go Down to the Beaten*, Chris Pitt, Racing Post Books, 2011 page 126. Also telephone interview with author.

156   Nick Gaselee, 'I had gone to the middle ...' – telephone interview with author.

156   Stan Mellor, 'He used to get ...' – face-to-face interview with author.

156   'It was like a battlefield ...' – writers and publications responsible for these metaphors included: the *Evening News and Star*, John Lawrence in the *Sunday Telegraph* and, later, *Horse and Hound*, Dick Francis (*Sunday Express*), Peter Wilson (*Daily Mirror*) and Tom Forrest (*Sunday Express*).

157   Cloud of steam – *Liverpool Daily Post*, 10 April 1967.

157   Pat McCarron, 'Everybody was just panic-stricken ...' – telephone interview with author.

157   Mellor, 'They were on the inside ...' – face-to-face interview with author. Mellor would go on to win two races in a week on Popham Down in 1969.

158   John Lawrence was using – and had been ejected from – the saddle with which Fred Winter rode to victory in the race on Kilmore in 1962 – *Liverpool Daily Post*, 8 April 1967.

158   Michael Daley – email correspondence with author.

158   Broderick, 'Give us a leg-up ...' – *Go Down to the Beaten*, Chris Pitt, Racing Post Books, 2011, page 127.

158 Kirtle Lad won the 1968 Yorkshire Grand National, but was killed at Market Rasen in his next race.

159 Hayhurst, 'landed sprinting ...' – telephone interview with author.

159 Demented serpents – *Horse and Hound*, 15 April 1967.

159 Three horses cleared the 23rd at the first time of asking – four if you include the riderless April Rose. Rondetto fell there again the following year.

159 Johnny Haine died in 1998.

150 Gaselee, 'went right up the horse's neck ...' – telephone interview with author.

160 David Mould, 'My brain was telling me ...' – telephone interview with author. As can happen in racing, Mould seems to have had a tempestuous relationship with Peter Cazalet, Different Class's trainer. Cazalet was a 'tyrant', he told me. 'Very fair, but what a tyrant. The rows we used to have! He used to sack me every week. I used to go to the Queen Mum and say, "He sacked me again." She got me my job back every week.'

160 Pat Buckley, 'I was exactly where I wanted to be ...' – telephone interview with author. In the 1968 Grand National, Buckley rode Rutherfords to fourth place. He said, 'He was a very good horse. He had his own mind about racing: some days he would, some days he wouldn't.'

161 Eddie Harty, 'It all happened in front of me ...' – telephone interview with author.

161 McCarron, 'I was in the next parish ...' – telephone interview with author.

Chapter 22

162 John Pinfold – face-to-face interview with author.

162 Michael O'Hehir – as the commentator said subsequently, 'If I hadn't had the good fortune to be standing there and to go over and ask Johnny Buckingham what that horse was, when all the horses fell and this lone one came along, I'd have been going through a racecard wondering, "What is that thing in black?"' His account can be listened to at: http://www.youtube.com/watch?v=5kA_FmPuXz4

162 John Buckingham, 'I just galloped into them ...' – face-to-face interviews with author; *Financial Times*, 5 April 2003; *Tales from the Weighing Room*, John Buckingham, Pelham Books, 1987, page 23.

163 Buckingham's winning ride at Market Rasen – *Horse and Hound*, 15 April 1967 (article by John Lawrence).

163 Pat Taaffe, 'I think if you'd asked me ...' – *My Life and Arkle's*, Pat Taaffe, Stanley Paul, 1972 page 70.

163 Josh Gifford, 'Jumping like a buck ...' – Gifford gave an account of the incident to the Midlands Grand National Club's 2011 Grand National preview night in Stirchley. The event was organised by author Chris Pitt.

163   Brian Fletcher, 'I was thrown off the horse …' – telephone interview with author.

164   Tommy Carberry, 'This carry-on …' – telephone interview with author.

164   Jackie Cullen, who won the 1973 Irish Grand National, was found dead at home with gunshot wounds in 2001.

164   Fredith's Son – *My Life and Arkle's*, Pat Taaffe, Stanley Paul, 1972, page 76.

164   Francis Shortt, 'Not going all that sweetly …' – telephone interview with author.

165   [Shortt] 'had time to pick his passage' – *Irish Field*, 15 April 1967.

165   Shortt got over at third attempt – telephone interview with author.

165   Terry Biddlecombe, Greek Scholar 'always wanted to please' – face-to-face interview with author.

165   Biddlecombe, 'Come on lads! …' – *Go Down to the Beaten*, Chris Pitt, Racing Post Books, 2011, page 127.

165   Pinfold, 'I did take one …' – face-to-face interview with author.

165   Kempton leapt onto a table – face-to-face interview with author.

165   Mac Bennellick – *Sunday Express*, 9 April 1967; *Havering Recorder*, 14 April 1967.

165   Chipping Warden football matched halted – telephone interview with Alison Grant, Buckingham's sister-in-law.

166   Cyril Watkins retreating to the garden – *Sunday Express*, 9 April 1967.

166   Dennis Lewell – email correspondence with Lewell's friend Graham Sharpe.

166   Eric Brown – telephone interview with author.

166   Buckingham cast as bandit escaping with the loot – *A Horse Called Freddie*, Vian Smith, Stanley Paul, 1967, page 138.

166   This hole in the 28th fence may well have been punched by Ronald's Boy, whose race was ended there on the first circuit when it was the 12th.

167   George Pottinger hitting car dashboard – telephone interview with his son Piers.

167   Packed Home's broken pedal bone – telephone interview with Tommy Carberry, his jockey.

167   This second loose horse may have been Leedsy.

Chapter 23

168   An exultant Clifford Booth … – face-to-face interview with author.

169   John Kempton, table 'creaked and groaned …' – face-to-face interview with author.

169   Tony Hutt's extra journey – face-to-face interviews with Geoff Stocker, the other driver used by the Kemptons, and Colin Hemsley, head lad.

169   Iris Watkins, I had to 'hide my face …' – *Sunday Express*, 9 April 1967.

169   Mac Bennellick, 'Thank God…" – ibid.

169   Dinner at the George – email correspondence with Zelda Blackadder, family friend.

169 Ann Buckingham, 'He's won ...' – *Daily Express*, 30 March 1968.

170 Josh Gifford, 'I thought I'd catch him ...' – Account given to Midlands Grand National Club's 2011 preview night.

170 Brian Fletcher won the race on Red Alligator in 1968 and Red Rum in 1973 and 1974. During a telephone interview, Fletcher told me he had walked the course 'three or four times'. Such attention to detail, combined with a knack – 1967 excepted – for being in the right place at the right time (or at least not being in the wrong place at the wrong time), help to explain Fletcher's exemplary Aintree record.

171 David Nicholson, 'tremendously determined ...' – *Tales from the Weighing Room*, John Buckingham, Pelham Books, 1987, Foreword.

171 Tim Brookshaw's 'few bob' on Honey End – *Daily Mirror*, 5 April 1967.

172 Josh Gifford's lost bet – account given to Midlands Grand National Club's 2011 preview night.

172 Absence of winning owners in 1962 and 1963 – *Go Down to the Beaten*, Chris Pitt, Racing Post Books, 2011, page 95; *The Times*, 1 April 1963.

172 Light-hearted suggestion of Popham Down's owner – face-to-face interview with Georgina Galt.

172 Anne, Duchess of Westminster present – *Sunday Telegraph*, 9 April 1967.

173 Nobby Howard escorting Gregory Peck – telephone interview with author.

173 Gifford puts half-a-crown in the champagne cork – *Tales from the Weighing Room*, John Buckingham, Pelham Books, 1987, page 29.

173 Envelope addressed to 'The Winner ...' – ibid.

173 John Pinfold – face-to-face interview with author.

173 Michael Daley – email correspondence with author.

173 Clement Freud's house burgled – the *Sun*, 10 April 1967.

174 Buckingham's landlady suggests a night out in Liverpool – *Daily Express*, 30 March 1968.

174 Flags and paint at Buckingham's house – *Tales from the Weighing Room*, John Buckingham, Pelham Books, 1987, page 30.

174 'None of the usual riotous scenes ...' – *Liverpool Daily Post*, 8 and 10 April 1967.

Chapter 24

176 Peggy's story – email correspondence with Christopher Morris.

176 £10 each-way – this means one £10 bet on the horse to win at the bookmaker's advertised odds (in Foinavon's case, 100/1) and one £10 bet on the horse to finish in the first four, usually at a quarter of the advertised odds, i.e. 25/1.

176 As Morris recalls, Peggy's tips were not very successful in other years. Then again, picking the winner from a forty-plus horse field is a much more difficult proposition than choosing the winning team in a football match.

177 Several million people bet on the National – in November 1959 Richard Stanley, MP for North Fylde, stated in parliament that over 50 per cent of the adult population had a bet on the Derby, the other race on the calendar to attract mass interest from individuals not otherwise interested in horse racing.

177 Peter Chapman, 'Tony came running back …' – email correspondence with author.

177 Tote's 445/1 payout – telephone interview with Grand National historian Reg Green.

178 New Betting and Gaming Act – The House of Commons second reading debate can be consulted at: http://hansard.millbanksystems.com/commons/1959/nov/16/betting-and-gaming-bill

178 7,000 betting-shops opened in May 1961 – *BOS* magazine, May/June 2011, page 21.

179 Cyril Watkins's ante-post bets of £16 each-way – *Sunday Express*, 9 April 1967.

179 Iris Watkins's winnings – *Sunday Times*, 9 April 1967.

179 In April 1967, you could have bought a dozen Hillman Minx family saloon-cars and still had plenty of change from £10,000.

179 William Hill, 'We could not …' – *Sports Mail*, 8 April 1967.

179 John Banks's £25,000 Grand National earnings – *Sunday Post*, 9 April 1967.

179 Lucy Geddes – email correspondence with Joan Smith, Lucy Geddes's daughter.

180 Helen Dillon – email correspondence with author.

180 Vivian Humphries – telephone interview with Darren, Humphries's son.

180 Nan Toone – *Daily Mirror*, 10 April 1967.

180 Martyne Millington – ibid.

180 Cream cakes at Royal Berkshire Hospital – email correspondence with ex-employee Eileen Spragg.

181 Alison Grant – telephone interview with author.

181 Patricia Rogers's weblog on Foinavon can be viewed at: http://patricia1957.wordpress.com/2010/02/23/1967-the-year-i-won-the-grand-national/

181 John Warham – telephone interview with author.

181 Nigel Everett – face-to-face interview with author.

182 House in Criccieth – email correspondence with Ian Atkinson. A reference to the house on www.criccieth-history.co.uk says it is "pink-stuccoed" and was "once owned by the Bird's Custard family". I am told this information comes from *Criccieth, a Heritage Walk*, a recently republished book by Eira and James Gleasure.

182 House in Yorkshire – email correspondence with Joyce Balding, friend and neighbour of the Sowerbys.

182 Chay Blyth, 'Had to have a bit on' – *Sporting Life*, 10 April 1967.

182 David Radford – letter to author.

182 Sussex man with correct 1-2-3 – *Sunday Times*, 9 April 1967.

182   Jack Haggerty – *Sunday Post*, 9 April 1967.

182   Ernest Sharps – *Racing Post*, 4 April 1997.

182   Alan Whitehead – email correspondence with author.

183   Bob Knight – email correspondence with Knight's sons, Martin and Steve.

183   Banbury bookie's bad luck – telephone interview with Paul Lambourne.

183   Alan Sweeney – email correspondence with Graham Sharpe, Sweeney's friend.

184   Everton fans' sweepstake – telephone interview with Michael Walters.

Chapter 25

185   Foinavon 'lame as anything' – face-to-face interview with stable lad Clifford Booth.

186   The suspensory ligament is situated between a horse's flexor tendon and the lower part of its cannon bone, which is like its shin. Head lad Colin Hemsley recalls that they always had to take great care with Foinavon's suspensories.

186   'The one-speed winner …' – *Daily Mail*, 10 April 1967.

186   'A dozen packets of Polos' – *Daily Telegraph*, 10 April 1967.

186   John Kempton: Foinavon jumps 'like a cat' – *Daily Mail*, 10 April 1967.

186   Other horses getting agitated – face-to-face interview with Colin Hemsley, head lad.

187   Jack Kempton taking back his £3 – face-to-face interview with Clifford Booth.

187   Michael Phillips, 'A sad chapter …' – *The Times*, 10 April 1967.

187   Peter Wilson, 'Rarely seen …' – *Daily Mirror*, 10 April 1967.

187   Hotspur, 'Most visitors …' – *Daily Telegraph*, 10 April 1967.

187   'The most fantastic moment …' – *News of the World*, 9 April 1967.

187   Don Cox, 'We must accept …' – *Sun*, 10 April 1967.

187   Spotlight column – *Daily Mirror*, 10 April 1967.

188   Mullingar's 'lazy horse' headline – telephone interview with Kieran O'Donnell, local resident.

188   John Lawrence article – 'One Big Hard Luck Story …' – *Horse and Hound*, 15 April 1967.

188   Newsreel footage of the 1928 Grand National may be viewed online at: http://www.britishpathe.com/video/the-worlds-greatest-race/query/ 1928+grand+national

189   'So as to reduce …' – *The Times*, 2 April 1928.

190   Buckingham's champagne celebration – *Daily Mirror*, 10 April 1967.

190   At London Palladium – face-to-face interview with author, also *Tales from the Weighing Room*, John Buckingham, Pelham Books, 1987, page 30.

190   Buckingham meeting Ron Atkins and Bruce Gregory at Plumpton – ibid., page 33.

191   Autograph/barber's shop incidents – ibid., page 33.

191 Watkins's to keep Foinavon 'for ever' – *Evening Post*, 8 April 1967.

191 Watkins parties – various sources, including Zelda Blackadder, family friend, and Paul Nixon, nephew.

191 Mac Bennellick, a 'Face in the News' – *Havering Recorder*, 14 April 1967.

191 Watkins and Bennellick visiting Compton – face-to-face interview with Clifford Booth.

Chapter 26

193 'The first horse …' – *Daily Mail*, 26 April 1967.

193 Reception details taken from contemporary reports, head lad Colin Hemsley and horsebox-driver Geoff Stocker.

193 Visit to Elm Park, Reading – *Evening Post*, 22 April 1967.

193 Other 'celebrity' appearances by Foinavon – sources include Geoff Stocker, the *Stratford-upon-Avon Herald* and the *Daily Express*.

194 Clifford Booth, 'We had it all held up …' – face-to-face interview with author.

194 'Since Foinavon surprised everybody …' – *Daily Express*, 26 April 1967.

194 Cyril Watkins, 'He is the most popular horse …' – *Daily Mail*, 26 April 1967.

195 John Kempton, 'It was always …' – face-to-face interview with author.

195 Donald Campbell was attempting to break the world water-speed record.

195 Kempton advertising for more horses to train – *Evening News & Star*, 17 August 1967.

196 One of the Kempton-trained winners, Kelvinnie, was carrying Cyril Watkins's black, red and yellow colours. Ironically, the jockey beaten into second place was John Buckingham.

196 Bassnet – one of the first-fence fallers at Aintree.

196 All horse racing in Britain cancelled – *The Times*, 29 November 1967.

Chapter 27

197 Cheshire lost nearly a third of its cattle – *The Times*, 22 January 1968.

197 William Hill £1 million a week turnover drop – *The Times*, 29 November 1967.

197 Tophams request for extended Grand National qualification period – minutes of Tophams Ltd board meetings, volume XIII.

197 102 entries for 1968 National – *The Times*, 26 January 1968.

198 Wilson's broadcast can be listened to at: http://news.bbc.co.uk/onthisday/hi/dates/stories/november/19/newsid_3208000/3208396.stm

198 Discussion with Colonel Livingstone Learmouth – minutes of Tophams Ltd board meetings, volume XIII.

198 Master of Art did run in the 1968 Grand National, falling at the 27th fence.

198 The landscape had turned white … – face-to-face interview with Colin Hemsley, the Kemptons' head lad.

199 A bitterly cold day at Ascot – *The Times*, 23 February 1968.

199 Three days before the Wetherby race, on 6 March, it was announced that Honey End, the 1967 Grand National runner-up, would not be returning to Liverpool in 1968, 'owing to training trouble' (*Sporting Life*, 7 March 1968). He had not run since finishing last in the Hennessy Gold Cup, the last big race before the sport was halted by the foot-and-mouth epizootic, at Newbury on 25 November. He would eventually avenge his defeat by Foinavon in the 1967 National, closer to home, in Sussex.

200 John Buckingham forced to sit out 1968 Grand National – *Tales from the Weighing Room*, John Buckingham, Pelham Books, 1987, page 35.

200 Phil Harvey gets the Aintree ride – in the racecards published by the *Liverpool Daily Post*, Johnny Lehane was listed on Monday as Foinavon's jockey. By Tuesday, this had changed to either Lehane or Harvey and on Thursday 28 March, two days before the race, to just Harvey.

200 Jenkins's 'nasty but necessary' Budget – *The Times*, 20 March 1968. The attention of Cyril Watkins and Mac Bennellick, Foinavon's football pools concessionaire owners, would also have been captured by an increase from 25 to 33 per cent in the duty levied on the pools and fixed-odds football betting.

200 'A much better atmosphere …' – *The Times*, 1 April 1968.

201 'Summer in spring …' – *The Times*, 30 March 1968.

201 Liverpool bus strike – *Liverpool Daily Post*, 28 March 1968.

201 Grand National bus ticket advertisements – minutes of Tophams Ltd board meetings, volume XIII.

201 Hemsley sleeping in horsebox – face-to-face interview with author.

201 John Kempton, 'About 10 million to one …' – *Evening News & Star*, 28 March 1968. Mandarin's assessment in the *Liverpool Daily Post* before the race was fairly typical. Another win for Foinavon and 'I'll give up betting for life,' he wrote.

202 Computer flunked the test – in the machine's defence, it got the seventh and eighth placed horses (Highland Wedding and Reynard's Heir) spot on. It also included the real-life second-, third- and fourth-place finishers in its first ten, but in ninth, first and second places.

202 Julian Critchley on colour television – *The Times*, 3 July 1967.

202 RCA to begin tube production – *The Times*, 6 July 1967.

203 Stan Mellor, 'He didn't know …' – face-to-face interview with author. Mellor had himself chipped three vertebrae in a fall at Newbury three weeks earlier.

203 Brian Fletcher, 'In today's world …' – telephone interview with author. Fletcher acknowledged after the 1968 race that he had been 'glad to get over the 23rd without any trouble' (*Liverpool Daily Post*, 1 April 1968).

203 David Mould, 'He didn't get the trip …' – telephone interview with author.

203 Phil Harvey, 'A hard old ride …' – telephone interview with author. There was open disagreement about what actually happened in the incident, which took place a stride or two beyond the fence. *Sporting Life* reported that Foinavon had fallen 'bringing down Ronald's Boy and Bassnet'. But this prompted Foinavon's co-owner, Mac Bennellick, to ring the newspaper up on Monday, 1 April to assert that it was Bassnet who had fallen and brought down Foinavon. The newspaper approached Alec Kilpatrick, Bassnet's trainer, who said Bassnet landed perfectly at the water, took one stride, at which point Foinavon ran into him. *Sporting Life* published a short story on the exchange on 2 April, concluding, 'Well they say no two people ever report the same incident in the same way – you pays your money and you takes your choice.'

204 Hemsley's bucket – face-to-face interview with author.

204 Andrew Wates, 'Like being catapulted …' – Telephone interview with author.

Chapter 28

205 Four mares in every five … – the *Irish Field* of 18 May 1968 wrote as follows, 'In covering season 1966, when 23, the 44 mares who visited him returned a fertility rate of 81.08 per cent … He was champion National Hunt sire in three of the last four seasons, his stock winning 164 races value £173,539 in those years.'

206 Dermot Whelan, 'His hock was shaking …' – face-to-face interview with author. Of 89 horses listed in the 1968 obituary of stallions, only nine were older than Vulgan and three the same age.

206 A month after the 1968 Grand National, Foinavon had run for the one and only time at Teesside Park. He fell, though on this occasion jockey Phil Harvey reports that he was going well. 'He was running with enthusiasm and his jumping was brilliant,' he told me. Even where he came down, he jumped the fence 'perfectly', but crashed to the ground on landing. 'He hit the deck as if he had dropped dead,' Harvey says.

206 'Foinavon's first …' – *Sporting Life*, 19 September 1968.

207 'It will probably be …' – *Sporting Life*, 25 September 1968.

207 Duels with Honey End – Foinavon had also come off second-best in the pair's first meeting, at Devon & Exeter on 3 August 1966.

207 'Foinavon had a poor season… ' – *Sporting Life*, 24 September 1968.

207 Mistake at the water… – *Sporting Life*, 25 September 1968.

207 Gifford's foot stuck in stirrup – *Sporting Life*, 25 September 1968.

208 Deciding when to stop – Gifford, who retired at 28 only two years after he was last champion, is one of those who probably did get it right. This followed a typically blunt conversation with his trainer, Ryan Price, which ended with the two striking a gentlemen's agreement for Gifford to take over the yard.

208 Anne, Duchess of Westminster, 'Not even Arkle... ' – *Arkle – the Classic Story of a Champion*, Ivor Herbert, Aurum Press 2003, page 206. Foinavon's old stable companion was denied a long retirement, succumbing to arthritis, or an arthritis-like condition, on 31 May 1970.

208 Mill House was retired in January 1970.

208 Foinavon found lame at Wincanton – *Sporting Life*, 5 October 1968.

209 Admiral Pennant declared to run in three races – *Sporting Life*, 12 October 1968.

209 Admiral Pennant impedes his rivals – *Sporting Life*, 14 October 1968. Notwithstanding this report, John Buckingham has no recollection of a loose horse being involved.

209 John Buckingham, 'The crowd were going mad... ' – face-to-face interview with author.

Chapter 29

210 Vincent O'Brien, 'A horse is like a car ...' – *Great Racehorse Trainers*, Tim Fitzgeorge-Parker, Pelham Books, 1975, page 101. O'Brien won a hat-trick of Grand Nationals between 1953 and 1955 and much else besides before transferring his attentions solely to the Flat.

210 Nijinsky – winner of the English Triple Crown (2,000 Guineas, Derby, St Leger) in 1970.

210 Popham Down had won the race in 1964 and 1965, and finished third in 1966 in a running won by Kilburn.

210 Domacorn – *Winner's Disclosure*, Terry Biddlecombe with Pat Lucas, Stanley Paul, 1982, pages 133–4.

210 'Putting up the price of Christmas' – *The Times*, 23 November 1968.

210–11 John Buckingham and Spanish Steps – *Tales from the Weighing Room*, John Buckingham, Pelham Books, 1987, page 38. Spanish Steps, who had the misfortune to run up against horses of the calibre of Red Rum, L'Escargot and Crisp at Aintree, nonetheless notched up two fourths and a third in the Grand National between 1973 and 1975. He duly won that afternoon at Ascot. John 'Jack' Cook, who rode the outsider Ross Sea in Foinavon's National in 1967, won the race four years later aboard Specify in a particularly tight finish. He died in 1999.

211 Buckingham, 'It broke my heart' – telephone interview with author.

211 Breakthrough year for Pitman – on 10 January 1969, he edged out David Mould and Terry Biddlecombe by a short head and a head respectively on a horse called Soloning in a big hurdle race at Newbury. 'I felt I had arrived,' he wrote. In March, he partnered Steel Bridge to second place in the National.

211 Pitman's 'incredibly hard' ride – face-to-face interview with author.

211 'Geordie' Mawson taken by surprise – telephone interview with author.

211 Persian War – winner of a hat-trick of Champion Hurdles between 1968 and 1970.

212 John Buckingham, 'He jumped the water ...' – interviews with author.

213–14 Foinavon's 'grazing hours' with Seas End – *Daily Express*, 4 April 1970.

Chapter 30

214 Colin Hemsley, 'If you give a racehorse ...' – face-to-face interview with author.

214 Details of upheaval at the yard and Foinavon's final months gathered from interviews with Hemsley and John and Trish Kempton.

215 John Kempton, 'We had the bright idea...' – face-to-face interview with author.

215 Kempton, 'We went from...' – face-to-face interview with author.

215 Hemsley answers a knock on his door – face-to-face interview with author.

216 'Geordie' Mawson, 'He was the type of horse...' – telephone interview with author.

216 Mawson, 'I got him out very quickly ...' – telephone interview with author.

216 Mawson, 'I always believed ..."' – telephone interview with author.

217 John Buckingham, 'Almost a sacred place ...' – *Tales from the Weighing Room*, John Buckingham, Pelham Books, 1987, pages 74 and 56.

217 Tiggy Partridge, 'Quite a recluse ...' – telephone interview with author.

218 Partridge/Aubin on auction of Yew Tree Farm – telephone interview with author.

218 'The Great Pools Swindle' – *News of the World*, 25 March 1973.

219 Michael Litchfield, Bennellick 'quite shabbily dressed' – telephone interview with author.

219–20 Bennellick's Ashford farm and details of later life – exchange of emails with Chris Compton, Bennellick's daughter-in-law.

220 Grand National trophy – thanks chiefly to the efforts of Jane Clarke, the course's Grand National historian, this is now at Aintree minus its original green base.

220 Limit on size of National field – since 1984, the maximum has been forty runners and pressure was building at time of writing to have this reduced further.

Appendix A – Field for the 1967 Grand National

Horse	Jockey	Weight	Starting price
1. What a Myth	P. Kelleway	12st 0lb	20/1
2. Freddie	P. McCarron	11st 13lb	100/9
3. Rondetto	J. Haine	11st 7lb	33/1
4. Different Class	D. Mould	11st 2lb	100/8
5. Solbina	E. Harty	11st 2lb	25/1
6. Kapeno	Mr N. Gaselee	11st 1lb	25/1
7. Anglo	B. Beasley	11st 1lb	100/8
8. Kilburn	T. Norman	11st 0lb	100/8
9. Limeking	P. Buckley	10st 13lb	33/1
10. Bassnet	D. Nicholson	10st 11lb	10/1
11. Rutherfords	J. Leech	10st 11lb	28/1
12. Forecastle	N. Wilkinson	10st 10lb	50/1
13. Greek Scholar	T. Biddlecombe	10st 9lb	20/1
14. Meon Valley	A. Turnell	10st 7lb	66/1
15. Honey End	J. Gifford	10st 4lb	15/2F
16. Ross Sea	J. Cook	10st 3lb	66/1
17. Castle Falls	S. Hayhurst	10st 3lb	50/1
18. Lucky Domino	J. Kenneally	10st 5lb	66/1
19. The Fossa	S. Mellor	10st 2lb	100/8
20. Norther	Mr J. Lawrence	10st 0lb	50/1
21. Packed Home	T. Carberry	10st 0lb	100/1
22. Dorimont	R. Pitman	10st 0lb	100/1
24. Kirtle Lad	P. Broderick	10st 3lb	28/1
25. Popham Down	M. Gifford	10st 0lb	66/1
26. April Rose	Maj. P. Bengough	10st 8lb	66/1
27. Vulcano	J. Speid-Soote	10st 0lb	40/1
28. Dun Widdy	Mr J. Edwards	10st 10lb	100/1
29. Aussie	F. Shortt	10st 0lb	50/1
30. Penvulgo	J. Lehane	10st 0lb	50/1

31.	Leedsy	S. Murphy	10st 5lb	50/1
32.	Princeful	R. Edwards	10st 2lb	100/1
33.	Game Purston	K. White	10st 0lb	66/1
34.	Red Alligator	B. Fletcher	10st 0lb	30/1
35.	Ronald's Boy	Mr P. Irby	10st 13lb	100/1
36.	Border Fury	Mr D. Crossley-Cooke	10st 2lb	100/1
37.	Harry Black	R. Reid	10st 0lb	100/1
38.	Foinavon	J. Buckingham	10st 0lb	100/1
39.	Aerial III	Mr T. Durant	10st 9lb	100/1
40.	Scottish Final	Mr B. Howard	10st 0lb	100/1
41.	Quintin Bay	J. Cullen	10st 0lb	50/1
42.	Tower Road	R. Williams	10st 0lb	40/1
43.	Barberyn	N. Mullins	10st 1lb	100/1
44.	Bob-a-Job	C. Young	10st 0lb	100/1
45.	Steel Bridge	E. Prendergast	10st 0lb	100/1

Appendix B – Timeform Rating of the 44 Runners

1.	What a Myth 167		23.	Packed Home 130?
2.	Freddie 163		24.	April Rose 129
3.	Anglo 158		25.=	Aussie 128
4.	Kilburn 156			Popham Down 128
5.	Different Class 155		27.	Princeful 127
6.	Kapeno 152		28.	Vulcano 125
7.	Bassnet 151		29.	Leedsy 124
8.	Solbina 150		30.	Penvulgo 123
9.	Rondetto 150?		31.	Border Fury 122
10.	Rutherfords 147		32.	Ronald's Boy 120
11.	Limeking 145		33.=	Barberyn 117
12.=	Forecastle 144			Dun Widdy 117
	Greek Scholar 144			**FOINAVON 117**
14.	Honey End 143			Scottish Final 117
15.=	The Fossa 142			Tower Road 117
	Meon Valley 142		38.	Quintin Bay 113
17.	Castle Falls 137		39.	Steel Bridge 110
18.=	Kirtle Lad 135		40.	Bob-a-Job 99
	Norther 135			Lucky Domino ?
20.	Red Alligator 132			Ross Sea ?
21. =	Dorimont 131			Aerial III –
	Game Purston 131			Harry Black –

(Taken from Timeform Black Book – National Hunt Edition – 1966/67 season, No. 26. Unadjusted for handicap.)

Appendix C – Result of 1967 Grand National, Aintree 8 April 1967 over 4 miles and 856 yards

Winner Foinavon J. Buckingham 100/1
2nd Honey End J. Gifford 15/2F
3rd Red Alligator B. Fletcher 30/1
4th Greek Scholar T. Biddlecombe 20/1

5th Packed Home T. Carberry
6th Solbina E. Harty
7th Aussie F. Shortt
8th Scottish Final Mr B. Howard
9th What a Myth P. Kelleway
10th Kapeno Mr N. Gaselee
11th Quintin Bay J. Cullen
12th Bob-a-Job C. Young
13th Steel Bridge E. Prendergast
14th Castle Falls S. Hayhurst
15th Ross Sea J. Cook
16th Rutherfords J. Leech
17th Freddie P. McCarron
18th Game Purston K. White

Winner's time: 9 mins 49.4 secs

Appendix D – Poem sent to Foinavon after the race

This handwritten poem was received by Foinavon's trainer John Kempton after the race.

1967 Grand National by Carol Mills & Sally Williams

Four and forty chasers
Stand on Aintree's grass
Honey End and Freddie
And here comes Different Class

They're under starter's orders
And now they are away
To face the biggest fences
In the land today

The first fence, and two horses fall
The crowd shout, "Bassnet's gone"
Meon Valley's down as well
The rest go racing on

They come to mighty Becher's Brook
All jumping very well
Then they come to Valentine's
Where lots of horses fell

And now they're round the Chair again
They're racing past the stand
With brilliant colours flashing by
O isn't this race grand!

The next fence is the twenty third
Two leading horses stop
Brave Rutherfords and Kirtle Lad
Go crashing through the top

Their riders though have hit the ground
And many others too
Horses, jockeys everywhere
Not one of them is through

But who's this in the distance
Who was so far behind?
Foinavon is the horse's name
No winning chance in mind

He jumps and clears the others
And on his way he plods
His jockey, Jonny Buckingham
Is praying to the gods

The winning post has come in sight
Foinavon still is clear
No other horse can catch him now
The race's end is near

Four and forty chasers
Scattered round the course
Foinavon is the winner
Oh! What a lucky horse!

Appendix E – Foinavon Race Record (by year)

Key: F – Flat; B – Bumper; H – Hurdles; S/C – Steeplechase.

Date	Racecourse (Race name)	Length	Type	Jockey	Placing
1962					
18 May	Dundalk	2m	B	Mr A. Cameron	Unpl.
17 Jul	Killarney	1m3f	F	M. Kennedy	Unpl.
2 Aug	Galway	2m	B	Mr A. Cameron	3rd
8 Sep	Phoenix Park	2m	F	M. Kennedy	2nd
16 Nov	Cheltenham	3m	H	P. Taaffe	3rd
1963					
23 Feb	Leopardstown	2m	H	P. Taaffe	Unpl.
2 Mar	Naas	2m1f	H	P. Taaffe	Unpl.
14 Mar	Cheltenham (Spa Hurdle)	3m1f	H	P. Taaffe	Unpl.
15 Apr	Fairyhouse	2m2f	H	P. Taaffe	Unpl.
23 Nov	Leopardstown	2m1f	S/C	L. McLoughlin	Unpl.
1964					
1 Jan	Baldoyle	2m1f	S/C	P. Taaffe	4th
11 Jan	Leopardstown	2m3f	S/C	L. McLoughlin	Fell
18 Jan	Navan	2m	S/C	L. McLoughlin	3rd
30 Jan	Gowran Park	2m1f	S/C	P. Taaffe	2nd
1 Feb	Leopardstown	2m1f	S/C	L. McLoughlin	Fell
29 Feb	Naas	2m	S/C	P. Woods	Won
17 Mar	Baldoyle	3m	S/C	P. Taaffe	4th
29 Apr	Punchestown	2m	S/C	P. McLoughlin	Won
28 Nov	Navan	3m	S/C	P. Taaffe	3rd
16 Dec	Mullingar	3m	S/C	P. Woods	3rd

1965

2 Jan	Baldoyle	3m	S/C	P. Taaffe	Fell
9 Jan	Naas	3m	S/C	P. McLoughlin	Fell
16 Jan	Leopardstown	3m	S/C	P. McLoughlin	BD
6 Feb	Leopardstown (Foxrock Cup)	3m	S/C	S. Barker	Won
27 Feb	Leopardstown	2m3f	S/C	S. Barker	Fell
17 Mar	Baldoyle	3m	S/C	L. McLoughlin	Unpl.
20 Apr	Fairyhouse	3m	S/C	S. Barker	Unpl.

1966

1 Jan	Newbury	3m	S/C	J. Kempton	4th
5 Feb	Kempton Park	3m	S/C	J. Kempton	Unpl.
4 Mar	Haydock	3m4f	S/C	J. Kempton	Unpl.
15 Mar	Cheltenham	3m1f	S/C	J. Kempton	Unpl.
19 Mar	Sandown	3m5f	S/C	J. Kempton	PU
29 Mar	Sandown	3m5f	S/C	J. Kempton	4th
16 Apr	Cheltenham	4m	S/C	J. Buckingham	Unpl.
28 May	Towcester	3m1f	S/C	J. Kempton	3rd
30 Jul	Newton Abbot	3m1f	S/C	J. Kempton	Unpl.
3 Aug	Devon & Exeter	3m	S/C	J. Kempton	2nd
29 Aug	Huntingdon	3m1f	S/C	J. Kempton	2nd
14 Sep	Devon & Exeter	3m	S/C	J. Kempton	Fell
21 Sep	Ludlow	3m	S/C	J. Kempton	3rd
7 Oct	Ascot	3m1f	S/C	J. Guest	4th
27 Dec	Kempton Park (King George VI Chase)	3m	S/C	J. Kempton	4th

1967

20 Jan	Lingfield	3m	S/C	J. Kempton	4th
4 Feb	Kempton Park	3m	S/C	R. Atkins	2nd
11 Feb	Sandown	3m	S/C	J. Kempton	Unpl.
22 Feb	Ascot	3m	S/C	B. Gregory	Fell
3 Mar	Newbury	3m	S/C	R. Atkins	Unpl.
16 Mar	Cheltenham (Cheltenham Gold Cup)	3m2f	S/C	J. Kempton	Unpl.
27 Mar	Huntingdon	3m1f	S/C	D. Patrick	4th
1 Apr	Leicester	3m	S/C	B. Gregory	Unpl.*
8 Apr	Liverpool (Grand National)	4m4f	S/C	J. Buckingham	Won
1 Nov	Newbury	3m	S/C	J.Kempton	4th

* denotes race in which his stirrup-leather broke

1968

22 Feb	Ascot	3m5f	S/C	J. Lehane	Unpl.
9 Mar	Wetherby	3m4f	S/C	P. Harvey	4th
16 Mar	Sandown	3m5f	S/C	J. Lehane	PU
30 Mar	Liverpool (Grand National)	4m4f	S/C	P. Harvey	BD
27 Apr	Teesside Park	4m1f	S/C	P. Harvey	Fell
1 Jun	Towcester	3m1f	S/C	J. Kempton	PU
22 Aug	Devon & Exeter	3m1f	S/C	J. Buckingham	4th
4 Sep	Devon & Exeter	3m	S/C	J. Buckingham	3rd
18 Sep	Devon & Exeter	3m1f	S/C	J. Buckingham	Won
24 Sep	Plumpton	3m	S/C	J. Buckingham	2nd
12 Oct	Uttoxeter	3m	S/C	J. Buckingham	Won
23 Nov	Warwick (Crudwell Cup)	3m5f	S/C	R. Pitman	Unpl.

1969

1 Feb	Kempton Park	3m	S/C	J. Buckingham	Fell

Acknowledgements

More than 200 people, as I now realise, have helped to make this book. The vast majority are identified in the notes accompanying the text, but to some I owe a special debt.

Those closest to Foinavon were especially generous with the time they allotted me. John and Trish Kempton twice invited me into their home to leaf through their scrapbooks and probe their memories. Clifford Booth, Frank and Joan Whittle, Geoff Stocker, Jill Hemsley and Joy Smith all provided indispensable details and valuable insight. Colin Hemsley filled in the minutiae of day-to-day life at a small racing yard and fielded countless questions.

For details of the horse's early life in Ireland, I am indebted to John and Jill McCormack, and also Jim Dreaper, who allowed me free access to the famous yard near Dublin where Foinavon once kept company with Arkle and Ben Stack. Peter McLoughlin, one of just four men who knew what it was like to ride the horse to victory, was a generous and knowledgeable guide during that visit. Dermot Whelan, who knew Foinavon's celebrated sire Vulgan as well as any man, performed a similar service at the Blackrath Stud, where the Grand National winner was conceived.

For fleshing out the characters of those who owned Foinavon at the time of his great day at Aintree, I am especially grateful to four people: Chris Compton, Paul Nixon, Lyn Shelton and Zelda Blackadder.

I was privileged to meet, talk to, or correspond with around 50 former jockeys, including 25 who rode in that unforgettable 1967

Grand National. All responded graciously to my inquiries and almost all contributed something I could not have gleaned elsewhere. I wish to thank every one of them, not least those for whom that grey afternoon in Liverpool holds little by way of happy memories. If I may single out just two: the late, great Josh Gifford devoted an evening in front of a crackling fire to reminiscing about Findon and life with Captain Ryan Price; and Foinavon's best-remembered jockey, John Buckingham – in whose village I came, by chance, to live in the early 1990s – talked me through each one of his rides on the horse that catapulted him into the limelight, with the help of his meticulously kept rider's logbook.

Ossie Dale filled me in on life behind the scenes at Aintree in the 1960s, while Ray and Muriel Lakeland explained the trials and tribulations of outside broadcasts in what was still a pioneering age for television. Guy Thibault supplied details of Vulgan's early years in France.

I am no horse-racing specialist, so the help of a number of experts has been fundamental to this attempt to tell Foinavon's story. Brough Scott and Sir Peter O'Sullevan, two of our foremost racing authorities, were kindness itself whenever I approached them, supplying much invaluable background information. Grand National historian John Pinfold most generously allowed extended access to vital research materials as well as contributing a vivid eye-witness account of Foinavon's race. Tim Cox also helped with research and allowed me the run of his magnificent library. Mick Mutlow and Jane Clarke provided invaluable facts and figures. Chris Pitt, a writer and enthusiast who knows far more about the National than I ever shall, helped with contacts, context and confirmation of obscure details that were proving hard to verify, as well as an invitation to the Midlands Grand National Club. Pitt's book, *Go Down to the Beaten*, was also a valuable source.

A wealth of historical Grand National footage, some of which was very helpful to me, is available to view (or indeed buy) at www.britishpathe.com.

I am also particularly grateful to Scott Bowers of the Jockey Club, Phil Turner of Timeform and Bruce Millington of the *Racing Post*, as well as staff of the British newspaper library at Colindale, the Liverpool Record Office and the R.E. & G.B. Way bookshop near Newmarket.

Among the many others who responded more considerately to my inquiries than I had any right to expect were: Isabelle Jekey, Kara McCulloch, Georgina Galt, Capt. Charles Radclyffe, Toby Balding, Peter Chapman, Vincent Slevin, Derek Thompson, Julian Thick, Rob Marriott, Kieran O'Donnell, Anne Collyer, Edward Saunders, Raymond Deacon, John de Moraville, Patrick Foley, Graham Budd, Randy Reynolds, Phil Prosser, Richard Church and Louise Martin.

Notwithstanding this army of contributors, mistakes are, I fear, inevitable and responsibility for them is, of course, mine.

I would like to thank the team at Bloomsbury – including Holly MacDonald, Phil Beresford, Julian Flanders, Emily Sweet, Nick Humphrey, Helen Flood, Ellen Williams and, most of all, Charlotte Atyeo – for their sound advice and for making my long-harboured ambition to publish this book reality. Two other individuals played critical roles. One is my agent David Luxton; the other, Matthew Engel, former editor of the Wisden Sports Writing imprint, who backed the idea from the outset and whose kindness extended to casting his inimitable writerly eye over parts of the text, for which special thanks.

Finally, thank you to Duncan Mackay and Sarah Bowron, the nearest thing I have these days to journalistic employers, for their patience throughout the protracted business of composition. And of course to Edi and Molly for love and forbearance during long hours in the rat-hole.

Oh, and not forgetting Foinavon, John Kempton's funny horse.

Index